ARGUING
FROM
SOURCES

**EXPLORING
ISSUES
THROUGH
READING
AND
WRITING**

ARGUING
FROM
SOURCES

EXPLORING
ISSUES
THROUGH
READING
AND
WRITING

DAVID S. KAUFER
Carnegie Mellon University

CHERYL GEISLER
Rensselaer Polytechnic Institute

CHRISTINE M. NEUWIRTH
Carnegie Mellon University

Harcourt Brace Jovanovich, Publishers

San Diego   New York   Chicago   Austin   Washington, D.C.

London   Sydney   Tokyo   Toronto

⊞ PREFACE

We wrote this book to solve practical problems in teaching original argument from sources, more commonly known as the research or term paper. As longtime teachers of that genre, we made it our custom to ask students to work from sources on an issue of interest, to make responsible inferences from their sources, and then to compose an argumentative essay with fresh insight.

Despite our high expectations, we were seldom satisfied with the results. Rather than handling their sources resourcefully and extending the discussion in useful directions, our students regularly interpreted the assignment as a recitation exercise with optional commentary: tell the teacher about the sources and say what you did or didn't like about them. Our students' interpretation of research writing seemed far less challenging, exploratory, or fun than the assignment we had in mind.

Had we believed that our students were not ready to meet our challenge, we would have long ago abandoned our goals as naive. But as we tried to explain to students the challenge they were missing, it became increasingly clear that the fault lay as much with us as with them. We did not know how to define that challenge.

As everyone who teaches composition knows, writing represents a marvelous opportunity to experiment with authorship—to take a self-rewarding intellectual journey. And yet we found ourselves lecturing students on how to locate sources in the library, how to cite them accurately, how to take notes, and how to polish a rough draft—research writing minus the challenge and the joy.

Out of these concerns, we began a three-year investigation into the tacit expectations that we, other teachers, and experienced writers bring to research writing. Our goal was to try to define the challenge for students without taking the challenge away. We felt that if we could make that challenge more explicit, we could let students in on our secrets, give them better motivation, and offer them better support and feedback.

The result is *Arguing from Sources,* a book organized around a sequence of reading and writing activities that require would-be authors first to summarize the positions of others, next to synthesize these positions, then to analyze these and other potential positions in order to arrive at some conclusions, and, finally, to elaborate their conclusions into an original argument of their own—the four standard academic writing tasks, to which Parts Two through Five of this book correspond.

Arguing from Sources has several unique features:

- It uses linked assignments. We have assumed that the knowledge and texts that students produce in one phase can be carried over into the next. Thus, summarizing prepares the intellectual ground for synthesizing; synthesizing, for analyzing; analyzing, for contributing. Working through the book from beginning to end will give students a sense of how their thinking must grow and change as they move from reading sources to composing original arguments.

- It presents a series of visual structures for thinking: a line of argument, a grid of common points, a synthesis tree. We have found that these visualizations help students see more clearly how their thinking must develop as they progress through the cycle of reading and writing.

- It focuses on the interaction of structure and content. Structures of argument are presented as methods that help writers organize, explore, and, eventually, master the content associated with an issue. While we don't teach content per se, we do teach students how to deal with an issue-related content in order to design interesting and fresh arguments. The book focuses on a single issue—wilderness—chosen for its relevance and its interest for students.

Every chapter contains "For Class" and "For Your Notebook" exercises. The "For Class" exercises are designed to give students a chance to practice their skills on the wilderness issue. The "For Your Notebook" exercises are designed to help students progress on an issue of their own choosing. The book concludes with a short glossary of the boldface terms defined in the text and an appendix on documenting a research paper.

The book is intended for students who have mastered the basic conventions of reading and writing. It can be used in lieu of a standard textbook on research writing or as a supplement to one; in a course on argument or critical thinking, especially reasoning from cases; as a handy reference for content teachers who assign the major term paper or who wish to structure and sequence writing assignments; and, finally, as a writing-across-the-curriculum textbook, introducing students to the social dynamics of academic communities.

Acknowledgments

Arguing from Sources represents one of the fruits of the WARRANT project, with goals of conducting research, building a curriculum, and designing a computer system to support the reading and writing of issue-centered argument. The project was funded by the Fund for the Improvement of Post-Secondary Education, without whose support we could not have worked. We thank Steve Ehrmann, our original project director, and Rusty Garth, our final one, for their encouragement.

The basic outline of the book was developed over a period of three years by Kaufer and Geisler, drawing on his work teaching an experimental course and on her research on expert/novice differences in arguing from sources. Kaufer and Geisler together developed the overall framework for Parts Two through Five. Geisler, with help from Kaufer, developed the specific strategies for Parts Two and Three ("Summarize" and "Synthesize"). Kaufer, with help from Geisler and Neuwirth, developed the specific strategies for Parts Four and Five ("Analyze" and "Contribute"). Neuwirth, with help from Kaufer and Geisler, was responsible for the Instructor's Manual.

We wish to thank our colleagues at Carnegie Mellon University and Rensselaer Polytechnic Institute, who have given us stimulating environments in which to think and work. We are particularly indebted to Preston Covey, director of Carnegie Mellon's Core Curriculum and Center for Design of Educational Computing, for the original inspiration to examine case-based reasoning and to Richard Young, whose vision of what invention and problem solving are has been a continual source of inspiration to us. We are also grateful to the reviewers of the manuscript, William L. Sipple of Robert Morris College and John N. Snapper of Calvin College.

In addition, we would like to give special thanks to those whose reading, teaching, and talking refined our work: Michael Palmquist, for trying to teach from our earlier manuscript and for his many editorial comments; Sister Barbara Sitko, for a careful reading of drafts of "Summarize" and "Synthesize" and for her focus on acts of interpretation; Michael Halloran, for his insightful reading of an earlier draft of "Summarize" and subsequent discussion of the metaphor of conversation; Charlotte Wilson, for her comments on an earlier draft; Michele Matchett, whose work on wilderness gave us the student essay in "Contribute"; Armar Archbold, for helping us understand what it meant to synthesize; Denise Troll, for her reading of earlier drafts of "Analyze" and "Contribute"; Joel Ness, for his graphic designs; Susan Bouldin, for her careful proofreading; Mary Ellen Lane, for her help in proofreading and collating the glossary; Ann Penrose and Alexander Friedlander, for their work in collecting the data on which this book was based; Paul Nockleby, for his confidence in our project; Natalie Bowen, for her careful attention to our meaning and style; and Marlane Miriello, our editor at Harcourt Brace Jovanovich, for bringing this book to press.

Finally, we would like to thank our immediate families—Barb and Aaron, Mark and Naomi Elizabeth—whose endurance through this project has outpaced our own.

D. S. K.

C. G.

C. M. N.

⸬ CONTENTS

ARGUING
FROM
SOURCES

**EXPLORING
ISSUES
THROUGH
READING
AND
WRITING**

PART ONE
INTRODUCTION

▦1 GET STARTED

*The most promising words ever written on the maps of
human knowledge are* terra incognita—*unknown territory.*

—Daniel J. Boorstin, *The Discoverers*

Throughout history, explorers have relied on incomplete maps of uncharted territories. Columbus started with maps portraying the New World as India. Lewis and Clark started their westward expedition with poorly specified maps of the Missouri River. To make their journeys, explorers go through four phases: (1) they consult the maps of others; (2) they explore similarities and differences among maps; (3) they make the journey themselves; (4) they return to design a new map. The exploration process involves designing and redesigning structures in order to accommodate what is learned from new explorations.

What is true for exploring physical territories is also true for exploring issues. Like physical exploration, the composition of argument involves the structuring and restructuring of maps through an issue—not physical maps but mental maps. Authors are constantly designing and redesigning their mental maps of an issue in order to make their exploration as rich, productive, and up-to-date as possible.

In this book, we'll teach you how to structure and restructure the ideas you'll use in composing written arguments. The major parts of this book correspond to the four phases of exploration:

- In Part Two, Summarize, you'll design a structure called a **line of argument** from an author's text. The line of argument you design for a particular author helps you outline a written summary of that author's position. You will write summaries of the texts of individual authors to teach yourself and others where each author stands and what his or her reasons are for standing there.
- In Part Three, Synthesize, you'll design structures called grids of common points and synthesis trees from the lines of argument of multiple authors. Your synthesis tree becomes the outline of a written synthesis, which you will use to teach yourself and others similarities and differences among these authors' positions on a single issue.
- In Part Four, Analyze, you'll reach your own conclusions on the issue by

exploring and evaluating possible as well as previous positions. Your written analysis will teach yourself and others about strengths and faults in alternative approaches to the issue, and it will give you a chance to get feedback on your conclusions.

- In Part Five, Contribute, you'll elaborate your conclusions into an original line of argument and, eventually, an original essay or contribution. Your original argument will teach you and others why one should stand on the issue where you have decided to stand.

CHOOSE YOUR ISSUE

What you choose as your issue carries important consequences. Your choice will set the boundaries of the territory you explore. Finding out too late that you've chosen the wrong issue is painful. The extra few hours you spend at the beginning of your project worrying about your choice of issue may save you hundreds down the road. An issue is a topic, so when you choose an issue, you are also choosing a topic. A topic is any subject matter about which you can read, think, write, and which you can discuss. Not all topics are issues, however. The following section explains the difference.

What Is an Issue?

An **issue** is a topic that sparks controversy within a community of speakers, readers, and writers. More specifically, an issue is a topic that creates a *tension* in the community, a discontent or dissatisfaction with the status quo. If the tension is commonly acknowledged by the community and judged important enough to command its attention, the topic that created it is recognized as an issue. Members of the community attach a social value to seeing the issue resolved. Not all topics warrant such favored attention. But when they do, they become issues.

To understand better the difference between a topic and an issue, consider carrot soup. Carrot soup is a topic that we can discuss and even disagree about. Imagine the following exchange:

Mary: "Carrot soup is wonderful."
John: "Carrot soup is awful."

Mary and John are having a discussion. The discussion probably won't go very far because there's not much left to discuss once their opinions are exchanged. Moreover, Mary and John's discussion of carrot soup doesn't have visible consequences for anyone but Mary and John. Mary may be trying to convince John to reconsider a soup he gave up at age six, but no one beyond John will be much affected even if he has a change of heart. John's decision to try or not to try carrot soup carries no consequences for a larger community.

When you are looking for an issue to explore, you need to make sure you have more than a topic. Unlike carrot soup, your issue must do more than generate differences of opinion—it should be able to sustain a discussion with consequences for a larger community. To see what this means exactly, consider how carrot soup might become an issue. Suppose one researcher claimed to link carrot soup with cancer. Other researchers disagreed. Evidence and reasons would be marshaled by all concerned and at least some people outside of the disagreeing parties would be affected by the outcome of the debate. Under these circumstances, carrot soup would become an issue.

Types of Issues

As you search through issues, you'll find differences that you should keep in mind when deciding on one to explore.

General versus Specialized Issues   Some issues have important implications for every competent adult in a society. That is, the community affected by them includes just about everyone. Nuclear arms, gun control, abortion, and capital punishment are examples. Such issues are referred to as *general* issues because they are seen as affecting the general public.

Other issues affect only subgroups or communities that are narrower in scope than the general public. Issues affecting academic communities (issues in physics, chemistry, biology, the teaching of writing) and professions (lawyers, doctors, plumbers, bakers) fall into this category. These issues are known as *specialized* issues because they address communities more specialized than the general public. The rise of the labor movement in the 1930s and the feasibility of developing superconductors for tomorrow's computers are examples of specialized issues.

To explore specialized issues as an author, you need specialized knowledge. As you search through issues for your own research project, ask yourself whether the issue is general or specialized. If specialized, ask yourself whether you have the background necessary to summarize, synthesize, analyze, and contribute new information. You can't expect to be an original author in an area that you are struggling to learn for the first time. As a student writer simply looking for a subject on which to practice composing argument, you should stick with general issues.

Literate versus Oral Issues   Normally, you can assume that all the sides taken in an issue will be *written down,* committed to print in newspapers, articles, or books. In such issues, called *literate* issues, the debate is channeled through formal written argument. These arguments circulate within a community—that is, authors in the community carefully plan written responses to the arguments of previous authors. The library is obviously the best place to learn about literate issues.

However, not all issues are literate issues. In some issues, called *oral* issues, only one side composes a formal position and commits it to writing. The other side (or sides) may prefer other methods of getting their position across. They may boycott, go on strike, filibuster, negotiate, tear up a contract, refuse to talk—but not, for one reason or another, express their position formally as authors. On some issues, furthermore, neither side may express their views in writing. In oral issues, you must rely on word of mouth as well as reading to get a balanced perspective.

Suppose you decide to address the issue of hunting. Is hunting moral or not? You do your library research and find that for every ten authors who deplore hunting, only one seems to defend it. Is the ratio between antihunters and prohunters really ten to one? Not necessarily. The ten-to-one ratio describes only the *antihunters who write formal essays* versus the *prohunters who write formal essays*. Prohunters may prefer to express themselves in ways different from formal written argument—in, say, angry phone calls to members of Congress and financial donations to hunting lobbies.

When you deal with an oral issue, the library is not likely to tell you the whole story, and it won't give you the balance of views and perspectives you'll want your research to include. To get that balance, you'll often need to play the role of journalist or field reporter—corresponding, telephoning, and conducting face-to-face interviews with representatives of various sides. These are useful roles to play even if your issue is literate, but they become essential when your issue is oral.

In your library research, if you cannot find a good balance of alternative positions on the issue you have chosen, you should suspect that the issue might be oral and that to explore it further, you'll have to search beyond the library. In this book, summarizing a conflicting range of positions is a skill we teach. Therefore, you will do better to focus on literate issues, because the library makes all sides of such issues available to you.

Local versus Nonlocal Issues   Some issues affect only your school, your neighborhood, your town, city, county, or state. Other issues affect your region, your country, or the world. Issues with narrower scope are *local* in comparison with issues of broader scope; issues with wider scope are *nonlocal* in comparison with issues of narrower scope. There are trade-offs in choosing between local and nonlocal issues.

You are likely to be more familiar with and more personally affected by local issues (your school's grading system, its food service, the traffic lights on campus). Consequently, you may find you can write about them with greater authority and commitment. At the same time, local issues are less likely to be literate issues. You probably won't find many periodicals and books discussing issues on your campus. If you want to make sure to address a literate issue (one relying on abundant and balanced scholarship), you should not pick a local one.

Nonlocal issues have the opposite qualities. You are less likely to have been directly touched by issues that affect large populations. So you will probably find it more difficult to write about such issues with a sense of personal experience and authority. But because nonlocal issues are more likely to be literate issues, and because we are most concerned in this book to teach you how to address literate issues as an author, you would do well to select nonlocal issues. Your library should offer ample resources for you to decide where you stand on such issues.

ENTER YOUR ISSUE

Even when you know some formal characteristics of the issue you are looking for (general, literate, nonlocal), you still need a way of deciding what issue to choose. You also need a way of finding your potential commitment to the issue. This section discusses various doors you can open to find your way into it.

Go In from a Topic

Like death and taxes, many topics imply or can become linked with issues. Consequently, entering an issue through a topic is often possible. Try to produce topics from your experience and your reading that may become issues. Reference materials in the library, which we discuss more fully in the next chapter, contain many such topics. To test your topic as an issue, see if you can identify a community that carries on a longstanding disagreement about it. Ask yourself whether you feel part of that community, are willing to learn about it, to join it. If you do, your topic will function as an issue worthy of your consideration.

Go In from a Problem Case

A **problem case** is a concrete situation whose existence raises discontent or dissatisfaction for a community. Members of the community share the goal of wanting to see these cases resolved, of wanting to see their dissatisfaction relieved. However, they can't agree on the best way to resolve these cases—they can't agree on solutions. Or they can't agree on what's causing the problem in the first place—they can't even agree on how to define the problem. Often, they can't agree on either. Their disagreement is what sustains the issue.

A useful way to enter an issue is through the problem cases associated with it. There is no more convincing way to enter an issue than to feel, firsthand, the dissatisfaction that a larger community also feels. Let's consider some examples:

One student writer, Mary, realized that from childhood she had always been intrigued by the childhood taunt "Sticks and stones can break my bones, but names will never hurt me!" Mary had always thought this slogan was wrong, because names *can* hurt—as she knew from her experience when people had hurled names at her. Using this problem case as a door for entering an issue, Mary discovered a community that discussed this "hurt" as an issue called "libel and slander." She thus decided to focus her library search on that issue.

Another student writer, Jerry, had been raised as a Roman Catholic and had followed the Church teachings on abortion. He believed that a woman should not get an abortion under any circumstances. What bothered Jerry was knowing that if his own girlfriend were to become pregnant, he would probably insist that she have an abortion. Jerry didn't know how to reconcile his opposing beliefs. His girlfriend's possible pregnancy formed a problem case that threw him into a state of uneasiness and dissatisfaction. He thus decided to focus his library research on the abortion issue, which could help him work through his problem case.

A third student writer, John, knew a person in his home town who had shot and killed his father and grandfather after getting into a heated argument with them. John knew very little about the gun control issue beyond slogans, but he had wondered since that tragedy whether gun control legislation could have prevented it. John felt he could answer a question that had stayed in the back of his mind for years by entering the gun control issue.

A fourth student, Marsha, had had a falling out with her friend Rita, who had been having family problems that prevented her from concentrating on her courses. She was failing her assignments and jeopardizing her grade point average. Marsha had advised Rita to discuss her problems with her teachers, but Rita had too much pride and refused. Acting "for Rita's own good," Marsha went to Rita's teachers and told them about her family situation. When Rita learned what Marsha had done, she accused Marsha of betraying her and she ended the friendship. Marsha was hurt and confused and wondered whether she had done the right thing. She discovered that a community addressing an issue called "paternalism" tried to discuss and resolve problem cases like her own.

A fifth student, Bruce, was having a conversation with a roommate when the name of Brooke Shields came up. Bruce's roommate remarked that Brooke had played a daughter of a prostitute in the movie *Pretty Baby,* when she was only twelve years old. Bruce's roommate quipped that Brooke was old enough to act in the movie but not old enough to see it. This quip stayed with Bruce as an interesting problem, and motivated him to pursue the issues of child acting laws and the movie ratings system.

In each case, the student was able to enter the issue by noticing, on a small scale, tensions that a larger community felt on a larger scale. Noticing is an indispensable, but seldom advertised, skill of argument. We often think of arguments as ways to generalize about issues. Seldom do we think of arguments as providing ways to see issues in the fine detail that makes them real and pressing. And yet it's the concrete detail—our ability to notice it and our need to account for it—that teaches us how to evaluate the arguments addressed to an issue and to develop our own.

Go In from a Text

Among the more common ways to enter an issue is through a text, which may be a newspaper or magazine article, as well as a book. A text that addresses an issue will often teach you about problem cases associated with it. From the text's statement of problem cases, you may decide that you would like to follow (and eventually lead) the discussion on these cases, about how to see them resolved. A text can thus give you the impetus to pursue an issue further. Many students find interesting issues by going to the library, browsing through texts, finding a text that makes them unusually interested and excited, and then committing themselves to the larger issue addressed by the text.

Go In from a Community

A final way to enter an issue is through the communities to which you already belong. Examine your own life as you presently live it. You are not without communities or commitments to them. You are the citizen of a nation. You are a prospective member of one or more professions. You represent an age group, an income group, a race, a religion, a sex, a family. You are married or unmarried, or in the process of moving from one state to another. You are a parent or prospective parent. You are a baseball fan or a baseball idiot. You like the outdoors, or you fancy yourself a couch potato.

Your actual or anticipated membership in all these groups already defines a set of interests for you. Your membership bequeaths you a set of problem cases that you must take responsibility for whether you know about them or not, whether you want to take responsibility for them or not. It also bequeaths you a set of topics and texts to help you follow the discussion among those who share your responsibilities.

For Class 1.1

1. List the issues you have written about in previous writing courses. Classify these issues as general or specialized, literate or oral, and local or nonlocal. In class, discuss why issues that are general, literate, and nonlocal are best for learning about the four phases of exploration discussed above.
2. In class, discuss topics that might turn into issues you want to pursue; problem cases from your own experience; texts you have read; groups to which you belong.

For Your Notebook #1

Choose your issue. Unless your teacher tells you otherwise, look for issues that are general, literate, and nonlocal. Find your issue by searching through topics, problem cases, texts, and the communities to which you already belong.

⊞ 2 PLAN YOUR RESEARCH

GET YOUR BEARINGS

When you choose an issue, you commit your time, energy, and experience to working on a solution to a controversy that concerns a community of people. To follow through on this commitment, you will need to explore your own values, goals, and experience as well as those of the authors who have already written on the issue. As an individual author, you seek to discover a way to make an original contribution to this community.

Before you set out on this journey of exploration and discovery, however, you need to get your own bearings on the issue. Essentially this involves a two-sided process: exploring the problem cases that have drawn you to the issue and exploring the key words the community has used to discuss the issue.

Explore Problem Cases

As we said in Chapter 1, a problem case is a concrete situation that, for some reason or another, bothers you or someone else in your community. Something about this situation causes you or someone else to be discontented. Something about it makes it a problem. At the heart of every issue is a set of problem cases.

Involving yourself in an issue means being concerned enough about a set of problem cases to work toward eliminating them. By creating an original argument, you will be suggesting a way for your community to handle a set of cases. According to your argument, they will reduce or eliminate these cases, if they follow your suggestions. Original argument, then, is a cooperative endeavor—a task in which you join a community in search of a better way of handling a set of situations.

To create an original argument, you must first get your bearings on your problem cases. Ask yourself, What are the concrete situations that bother me? What are the situations my argument will try to resolve?

9

To describe each problem case completely, you need to include four kinds of information:

ASPECTS OF A PROBLEM CASE

Agent: Who is doing something that causes the problem?
Action: What are they doing?
Goal: Why, from their perspective, are they doing it?
Result: What is the outcome of their action?

Your problem cases may come from one of two sources. First, they may arise from your own personal experience. Mike, for example, decided to re-search the 55-mph speed limit after receiving a speeding ticket in his home state of Massachusetts. It's not hard to see why the following problem case bothered him:

A PROBLEM CASE FROM PERSONAL EXPERIENCE

Agent: The Massachusetts state police
Action: fined me for driving 57 mph in a 55-mph zone
Goal: in order to increase traffic safety.
Result: As a result, I had to make a special trip home to go to court and I now have a driving record.

Problem cases may also come from something you've read or heard about. A situation described by someone else may stick in your mind; for some reason, you find it bothersome. In effect, you find yourself sharing the concerns of others who've noticed the situation before you. You want to join them in the search for a solution.

For example, one problem case that attracted us to the wilderness issue was first described by Eric Julber in an essay he wrote for *Reader's Digest* in May 1972. As you'll see, Julber has included a striking portrait of what we will call "the problem case of the purists."

LET'S OPEN UP OUR WILDERNESS AREAS

Eric Julber

The prevailing philosophy with regard to the use of some 40 million 1
acres of America's magnificent wilderness has become what I term "purist-
conservationist." The purist is, generally speaking, against everything. He is
against roads, campgrounds, ski lifts and restaurants. He has very strong
ideas about who deserves to enjoy natural beauty and, ideally, would reserve
beauty for those who are willing and able to hike, climb, crawl or cliffhang
to achieve it. The purist believes that those who do not agree with him desire
to "rape the landscape."

The purist standards were embodied in the Wilderness Act of 1964, 2
which provides that in such areas there shall be "no permanent road . . . no
temporary road . . . no mechanical transport and no structure or installation." The practical effect of this philosophy, thus frozen into federal law,
has been to make many of the most beautiful areas of the United States "off
limits" to anyone who is not willing and able to backpack into them. Statistics show that this means 99 *percent* of Americans.

In 1965, there were 1,475,000 visitors to the Wilderness areas. In 1970, 3
the number of visitors had increased only to 1,543,000. This represents use
by less than one percent of our population. Moreover, a survey on behalf of
the President's Outdoor Recreation Resources Review Commission
(ORRRC) showed, by statistical analysis, that the users are the intellectual
and financial elite of our nation.

Reports the ORRRC: "In the sample of Wilderness users interviewed, 4
more than 75 percent had at least a college degree, and a high proportion
have done postgraduate work or hold advanced degrees. . . . Wilderness
users are disproportionately drawn from the higher income levels. Professional and semiprofessional people, and those in white-collar occupations,
account for approximately three quarters of those interviewed."

And what of ordinary Americans, those whose favorite recreations are 5
driving, sightseeing, easy walking and camping? What of the too-old, the
too-young, the timid, the inexperienced, the frail, the hurried, the out-of-

Eric Julber, "Let's Open Up Our Wilderness Areas," *Reader's Digest,* May 1972. Reprinted
with permission of the publisher and the author.

shape or the just-plain-lazy, all of whose taxes acquired and maintain the Wilderness areas?

For this group—99 percent of the American population—federal agencies   6 provide 73,700 acres of campgrounds and 39,100 acres of picnic sites: a total of 112,800 acres. And I believe that the areas provided to the common American are not the prime scenic areas; they are the fringes, the leftovers, the secondary scenic areas.

I feel I can speak with some authority as to purist philosophy, because I   7 was once a purist myself. I have carried many a 50-pound pack; I've hiked to the top of Mt. Whitney, there to think beautiful thoughts; I've hiked the 200-mile length of California's John Muir Trail, running from Yosemite to Sequoia. And even in later years, when the press of law practice kept me physically away from the wilderness, in spirit I remained a purist. Keep those roads and crowds out, I said!

But no more. Recently I paid a visit to Switzerland. What I saw there   8 made a non-purist out of me. Switzerland has, within the boundaries of a country half as large as South Carolina, one of the most astonishing concentrations of natural beauty on the face of the earth. Not only was I overwhelmed by Switzerland's beauty, but I was amazed to find that virtually every part of it was accessible and thoroughly used by people of all shapes and ages. It was, in fact, exploited to the ultimate—crisscrossed with roads, its mountain valleys heavily grazed and farmed, hotels and restaurants everywhere. Where the automobile cannot go, railroads take you; and when the going gets too steep for cogwheel trains, you catch an aerial tramway.

The most remarkable viewpoints in the country have been deliberately   9 made accessible by some kind of comfortable transportation. People from all over Europe sit on Switzerland's restaurant patios, 10,000 feet high, admiring the magnificent views—views that in America would be excluded from 99 percent of our population without days of the most arduous struggle.

The Swiss philosophy says: Invite people in; the more the better. The   10 purist says: Keep people out. The Swiss say: Let the strong climb if they choose (and many of them do), but let the children, the aged, the hurried or just-plain-lazy ride.

I, who have now done it both ways, say: My thoughts were just as   11 beautiful on top of Switzerland's Schilthorn—9,757 feet up; restaurant lunch of fondue, wine, strawberry pastry and coffee; reached by 30-minute tram ride—as they were on top of Mt. Lyell in America's Yosemite—13,095 feet up; lunch of peanut-butter sandwich; reached by two-day hike. I conclude that the purist philosophy which keeps Americans out of their own land is an unwise misuse of our wilderness resources.

Let me propose an alternative philosophy. For want of a better term, call   12 it an "access" philosophy. Consider as an example Muir Trail in California, with its magnificent Wilderness scenery—peaks, meadows, hundreds of lakes, streams, even glaciers. Its southern end is 212 miles from Los Angeles, its northern end 215 miles from San Francisco. Under present purist conditions, the Muir Trail is inaccessible to all except the hardiest, for only two roads touch it between its two ends. To reach its most beautiful parts you have to hike over mountain passes averaging 10,000 feet in height, packing supplies on your back.

Under the "access" philosophy, I would install aerial tramways at three or four locations within easy driving distance of Los Angeles. These tramways would have large gondola cars suspended from cables between towers that can be up to a mile apart; the cars would move silently high above the landscape. At the terminal of each tramway—after, say, an hour's ride—there would be restaurant facilities, picnic areas, observation points. A family could stay for a few hours or camp for weeks. General access would be year-round, as compared to the present 90-day, snow-free period.   13

Why not also put a tramway in Grand Canyon?   14

The visitor now cannot get from the South Rim to the North Rim (a distance of from 8 to 18 miles) without driving 217 miles around, and he cannot get to the bottom of the canyon (the most interesting part) except on foot or muleback. I would install an aerial tramway in an inconspicuous fold of the canyon, so that visitors could ride from the South Rim to the bottom, and from the bottom to the North Rim, thus getting a feel for its immense depths.   15

That brings up the ultimate argument that purists always fall back on: that the Swiss can do such things with taste, judgment and reverence for the landscape; that we Americans would botch it up. This is neither altogether true nor altogether false. We are capable of abominations, but we are just as capable of tasteful building as Europeans. Witness the beautiful aerial tramway at Palm Springs, Calif., which carries visitors to the slopes of Mt. San Jacinto. Built in 1963, after 15 years of battle with purists, this tramway has taken 2.5 million people to a lovely area which before was a full day's arduous climb away.   16

Surprisingly, the litter problem is often least great in precisely those areas where access is provided to beautiful spots. The Palm Springs aerial tramway, for instance, and Glacier Point in Yosemite are remarkably free of litter despite heavy visitation. This, I think, is because people will not litter when they feel others are watching; and also because purchasing a ticket on a tramway gives one a proprietary interest in keeping the premises clean.   17

It is my firm belief that if Americans were permitted access to Wilderness areas in the manner I have suggested, we would soon create a generation of avid nature lovers. Americans would cease to be "alienated" from their landscape, and would mend their littering tendencies. If you question any purist or wilderness buff, you will find that what initially "turned him on," in almost every case, was an experience in which he was provided access to natural beauty—be it in Glacier Park, Yellowstone, Grand Canyon or Yosemite (as in my own case)—by roads, bus or other similar non-purist means. Yet, if purists had had the influence 100 years ago that they have today, there would be no roads or other facilities in Yosemite Valley, and   18 the strong probability is that neither I nor millions of other Americans would ever have seen its beauties, except on postcards.

I believe that the purist philosophy is unfair and undemocratic, and that 19 an alternate philosophy, one of enlightened, carefully controlled "access," is more desirable and also ecologically sound. If the Swiss can do it, why can't we?

By pulling together the information scattered throughout Julber's first seven paragraphs, we can describe the problem case as follows:

THE TYPICAL PROBLEM CASE OF THE PURISTS

Agent: The purists, 1 percent of Americans, the intellectual and financial elite of the nation
Action: have reserved 40 million acres of wilderness only for those willing to backpack into them
Goal: in order to preserve their beauty.
Result: As a result, 99 percent of Americans are restricted to 112,800 acres of secondary scenic areas.

The problem case of the purists is, for Julber, a typical case, one that recurs time and again in different places and different areas. But Julber also mentions *particular* problem cases, situations that occurred in specific times and places. In his second paragraph, for example, he refers to the passing of the Wilderness Act of 1964:

THE PARTICULAR PROBLEM CASE OF THE WILDERNESS ACT

Agent: The purists, 1 percent of Americans, the intellectual and financial elite of the nation
Action: passed the Wilderness Act of 1964, which prohibited the building of roads, mechanical transport, and structures in 40 million acres of wilderness
Goal: in order to preserve their beauty.
Result: As a result, 99 percent of Americans are restricted to 112,800 acres of secondary scenic areas.

Notice that our description of this particular problem case simply makes some of the aspects of Julber's typical problem case more specific.

Whether the problem cases that attract you to an issue are typical or particular, they will all exhibit some tension, which, as we said in Chapter 1, is a conflict between two or more aspects of a situation—it is the source of the discontent. You can usually locate the tension in a case by trying to insert the word "but" at the most appropriate point in a description. In our description of Julber's typical problem case, for example, we can easily insert "but" before the result of the purists' action:

THE TENSION IN A PROBLEM CASE

Agent: The purists, 1 percent of Americans, the intellectual and financial elite of the nation
Action: have reserved 40 million acres of wilderness only for those willing to backpack into them
Goal: in order to preserve their beauty.

   But

Result: As a result, 99 percent of Americans are restricted to 112,800 acres of secondary scenic areas.

    Once you have written a description of a problem case, you may be able to think of a real or hypothetical case that eliminates the tension pinpointed by this "but." In paragraphs 8 through 11, for example, Julber contrasts the purists' problematic approach to the wilderness issue with the approach taken by the Swiss:

A HYPOTHETICAL CASE TO ELIMINATE THE TENSION

Agent: The Swiss
Action: have built roads, trains, and tramways
Goal: in order to provide access to their scenic beauty.
Result: As a result, people from all over Europe come to admire the magnificent views.

    Our description of this case has no need for a "but" because the tension between the agent and result found in the purist problem case has disappeared. Instead of 1 percent imposing their actions and goals on 99 percent, Julber describes how the entire Swiss people are taking actions with beneficial results for all Europeans. In this way, Julber has used the case of the Swiss to indicate how Americans should resolve the tension in the problem case of the purists.

For Class 2.1

    Complete the exercises below, dealing with Julber's description of how he would use his access philosophy to improve the situation in two particular problem cases, the Muir Trail case and the Grand Canyon case (paragraphs 12 and 15).

1. Examine Julber's descriptions of the Muir Trail case and the Grand Canyon case as they are now, *before* the adoption of his access philosophy. Then return to the description of his typical problem case of the purists outlined in the discussion above. Rewrite the description of this typical case (agent, action, goal, result) so that it applies to each of these two particular cases.

Which aspects of the typical case did you have to change in order to describe the two particular cases? Which aspects remain the same in both the typical and particular cases?

2. Write a description of the Muir Trail and Grand Canyon cases as Julber believes they would be *after* the adoption of his access philosophy. Remember to include the agent, action, goal, and result in each of your descriptions.

3. Compare your descriptions of the Muir Trail and Grand Canyon cases *before* and *after* adoption of the access philosophy. What aspects of these two cases would be changed by Julber's philosophy? How would these changes eliminate or reduce the tension in Julber's typical problem case?

4. As a class, generate a list of as many other problem cases in the wilderness issue as you can. Draw on both your personal experience and your reading.

Generate a List of Key Words

Once you have described your initial set of problem cases, it is time to research what other authors have written about them. To find texts by these authors, you must work as a detective, following a trail of leads known as key words.

A *key word* is a term used by an editor to group or index texts on related topics. An initial list of key words is a set of your starting hunches concerning the topics under which you might find your issue discussed. As you conduct your research, you will discover that some of these hunches are good, some have to be discarded, and some new ones have to be added.

Your initial list of key words should include three sets of words. One set comes directly from your problem cases. Because these cases have often been the focus of considerable publishing activity, you can use the names of persons, places, and events as key words in your research. For example, Julber refers to the following problem cases in his article. Any of these could prove to be helpful key words in a library search on the wilderness issue:

KEY WORDS FROM PROBLEM CASES IN WILDERNESS

Muir Trail
Grand Canyon
Wilderness Act of 1964
Switzerland
Mt. San Jacinto/Palm Springs
Glacier Point in Yosemite

A second set of key words comes from the general topics under which your issue might be discussed. If you know little about your issue, your hunches concerning these topics may be fairly wild. But if you are starting with something you've read, you can use topics mentioned by the author. Julber, for example, mentions the following general topics that we can use as key words in our library search on wilderness:

KEY WORDS FROM GENERAL TOPICS ON WILDERNESS

wilderness	transportation
recreation	landscape
scenic areas	backpacking
natural beauty	littering
access	ecology

A good rule of thumb to remember about general topics is "The more the better." Try to generate as many synonyms as you can think of. If you are stuck, talk to people who know something about the issue and listen for the topics they mention.

A third set of key words to add to your list is the names of authors or groups of authors who may have written about your issue. List the names of people you've heard interviewed on the nightly news or quoted in a report on your issue. These people have often published on their own on the same issue and—since they are quoted by others—they probably represent major positions you should know about.

Of course, if you know little about your issue, you won't be able to include the names of authors on your initial list, but remember to add them later as you come across them in your reading. Also keep in mind that some reports are written by committees rather than single authors and are thus indexed by committee name. For instance, because Julber mentions the President's Outdoor Recreation Resources Review Commission (ORRRC), we would include the name of this committee on our list of key words for the wilderness issue.

For Your Notebook #2

1. Get your bearing on your issue by exploring problem cases. Label this section of your notebook "My Problem Cases."

   - In your notebook, write a description of each of the problem cases you believe are involved in the issue you've chosen.
   - For each description, include as much as you can about each aspect of the case. If you are not sure of any of these facts, speculate on the possibilities: Who might have been involved? What kinds of actions must have been taken? Remember your goal here is to dredge your memory and understanding as deeply as possible.
   - Following each description, write about what has drawn you to the case. What is the tension you perceive? Why are you less than content to see it continue or happen again? What would have to change to make you more satisfied?

2. Make a list of the key words that might be associated with your problem cases. Include the names of particular problem cases, general topics of discussion, and any authors you may have heard or read about. Label this section of your notebook "Possible Key Words."

ESTABLISH YOUR RESEARCH PRIORITIES

Once you have your bearings on an issue, you should search for other authors who have written on the issue before you. The positions taken by these authors, represented in a set of argumentative texts, establish what the concerns of your community are, what arguments have been made, and what evidence is accepted or in dispute. In response to these texts, you will eventually develop your own position. That is, against the background of their "conversation," you will endeavor to say something new.

A search for texts on your issue will inevitably take you to your university or local library. The texts housed there are basically of two kinds: books and periodicals. Books are extended works by a single author or group of authors, published in hard- and softcover in specific years or editions. Periodicals are collections of shorter pieces put together by an editor and issued at set intervals over a number of years.

The particular objects of your search are the argumentative texts that represent major positions on your issue. An **argumentative text** is one in which an author takes a position on an issue and tries to convince you to accept it. Sometimes an author or group of authors take an entire book to put forward a position. More often, they set forth their positions in single chapters of edited books or in individual articles published in periodicals.

In putting together a set of argumentative texts, you must be careful not to include texts that are merely informative. An informative text is one in which an author simply surveys what is currently known or believed about an issue. While these texts may be helpful in supplying key words or background information for your research, they do not present specific positions on the issue.

To see the difference between an argumentative and an informative text, consider what would happen if new research suggested that carrot soup was dangerous to your health. In such a situation, researchers would write texts on the "carrot soup issue." One might argue that carrot soup ought to be banned just like heroin. Another might claim that warning labels would be sufficient. These texts would be argumentative because they argue for specific positions the authors want you to accept and act on.

Other texts published on this issue, however, would simply inform readers of the controversy. A weekly news magazine, for example, would probably publish an article describing the positions taken by various researchers and possibly quoting one or two of them. This article would probably not, however, come out in favor of any of these positions, and thus it would not be argumentative.

As you are working on an issue, you will find informative texts helpful in suggesting major topics that have preoccupied your community. They may even mention the names of authors who have taken key positions. Add all of these to your key-word list, but keep in mind that, in themselves, informative texts don't represent positions you can respond to. They should not be included in your final set of argumentative texts.

Survey Your Resources

The books in your library are organized on the shelves (or *stacks*) according to topic and, within topic, according to author. Periodicals may be arranged in the same way or may be simply alphabetized according to the title of the periodical. In either case, each text in a library is assigned a unique call number that you must know in order to locate it.

The hub of your research activity is the reference area of your library. This area contains all of the resources you need to find texts on your issue in the library's stacks. This area also contains facilities for extending your search beyond your library's walls to other libraries in the area and around the country. At least four kinds of resources are available in this reference area: encyclopedias, indexes and abstracts, the card catalog, and—last but not least—the reference librarian.

Encyclopedias are sets of informative articles organized by topic and published in alphabetical order in multivolume sets. They range from the general encyclopedias you may have used in grade school to scholarly and specialized collections in specific areas such as the social sciences, education, and philosophy. For your purposes, the more scholarly and specialized encyclopedias are the most useful.

Entries located under key words in these encyclopedias will provide you with a broad overview of your issue. They usually survey the major arguments that have been made and will certainly suggest key words you can use in further searches. They may even provide you with a bibliography of the major works on your issue. Such a bibliography is a gold mine, because it provides you with citations to a core of important texts on your issue. With it you can concentrate on simply adding citations for the years since the most recent citation. Remember, however, that the entry itself is an informative text and should not be included in your final set of argumentative texts.

Indexes are bound lists of all the articles published in a group of periodicals during a particular time period. They are listed by topic, by author, or both. *Abstracts* are organized in a similar fashion but they also give you a one- or two-paragraph description of the text being indexed. Some abstracts also list books.

The editors of an index or abstract usually choose to include citations from periodicals that regularly publish in a particular field. For example, the editors of the *Public Affairs Information Service (PAIS)* choose to index periodicals that publish on public affairs. Similarly, the editors of the *Business Periodicals Index* select only periodicals that publish on business issues. Thus, in choosing which indexes and abstracts to consult, it is important to think about the range of special-interest groups in your issue. Many times, these special-interest groups take different perspectives and you will want to include all of them in your survey of major positions.

Special-interest groups interested in the wilderness issue, for example, publish in periodicals indexed in such areas as government, environment, business, law, and philosophy. A brief check in the library turned up at least nine indexes we could check:

INDEXES RELEVANT TO THE WILDERNESS ISSUE

Government Reports Index
Checklist of Official Publications of the State of New York
Environmental Protection Agency Reports: Bibliography Quarterly
Index to Legal Periodicals
Environmental Abstracts
Environmental Index
102 Monitor
Business Periodicals Index
Philosopher's Index

In your search, make sure to cover a range of indexes to avoid collecting an unbalanced set of positions. On the wilderness issue, for example, texts in the *Business Periodicals Index* would tell us very little about positions taken by ecologists. We would certainly want to counterbalance it with a look in the *Environmental Index*.

If you are unsure about the special-interest groups involved in your issue, you should check one of these major general indexes:

MAJOR INDEXES

A Reader's Guide to Periodical Literature (general interest)
New York Times Index (current events)
International Index (general scholarship)
Humanities Index
Social Sciences Index

Once you have located an index on the shelves, you will probably find that it consists of four paperback volumes a year, with a hardback volume issued at the end of each year. Some indexes now also distribute their volumes on microfiche.

To choose the right volume with which to begin a key-word search, start with the date when your issue began to attract attention and work your way forward to more recent dates. If you don't know much about your issue's time period, begin with the most recent year and work backward until you turn up citations. Whenever a particular key word seems to turn up a lot of citations, check it first when you turn to other volumes. Also, if you come across key words you hadn't thought of, add them to your list.

Card catalogs index the books in your library according to topic, title, and author. Use your key words to search by topic and by author. If the catalog cross-references other topics, make sure to add them to your list of key words. In your search, be on the lookout for two types of books. First, look for books by authors who make an extended argument on your issue. In the card catalog, these will be listed by topic and by the names of the authors. Second, look for edited books, which collect together a set of texts representing many different positions. In the card catalog, these will be listed by topic and by the names of the persons who put together or "edited" the collection.

The final resource available in the reference area of your library is the *reference librarian*. These librarians are trained to answer all of your questions concerning the location and use of the many services your library offers. Do not underestimate how helpful they are willing to be. They are the quickest guide to what is available in your library and where it can be found. Do not expect them, however, to think through your issue for you—only you can decide what you are looking for.

Record Citations

As you locate citations to texts on your issue, record the complete citation in your notebook, noting the title of the source providing the citation, the key word you used to find it, and the dates covered by the source.

A complete citation will include the following pieces of information:

INFORMATION FOR A COMPLETE CITATION

Author's name. Place the author's last name first. If the text has more than one author, include all of their names.

Title of the text. If the text is an entire book, underline it. If it is an article in a periodical or a chapter in a book, put it in quotation marks.

Title of the volume. If the text is an entire book, the title of the volume is the same and need not be repeated. But if the text is an article in a periodical or a chapter in a book, you must include the title of this volume separately. It should be underlined.

Editor's name. Edited volumes are always indexed by the name of the editor who put the collection together. If your text is a chapter in an edited collection, make sure to include the editor's name.

Publication Information. For books, the publication information includes place of publication, name of the publisher, and date of publication. For edited books, also include the page numbers of the text. For articles in periodicals, the publication information includes volume number, date of publication, and page numbers.

At this stage in your research, you will probably turn up many citations that you decide not to pursue. To save yourself time, you may want to photocopy especially long lists of these citations.

To save space, many indexes use abbreviations for the titles of the periodicals they index. Make sure you understand what these abbreviations stand for by looking them up, usually at the front of the yearly volume. Write them out in full even if you photocopy the citation itself.

For citations you find in the card catalog, make sure to record the call number of the volume so you can locate it later on in the stacks.

Classify Your Citations

If you have done a thorough job of surveying the resources in your library, you will probably end up with many more citations than you are willing or able to pursue. But don't make the mistake of rushing to the stacks to find the first five or ten citations you come across. Take the time to see the whole range of texts that have been published on your issue, and then carefully consider which of them to pursue.

In making a decision about a particular citation, try to determine three characteristics of the text being cited:

CHARACTERISTICS FOR CLASSIFYING CITATIONS

purpose
perspective
likelihood of providing further leads

The purpose of most texts written about issues is, as we have mentioned before, either argumentative or informative. You are looking, of course, for argumentative texts—although some good informative texts may be helpful at the start. The best clues to a text's purpose are the title of the volume in which it appears and the title of the text itself. Many periodicals specialize in one kind of text or the other; the title of such a periodical is often useful as a guide. The title of the text itself is also a useful clue. Some simply sound more informative or argumentative. Books are almost always argumentative in part or whole.

The perspective taken by a text refers to the special interests of its readers. For books, the best clue to perspective is the name of the publisher; publishers tend to specialize in one perspective or another. The Sierra Book Club, for example, publishes books for readers who are in favor of preservation. Academic Press publishes a wider range of opinion, but with a more scholarly tone. For periodicals, the best clue is provided by the title. You would expect, for example, that articles published in the *Oil and Gas Journal* would take a more conservative stand on preservation than the *Audubon Report*. At first, you will not recognize many of these clues, but with experience, you will be familiar with the publishers and periodicals that deal with your issue. Remember that your goal here is to select a range of perspectives to pursue.

The likelihood that a text will provide you with further leads is determined by the references it provides. Books and periodicals with bibliographies are almost always worth examining, especially at the beginning of your research. Even if the text itself is less than useful, its bibliography may make it worth pursuing. The presence of a bibliography is usually indicated in indexes and card catalogs by the abbreviation *bib.* or *bibl.*

For Class 2.2

The following citations on the wilderness issue were turned up in a search through the resources of our university library. In groups, review these citations for clues to their purpose, perspective, and likelihood of further leads. Place an asterisk in front of those you think would be worth pursuing.

Group A

1. Arthur, John. "Resource Acquisition and Harm." *Canadian Journal of Philosophy* 17 (1987): 337-347.
2. Kosloff, Laura H. "Water for Wilderness: Colorado Court Expands Federal Reserved Rights." *Environmental Law Reporter* 16 (1986): 10002-10007.
3. McQuade, W. "The Male Manager's Last Refuge." *Fortune* 112 (August 5, 1985): 38-42.
4. "Don't Call It 'the Barrens.'" *Audubon* 83 (July, 1981): 72+.
5. "The National Parks: A Plan for the Future." *National Parks* 55 (November-December, 1981): 10+.
6. "The End of American Wilderness." *Environmental Review* 9 (Fall, 1985): 197+.
7. United States Congress. House Committee on Interior and Insular Affairs. *Additions to the National Wilderness Preservation System,* Y 4.IN 8/14: 97-9, 1982.
8. Krutilla, John V., ed. *Natural Environments: Studies in Theoretical and Applied Analysis.* Baltimore: Johns Hopkins University Press, 1972.
9. Birch, Charles. *The Liberation of Life: From the Cell to the Community.* Cambridge: Cambridge University Press, 1981.
10. Shepard, Paul. *Nature and Madness.* San Francisco: Sierra Book Club. 1982.

Group B

1. Stanfield, Rochelle L. "Cowboys and Conservationists in Range War over Grazing Fees on Public Lands." *National Journal* 17 (1985): 1623-5.
2. Edelson, Stephen. "The Management of Oil and Gas Leasing on Federal Wilderness Lands." *Boston College Environmental Affairs Law Review* 10 (1983): 905-61.

3. "Countryside: Tomorrow Is Too Late." *Economist* 297 (October 26, 1985): 70.
4. "If the Sagebrush Rebel Wins, Everybody Loses." *Living Wilderness* 45 (Summer, 1981): 30+.
5. "Wildcatting vs. Wilderness." *Defenders* 57 (February, 1982): 30+.
6. "The Fight to Save Wild Alaska." *Audubon Report,* 1982.
7. Berglund, Berndt. *Wilderness Survival: A Complete Handbook and Guide.* New York: Scribner, 1972.
8. Schwartz, William, ed. *Voices for the Wilderness.* New York: Ballantine, 1969.
9. Gutkind, Erwin Anton. *Community and Environment: A Discourse on Social Ecology.* London: Watts, 1953.
10. Harrison, James D. *An Annotated Bibliography on Environmental Perception with Emphasis.* Monticello: Council of Planning Libraries, 1969.

Group C

1. Carroll, James R. "The California Wilderness Bill: A Tree-by-tree Compromise for 1.8 Million Acres." Map. *California Journal* 15 (1984): 492-4.
2. "BLM Seeks Comments on Lockup Plan in Utah." *Oil and Gas Journal* 84 (April 28, 1986): 44+.
3. "Establishing Backcountry Quotas: An Example from Mineral King." *California Environmental Management* 5 (July, 1981): 335+.
4. "Wildlife Preservation Encouraged by New Jersey, Pennsylvania Utilities." *Public Utilities Fortnightly* 116 (December 12, 1985): 61-2.
5. "A History of the Nature Conservancy." *Nature Conservancy News* 31 (July-August, 1981): 4+.
6. "Environmental Ethics and Nonhuman Rights." *Environmental Ethics* 4 (Spring, 1982): 17+.
7. "Battle over Bighorn." *Defenders* 57 (August, 1982): 2+.
8. Terrie, Phillip G. *Forever Wild: Environmental Aesthetics and the Adirondack Forest.* Philadelphia: Temple University Press, 1985.
9. Cragg, J. B., ed. *Advances in Ecological Research.* Volumes 1-17. New York: Academic Press, 1962-.
10. Nash, Roderick, comp. *Environment and Americans: The Problem of Priorities.* New York: Holt, Rinehart and Winston, 1972.

Group D

1. Goldman-Carter, Janice. "Federal Conservation of Threatened Species: By Administrative Discretion or by Legislative Standard?" *Boston College Environmental Affairs Law Review* 11 (1983): 63-104.
2. "Make Way for the Grizzly." *Economist* 299 (June 7, 1986): 34.
3. Gannes, S. "Improving on Nature." *Fortune* 112 (October 28, 1985): 173+.
4. "Predicting Costs of Eastern National Forest Wilderness." *Journal of Leisure Research* 13 (1981): 112+.
5. "Plan to Speed Forest Cutting Is Criticized." *Wall Street Journal* (June 29, 1982): 29.
6. "Privatization: An Idea Whose Time Must Wait." *American Forests* 88 (September, 1982): 36+.
7. Frome, Michael. *Battle for the Wilderness.* New York: Praeger, 1974.

8. United States Congress. Senate Committee on Energy and Natural Resources. *Additions to the Wild and Scenic River System.*, Y 4.En 2: 5.hrg: 99-980, 1987.
9. Maldonado, Tomas. *Design, Nature, and Revolution: Toward a Critical Ecology.* New York: Harper and Row, 1972.
10. Still, Henry. *Man: The Next 30 Years.* New York: Hawthorn Books, 1968.

For Your Notebook #3

Establish research priorities for your issue:

- Using the key words you generated in your last notebook exercise (#2), survey the resources in your library. For each profitable lead you come across, start a new page in your notebook by recording the title of the resource, the key word you used to find this lead, and, if appropriate, the dates covered by the resource.
- Record the citations given by each lead, making sure to get the complete citation. Look up any abbreviation you don't understand. If a bibliography is noted, make a note by the citation.
- Rather than copying by hand, you may wish to tape or paste a photocopy of the citations into your notebook. Make sure, however, that you know how to read the abbreviations.
- Classify each of your citations by noting its purpose, perspective, and likelihood of further leads. Mark with an asterisk those you want to pursue.

LOCATE AND EVALUATE YOUR SOURCES

Imagine your work so far as a scouting expedition through the territory of your issue. Think of the next phase as the chase. The work of locating and evaluating your sources is strenuous and time-consuming, so you should plan to spread it out over several trips to the library.

Create a Working Bibliography

You begin the task of locating and evaluating sources with the creation of a set of bibliographic notecards. Traditionally, these have been 3 × 5 cards, which can easily be separated and rearranged. Newer database technology also allows you to store and reorder this information by computer. Choose the format that works best for you in terms of convenience and the resources available in your library.

A set of bibliographic notecards provides you with a working bibliography for your search through the library. Each card should contain space for five kinds of information added in different phases of this search:

CONTENTS OF A BIBLIOGRAPHIC NOTECARD

Full citation
Name of the resource that provided you with the citation

Call number of the volume
Status of the text in your library's collection
Your evaluation of the text

Construct your set of bibliographic notecards from the lists of citations you created in the reference area. Use a separate notecard for each text you have decided to pursue.

Locate Your Sources

Separate your bibliographic notecards into two sets, one for citations to books, the other for citations to periodicals.

Arrange your book notecards alphabetically by author and take them back to the card catalog. Look up each volume and record the call number. If the volume is not listed, mark the notecard "Not in collection" and set it aside.

Arrange your periodical notecards alphabetically according to the first main word of the periodical titles. Look them up in your library's list of journal holdings, usually found near the reference librarian. If your library arranges periodicals by call number, record the call number on the notecard. If they are shelved by title, simply write "In the collection" on the notecard of each one you find.

Make sure the volume you want is actually in the collection. Occasionally, you will find only later or earlier volumes. If the volume you need is not listed, mark the notecard "Not in collection" and set it aside.

Finally, take all the cards for volumes in the collection and rearrange them by call number. Pull these volumes from the stacks one armful at a time. Mark the card of any volume you cannot find as "Not found" and set it aside. If your library has closed stacks, fill out requests for these volumes to be brought to you.

Evaluate Your Sources

As you pull each armful of volumes from the stacks, sit down and evaluate the usefulness of the texts they contain. For books containing an extended argument, scan through the table of contents, the preface, and the closing chapter. For edited volumes, scan the preface, table of contents, and several interesting chapters. For periodicals, scan the abstract and the introductory and concluding paragraphs.

For each text, ask yourself the following questions:

QUESTIONS FOR EVALUATING A REFERENCE

- Does the author discuss my issue or was my citation misleading?
- Does the author take a position on my issue or does the text simply inform?

- Does the author cover important topics in my issue or does the text seem obscure?
- Does the author represent a significant new perspective on my issue or do I already have a better representative?
- Does the author mention problem cases that concern me or does the text deal with situations I am not considering?
- Is the author an authority on the issue or is the text a superficial treatment?
- Does the author provide a useful bibliography or is the text undocumented?
- Was the text published in an important time period for my issue or does it predate crucial developments?

On the basis of your answers, decide whether or not to keep the text. Mark "To be read" on the notecards of those you decide are worth reading. Make a photocopy of chapters and articles and immediately transfer the citation information to the first page. Check out book-length texts.

If you decide not to keep a text, write a short description of its contents on the bibliographic notecard, mark the card "Not clearly relevant," and return the volume for reshelving. Keep these notecards in case you want to relocate the texts later.

Extend Your Reach

Volumes not included in your library's collection can often be obtained from other libraries using interlibrary loan or reciprocal borrowing privileges. Generally speaking, if you request a text through interlibrary loan, it will be delivered in seven to ten days. If you have reciprocal borrowing privileges, you may be able to get a text more quickly by going directly to another library in the area. Ask your reference librarian about the best way to obtain a text not in your collection.

Volumes listed in your library's collection but not on the shelves may be either on loan or lost. Check their status at the circulation desk. If they are on loan, you can ask that they be recalled. If they appear to be lost, you can ask the librarian to initiate a search.

For Class 2.3

With a group of classmates, locate and evaluate the texts given in one of the following working bibliographies on wilderness.

1. Create bibliographic notecards for each of the citations and check their availability in your library using the card catalog and journal listings.
2. Locate the volumes on the shelves. Check at circulation concerning any that are missing. For those not listed in the collection, fill out interlibrary loan requests.

3. Evaluate your finds. Photocopy or check out what you judge to be the most useful of these texts and be prepared to explain your choice to the rest of the class.

Working Bibliography A

1. Hargrove, Eugene C. "Foundations of Wildlife Protection Attitudes." *Inquiry* 30 (1987): 3-31.
2. Evernden, Lorne Leslie Neil. *The Natural Alien: Humankind and Environment.* Toronto: University of Toronto Press, 1985.
3. Carlstein, Tommy. *Time Resources, Society, and Ecology: On the Capacity for Human Interaction in Space and Time.* Boston: Allen and Unwin, 1982.
4. Calder, Nigel. *Eden Was No Garden: An Inquiry into the Environment of Man.* New York: Holt, Rinehart and Winston, 1967.
5. Wilderness Conference. *Wilderness and the Quality of Life.* Proceedings of the 10th annual conference. San Francisco: 1969.
6. Sprigge, T. L. S. "Are There Intrinsic Values in Nature?" *Journal of Applied Philosophy* 4 (1987): 21-28.
7. Runge, Carlisle Ford. "Energy Exploration on Wilderness: 'Privatization' and Public Lands Management." Bibl. *Land Economics* 60 (1984): 56-68.
8. "After the Lands Act: Timber and Mining Industries Voice Mixed Reactions." *Alaska Construction and Oil* 22 (September, 1981): 26 + .
9. "Wilderness: Lusting After the Last Acre." *Progressive* 46 (March, 1982): 30 + .
10. Elliot, Robert, and Arran Gore. *Environmental Philosophy: A Collection of Readings.* University Park: Pennsylvania State University Press, 1983.

Working Bibliography B

1. Clark, Stephen R. L. "Animals, Ecosystems, and the Liberal Ethic." *Monist* 70 (1987): 114-133.
2. Brooker, Richard. *Environmental Economy.* New York: Methuen, Inc., 1986.
3. Rolston, Holmes. *Philosophy Gone Wild: Essays in Environmental Ethics.* Buffalo: Prometheus Books, 1986.
4. Taylor, Gordon Rattray. *The Doomsday Book: Can the World Survive?* New York: World Publishing Company, 1970.
5. United States Congress. House Committee on Interior and Insular Affairs. *Federal Coal Leasing Policy and the Bisti Badlands Wilderness Property.* Y 4.In 8/14:98-12, 1984.
6. Harmon, David. "Cultural Diversity, Human Subsistence, and the National Park Ideal." *Environmental Ethics* 9 (1987): 147-158.
7. Austin, P. "Are Paper Companies Destroying the Maine Woods?" *Business and Society Review* 58 (Fall, 1986): 20-4.
8. "California vs. Berland: a Precarious Victory for Wilderness Preservation." *Columbia Journal of Environmental Law* 7 (1982): 179 + .
9. "Substitutability, Reversibility, and the Development-Conservation Quandary." *Journal of Environmental Management* 15 (July, 1982): 79 + .
10. Barbour, Ian G., ed. *Earth Might Be Fair: Reflections on Ethics, Religion, and Ecology.* Englewood Cliffs, N.J.: Prentice Hall, 1972.

Working Bibliography C

1. Dooley, Patrick K. "The Ambiguity of Environmental Ethics: Duty or Heroism." *Philosophy Today* 30 (1986): 48-57.
2. Attfield, Robin. *The Ethics of Environmental Concern.* Oxford: Basil Blackwell, 1983.
3. Ehrlich, Paul R., and Anne Ehrlich. *Extinction: The Causes and Consequences of the Disappearance of Species.* New York: Random House, 1981.
4. Hardin, Garrett James. *The Limits of Altruism: An Ecologist's View of Survival.* Bloomington: Indiana University Press, 1977.
5. Davis, Joseph A. "Millions of Acres in 20 States Win Wilderness Protection: Most Action Since 1964." Table. *Congressional Quarterly Weekly Report* 42 (1984): 2667-9.
6. Leepson, Marc. "Protecting the Wilderness." Bib. *Editorial Research Reports* (1984): 591-608.
7. "Industry Must Defeat Either-Or Syndrome to Gain Access to ANWR." *Oil and Gas Journal* 85 (December 1, 1986): 32-3.
8. "Yellowstone: The Incredible Shrinking Wilderness." *National Parks* 32 (January-February, 1982): 20+.
9. Farney, Dennis, and Robert E. Taylor. "Western Conflict: Federal Land Agency Is Tugged Two Ways in Wilderness Battle; BLM Is Caught in the Middle between Conservationists, Partisans of Development." Map. *Wall Street Journal* 207 (April 24, 1986): 1+.
10. Worster, Donald. *Nature's Economy: A History of Ecological Ideas.* Cambridge: Cambridge University Press, 1985.

Working Bibliography D

1. Adams, J. R. "The Curse of a Splendid View." *Forbes* 138 (December 1, 1986): 182+.
2. Lyle, John Tillman. *Design for Human Ecosystems: Landscape, Land Use, and Natural Resources.* New York: Van Nostrand Reinhold, 1985.
3. Hardin, Garrett James. *Exploring New Ethics for Survival: The Voyage of the Spaceship Beagle.* New York: Viking, 1972.
4. Nash, Roderick. *Wilderness and the American Mind.* New Haven: Yale University Press, 1967.
5. "Marching Backwards: The Department of Interior Under James G. Watt." *National Wildlife Federation Report.* April 29, 1982.
6. Blumm, Michael C. "Beyond Mitigation: Restoring Federally Damaged Salmon Runs under the Columbia Basin Fish and Wildlife Program." *Environmental Law Reporter* 14 (1984): 10011-16.
7. "The Future Development of Canada's North: A Legal and Political Perspective." *Alternatives* 10 (Spring-Summer, 1981): 43+.
8. "Oil and Gas Leasing in Wilderness—What the Conflict Is All About." *Sierra Club Bulletin* 67 (May-June, 1982): 28+.
9. Passmore, John. "Nature, Intellect and Culture." In *Philosophy and Culture.* Ed. Venant Couchy. Montreal: Editions Du Beffroi, 1986.
10. Dasmann, Raymond Fredric. *Environmental Conservation.* New York: Wiley, 1972.

For Your Notebook #4

Locate and evaluate sources for your issue:

- Create a set of bibliographic notecards for the references you asterisked in your last working session (#3). Separate them into books and periodicals.
- Check the availability of these references in your library's collection.
- Locate the volumes that should be in the collection.
- Evaluate the texts you have gathered.
- Evaluate the importance of your references not in the collection. Extend your reach to find those you decide are important to pursue.

PART TWO
SUMMARIZE

▞ 3 READ
AND MARK
THE TEXT

If you have selected argumentative texts on your issue carefully, each will represent a distinct position to which you may eventually want to respond as an author. When you read these texts, you must pay attention to two things in order to understand them: (1) What is the author saying? (2) Why is the author saying it?

To give this kind of attention to a text, you inevitably need to read through it at least twice. First you read to get an overall sense of the direction of the argument. Then you return to reread and make notes in the margin of your photocopies. Occasionally, your first reading of a text will show you that it's not what you expected—slightly off the issue or repetitive of a position you have already considered. In this case, you may decide not to reread it. In all other cases, however, leave enough time for both a first and second reading as described below.

READ FOR A SENSE OF DIRECTION

The goal of your first reading is to establish an overall sense of the direction of an author's argument. What is this author trying to get you to accept and act upon? What are the points the author is trying to make?

Points are statements of belief about the world that an author presents as true but that other authors might contest. An argumentative text can be looked at as a series of points laid out to get you from where you currently are to where the author wants you to be. In your first reading, you try to follow the line formed by these points.

Because authors don't want to lose you as a reader, they provide help in two ways. First, they often use *headings,* as we do in this book. Headings serve as roadsigns pointing to major points in the author's argument. Thus, you can use them to follow changes in the author's line of argument. In William Tucker's essay "Is Nature Too Good for Us?" (page 50), for example, Tucker has broken his text into ten sections, three of which have headings:

HEADINGS FROM TUCKER'S TEXT

Impossible Paradises
That Frontier Spirit
Not Entirely Nature

While these headings may not mean much before you read Tucker's essay, they are a good check of your understanding afterward. Once you have finished reading the essay, you should be able to paraphrase the points that Tucker makes about "impossible paradises," the "frontier spirit" and something that is "not entirely nature."

Not all authors divide their texts into sections using headings, but all do make use of a second aid for readers—*transitions*. Transitions are words or phrases that connect points in a text by indicating the relationship between what has gone before and what is to come. Different kinds of transitions mark different kinds of connections. When you encounter a transition, you must do some work to figure out what points the author is trying to connect. Authors can connect the current point to the immediately preceding point, to a point some distance back, or even to a point never stated directly in the text. The only way to decide is to think through the ideas: What connection seems to be the most likely given the author's direction so far?

In addition to identifying the points the author is trying to connect, you must also identify the nature of the connection. Some of the more common transitions appear in the following list, along with the connections they indicate:

COMMON TRANSITIONS

- *contrast:* on the other hand, but, even though, yet, despite, though, nevertheless, however, counter to, in contrast
- *addition:* also, in addition, and, as well, furthermore
- *example:* for instance, for example, illustrated by, one of
- *equivalence:* in other words, the same, once again
- *emphasis or unexpectedness:* even, still
- *cause or result:* thus, then, hence, because, as a result
- *comparative quality or quantity:* most, least
- *part-whole:* in part, largely, mainly
- *time order:* then, now, after, along with, at the same time as
- *dependency:* only after, since
- *reason:* naturally, at bottom, because
- *representativeness:* most notably, tellingly, indicative
- *truth content:* it may seem, it may appear, actually, really, ultimately
- *replacement:* instead, rather than, not simply

Transitions mark major signposts, intersections, and changes of direction in an author's argument; they serve as reminders of the route you're following. But keep in mind that every point in a well-formed argument is connected to the others—whether the connection is marked explicitly by a transition or not. Generally, authors will assume you can infer the appropriate connections between most points without transitions. If you can't see how the current point is connected to what you have read so far, backtrack to the last point you understood and try to go forward again. If that doesn't work, put a question mark in the margin. Often, your further reading will clarify the point.

As an example, in the opening section of "Is Nature Too Good for Us?" Tucker marks a few connections explicitly with transitions and leaves the rest implicit for us to figure out for ourselves. In the right-hand margin, we have indicated some of the connections we see:

CONNECTIONS IN TUCKER'S OPENING SECTION

Probably nothing has been more central to the environmental movement than the concept of wilderness. "In wildness is the preservation of the world," wrote Thoreau, and environmental writers and speakers have intoned his message repeatedly. Wilderness, in the environmental pantheon, represents a particular kind of sanctuary in which all true values—that is, all nonhuman values—are reposited. Wildernesses are often described as "temples," "churches," and "sacred ground"—refuges for the proposed "new religion" based on environmental consciousness. Carrying the religious metaphor to the extreme, one of the most famous essays of the environmental era holds the Judeo-Christian religion responsible for "ecological crisis."   *equivalence*   1

The wilderness issue also has a political edge. Since 1964, long-standing preservation groups like the Wilderness Society and the Sierra Club have been pressuring conservation agencies like the National Forest Service and the Bureau of Land Management to put large tracts of their holdings into permanent "wilderness designations," countering the "multiple use" concept that was one of the cornerstones of the Conservation Era of the early 1900s.   *addition*   2

Preservation and conservation groups have been at odds since the end of the last century, and the rift between them has been a major controversy of environmentalism. The leaders of the Conservation Movement—most notably Theodore Roosevelt, Gifford Pinchot, and John Wesley Powell—called for rational, efficient development of land and other natural resources: multiple use, or reconciling competing uses of land, and also "highest use," or forfeiting   *example*   3

addition

more immediate profits from land development for more lasting gains. Preservationists, <u>on the other hand</u>, the follow-   contrast
ers of California woodsman John Muir, have advocated protecting land in its natural state, setting aside tracts and keeping them inviolate. "Wilderness area" battles have become one of the hottest political issues of the day, especially in western states—the current "Sage-brush Revolt" comes to mind—where large quantities of potentially commercially usable land are at stake.

For Class 3.1

On pages 63–72 you will find Roderick Nash's essay "The Irony of Victory," originally published as the concluding chapter of his <u>Wilderness and the American Mind</u> (New Haven: Yale University Press, 1979). Do a first reading of the essay. As you read, take one of the sections of the essay (marked by lines in the text) and do the following:

1. For each of the transitions underlined in the text, write out the two points being connected and state the relationship between them.
2. Find five pairs of sentences that are not connected by transitions. Write them out and state what you think the author intended to be the connection between them.
3. Write a heading for your section that describes the point made by that section.

In class, compare your results section by section. Then discuss what you think is the general direction of Nash's argument. What does he want you, his readers, to accept and act upon?

For Your Notebook #5

Read through each of the argumentative texts that you have photocopied in your previous working sessions to establish an overall sense of direction for the arguments.

- Pay attention to the headings and transitions.
- Try to see the connections between the points the author is making.
- Put a question mark in the margin of any point or connection you cannot understand.

REREAD AND MARK THE TEXT

The goal of your second reading of an argumentative text is to deepen your understanding of the function and meaning of the points an author makes. To this end, you will mark each text in the way we've marked the first paragraph of Tucker's essay below. These markings include:

MARKINGS FOR A SECOND READING

1. labels for the sources
2. lines dividing topics
3. labels for topics
4. classifications of points
5. annotations for points

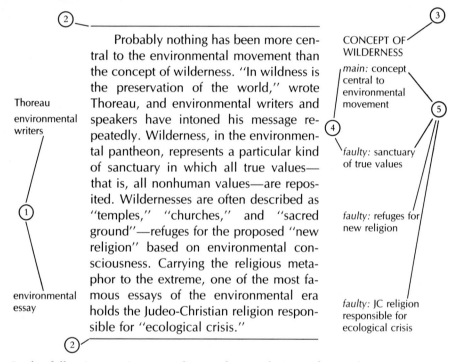

In the following sections, we discuss these techniques for marking.

Label Sources

Argumentative texts usually include two types of points: points made by the authors themselves and points made by other people and cited in the text. You can tell a lot about what authors take to be their community by the sources they cite. These sources are people to whom the author wants to respond. Sometimes this response is an agreement—the author quotes or paraphrases someone who supports his or her line of argument. More often, this response is a disagreement—the author characterizes a position which he or she wants you to reject.

The key to recognizing an author's use of sources is recognizing when the author is attributing an idea or action to someone else. For example, in the opening paragraph of his essay, Tucker attributes points to Thoreau (a specific author), to "environmental writers and speakers" (a group of authors), and to "one of the most famous essays of the environmental era" (an essay by a specific but unnamed author). All three of these serve as sources for Tucker.

LABELING TUCKER'S SOURCES

Thoreau

environ-

mentalists

Probably nothing has been more central to the environmental movement than the concept of wilderness. "In wilderness is the preservation of the world," wrote Thoreau, and environmental writers and speakers have intoned his message repeatedly. Wilderness, in the environmental pantheon, represents a particular kind of sanctuary in which all true values—that is, all nonhuman values—are reposited. Wildernesses are often described as "temples," "churches," and "sacred ground"—refuges for the proposed "new religion" based on environmental consciousness. Carrying the religious metaphor to the extreme, one of the most famous essays of the environmental era holds the Judeo-Christian religion responsible for "ecological crisis."

famous essay

To figure out who's included in an author's community, skim through the text and label the sources in the left-hand margin of the text as we have done above.

Cluster Points by Topic

While you can read nearly every sentence in an argumentative text as a separate point, authors generally divide their points into several sections, each addressed to a separate topic. The next step in marking an author's text is to identify these topics and mark these sections.

As discussed in Chapter 1, a topic is anything which can be talked about—an event, a belief, a person, a thing, a concept. If you imagine an argumentative text as a set of headphones through which you listen to a community's discussion, topics are the things you hear being talked about. As in any normal discussion, you may find several different points made about a single topic. Some of these may be the author's own points. Others may be the points of other people. Generally speaking, you can think of an argumentative text as a series of points clustered around a small set of topics.

To mark the topics in a text, draw lines to divide the points into clusters and insert labels for their topics in the right-hand margin. In the opening section of Tucker's essay, for example, we found three clusters of points centered around "the concept of wilderness," "the political edge of the wilderness movement," and "preservation versus conservation." As shown below, we have divided the text into these three clusters and inserted the labels in the right-hand margin.

Probably nothing has been more central to the environ-   concept of   1
mental movement than the concept of wilderness. "In wil-   wilderness
derness is the preservation of the world," wrote Thoreau,
and environmental writers and speakers have intoned his
message repeatedly. Wilderness, in the environmental pantheon, represents a particular kind of sanctuary in which all
true values—that is, all nonhuman values—are reposited.
Wildernesses are often described as "temples," "churches,"
and "sacred ground"—refuges for the proposed "new religion" based on environmental consciousness. Carrying the
religious metaphor to the extreme, one of the most famous
essays of the environmental era holds the Judeo-Christian religion responsible for "ecological crisis."

The wilderness issue also has a political edge. Since   political edge   2
1964, long-standing preservation groups like the Wilderness
Society and the Sierra Club have been pressuring conservation agencies like the National Forest Service and the Bureau
of Land Management to put large tracts of their holdings
into permanent "wilderness designations," countering the
"multiple use" concept that was one of the cornerstones of
the Conservation Era of the early 1900s.

Preservation and conservation groups have been at odds   preservation vs.   3
since the end of the last century, and the rift between them   conservation
has been a major controversy of environmentalism. The
leaders of the Conservation Movement—most notably
Theodore Roosevelt, Gifford Pinchot, and John Wesley
Powell—called for rational, efficient development of land
and other natural resources: multiple use, or reconciling
competing uses of land, and also "highest use," or forfeiting
more immediate profits from land development for more
lasting gains. Preservationists, on the other hand, the followers of California woodsman John Muir, have advocated
protecting land in its natural state, setting aside tracts and
keeping them inviolate. "Wilderness area" battles have become one of the hottest political issues of the day, especially
in western states—the current "Sagebrush Revolt" comes to
mind—where large quantities of potentially commercially
usable land are at stake.

For Class 3.2

Return to Nash's essay (page 63) and label the topics discussed in each of the sections. Put these labels in the right-hand margin.

Compare your labels with those of your classmates. Did you all "hear" the same discussion in Nash's text?

Classify the Points

As already mentioned, each topic in an argumentative text represents a cluster of discussion on an issue. And, as you might expect, the way this discussion is presented is colored by the author's particular perspective on the issue. That is, authors don't simply report on what they believe and what other people in the community believe. Rather they want to convince you to accept some beliefs and reject others.

Seeing the difference between these kinds of points is crucial to your success in reading an argumentative text. In order to ensure this success, you will find it helpful to think of the organization of an author's argument as a structure that includes three kinds of points:

THE MAIN PATH/FAULTY PATH STRUCTURE

1. points lying along the **main path** of the argument—points that the author wants you to accept and act on.
2. points lying on **faulty paths**—points that the author wants to make sure you avoid or reject.
3. points lying on **return paths**—points that the author provides as reasons for rejecting the points on faulty paths.

To understand the direction of an author's line of argument, you must, above all, distinguish among points lying on these three different kinds of paths. This basic three-part structure can be visualized as shown below:

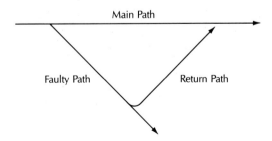

As part of your second reading of an argumentative text, insert labels for the paths in the right-hand margin for each major point you find. Work topic area by topic area. Ideally, each topic area will contain at least one point lying on the main path, one or more points lying on faulty paths, and at least as many points lying on return paths. This pattern will vary, of course, but you can use some of the many clues authors give concerning their attitudes toward points as a guide. Some of these clues are discussed in the sections below.

Identifying the Main Path   The most common way for authors to identify points lying on the main path of their argument is the directness with which these points are stated. Points that authors present directly as facts, without comment, usually lie on the main path. In Tucker's second paragraph, for example, he makes the following point directly and without comment:

POINT PRESENTED DIRECTLY

> Preservation and conservation groups have been at odds since the end of the last century.

The directness of his point suggests it lies on Tucker's main path. It is an important one he wants his readers to accept and act on.

Occasionally authors go out of their way to give you stronger clues concerning their identification with a particular point. Such phrases as "I believe" or "we must" posit a strong self-identification with a point. These points invariably lie along the main path of the argument and are usually quite significant. Tucker, for example, closes his essay with the following statement:

POINT PRESENTED WITH SELF-IDENTIFICATION

> <u>We</u> must recognize the part we play in nature—that the "land is <u>ours.</u>"

This self-identification leaves little doubt that this point lies on the main path of Tucker's argument.

A third clue that a point lies on the main path of an author's argument is an author's approval or praise. If an author describes a position in glowing terms, you can be sure that it is on the main path. Here, for example, is how Tucker describes the policy of stewardship in his final paragraph:

POINT PRESENTED WITH APPROVAL

> That is the <u>legitimate</u> doctrine of *stewardship* of the land.

Approval is a powerful signal of an author's attitude toward a point. It can even overcome the normal suspicion attached to a point attributed to someone else. If, at the same time the point is attributed, it is also approved, the overall effect is to place the point on the main path. Thus, for example, Tucker approves of the policies of "multiple use" and "highest use" at the same time he attributes them to the conservationists:

POINTS ATTRIBUTED AND APPROVED

> The leaders of the Conservation Movement—most notably Theodore Roosevelt, Gifford Pinchot, and John Wesley Powell—called for rational, efficient development of land and other natural resources: multiple use, or reconciling competing uses of land, and also "highest use"—forfeiting more immediate profits from land development for more lasting gains.

A final clue that an author is placing a point on the main path is the use of a *problem/solution framework.* Whenever authors describe a point in such terms as "the essential problem," or "the real solution," they are signaling that it lies on their main path. It is something they want you to accept and act on. A deft example of this technique occurs toward the end of Tucker's essay:

POINTS PRESENTED IN A PROBLEM/SOLUTION FRAMEWORK

> It is this undeniable paradox that forms the real problem of setting up "wilderness." Only when we have created a society that gives us the leisure to appreciate it can we go out and experience what we imagine to be untrammeled nature. Yet if we lock up too much of our land in these reserves, we are cutting into our resources and endangering the very leisure that allows us to enjoy nature.
>
> The answer is, of course, that we cannot simply let nature "take over" and assume that because we have kept roads and people out of huge tracts of land, then we have absolved ourselves of a national guilt. The concept of stewardship means taking responsibility, not simply letting nature take its course.

As this passage indicates, authors usually combine several clues to indicate their attitude toward a point. In addition to the problem/solution framework, Tucker also uses approval ("undeniable"), self-identification ("we cannot"), and direct presentation ("stewardship means taking responsibility").

Identifying Faulty Paths   Points that lie along faulty paths in an author's argument would lead you off the author's main path if you accepted them. These are the points the author wants you to reject or avoid.

You might wonder why authors bring up faulty paths. After all, you might think, aren't they just calling my attention to counterarguments that I might not have thought of? Wouldn't I be more convinced, more likely to accept their points, if they never mentioned their alternative positions at all?

The key to understanding why authors bring up points on faulty paths lies in the nature of belief and action. Suppose you had to give someone directions to your house. You've done this many times before, and you know the best—the main—path to get to your street. But you also know that, at an important intersection, many people get confused and take the wrong turn.

What do you do? Do you give your friends directions that describe only the main path you want them to take? Or do you include something about the faulty path you want them to avoid? If you're like most people, you will include both types of information:

DIRECTIONS INCLUDING BOTH MAIN AND FAULTY PATHS

"When you get to the intersection of Murray and Forward, you'll see two streets going off to the right, one sharply, the other more gently. The gentle right puts you on the freeway downtown. You don't want to go that way. Instead take the sharp right. That'll bring you to my house."

In a similar manner, authors who want to make sure you stay on their main path through an issue take the time to describe faulty paths that may distract or mislead you. By warning you about these potential wrong turns, they try to ensure that you will not be misled.

The clues for faulty paths are the opposite of those for main paths: fault-finding, attribution, unrequired quotation, and parody. *Faultfinding*, the opposite of approval, is probably the most obvious clue. We can have little doubt of Tucker's perspective, for example, in the following passage when he uses several terms to find fault with the preservationists' position:

POINT PRESENTED WITH FAULTFINDING

It seems to me that the wilderness ethic has actually represented an attempt psychologically to reopen the American frontier. We have been desperate to maintain belief in unlimited, uncharted vistas within our borders, a preoccupation that has eclipsed the permanent shrinking of the rest of the world outside. Why else would it be so necessary to preserve such huge tracts of "roadless territory" simply because they are now roadless, regardless of their scenic, recreational, or aesthetic values? The environmental movement, among other things, has been a rather backward-looking effort to recapture America's lost innocence.

A more subtle sign that a point lies on a faulty path is the use of *author attribution*. We have already seen a masterly example in Tucker's opening paragraph:

POINT PRESENTED WITH AUTHOR ATTRIBUTION

Probably nothing has been more central to the environmental movement than the concept of wilderness. "In wilderness is the preservation of the world," wrote <u>Thoreau</u>, and <u>environmental writers and speakers have intoned his message repeatedly.</u> Wilderness, in the environmental pantheon, represents a particular kind of sanctuary in which all true values—that is, all nonhuman values—are reposited. Wildernesses are often described as "temples," "churches," and "sacred ground"—refuges for the proposed "new religion" based on environmental consciousness. Carrying the religious metaphor to the extreme, <u>one of the most famous essays of the environmental era</u> holds the Judeo-Christian religion responsible for "ecological crisis."

This kind of attribution is one of the most common ways authors have to introduce distance between themselves and a point. If you see an author attribution, you should suspect the point is on a faulty path unless other clues, such as praise, suggest a greater identification.

In addition to author attribution, authors also use unrequired quotation to introduce distance from a point. *Unrequired quotation* is the use of quotation marks around words or phrases that are not directly attributable to a particular author. These phrases have entered into common use and need not be quoted to show that they are another author's words. When authors nevertheless put them inside quotation marks, they are suggesting that the quoted material is somehow suspect. Tucker uses this technique to cast doubt on the environmentalists' position:

POINT PRESENTED WITH UNREQUIRED QUOTATION

Probably nothing has been more central to the environmental movement than the concept of wilderness. "In wilderness is the preservation of the world," wrote Thoreau, and environmental writers and speakers have intoned his message repeatedly. Wilderness, in the environmental pantheon, represents a particular kind of sanctuary in which all true values—that is, all nonhuman values—are reposited. Wildernesses are often described as <u>"temples," "churches,"</u> and <u>"sacred ground"</u>—refuges for the proposed <u>"new religion"</u> based on environmental consciousness. Carrying the religious metaphor to the extreme, one of the most famous essays of the environmental era holds the Judeo-Christian religion responsible for <u>"ecological crisis."</u>

None of these terms are attributable to a specific author; thus they need not be quoted. The effect of the quotation marks is to create distance between them and Tucker, to suggest that they are somehow faulty.

The final technique for distancing, *parody*, is the use of inappropriately formal or informal language. When Tucker uses the words "intoned," "pantheon," "sanctuary," "all true values," and "reposited" in his opening paragraph, he is using parody:

POINT PRESENTED WITH PARODY

> Probably nothing has been more central to the environmental movement than the concept of wilderness. "In wilderness is the preservation of the world," wrote Thoreau, and environmental writers and speakers have <u>intoned</u> his message repeatedly. Wilderness, in the environmental <u>pantheon</u>, represents a particular kind of <u>sanctuary</u> in which <u>all true values</u>—that is, all nonhuman values—are <u>reposited</u>. Wildernesses are often described as "temples," "churches," and "sacred ground"—refuges for the proposed "new religion" based on environmental consciousness. Carrying the religious metaphor to the extreme, one of the most famous essays of the environmental era holds the Judeo-Christian religion responsible for "ecological crisis."

All of these terms of high, usually religious, seriousness seem out of place in describing wilderness. Parody is Tucker's signal not to take wilderness as seriously as the preservationists do.

Identifying Return Paths   Simply describing points on faulty alternative paths is not sufficient to ensure that you do not accept them. Authors of argumentative essays have to do more. They must offer you reasons. These reasons lie on what we call the return paths of an author's argument. They provide you with the routes by which you can get from a faulty path back onto the author's main path.

An author may give you more or less extended reasons for rejecting a point on a faulty path. These reasons range from a single negative "faultfinding" word to extended descriptions. No matter the length, however, you should pay attention to these reasons. Later, when you are trying to decide what you actually believe, you will want to consider these reasons once again.

Points on return paths usually fall into one of two categories: (1) explanations of the negative effects of a position, and (2) failure of a position to meet important criteria. Explanations of negative effects are historical explanations. They detail the past, present, or future consequences of accepting and acting on the points offered by others. Tucker, for example, spends an entire section of his essay (paragraphs 11–16) detailing the negative effects preservation has had on the U.S. balance of international trade in energy and minerals.

All of the negative effects Tucker details—the land locked up without adequate resource inventories, the increase in timber prices and timber imports, the expense and inefficiency of mineral exploration in the Overthrust Belt—he offers as reasons for rejecting the preservationist policy.

Failure to meet criteria is a second category of points authors often offer on return paths. Authors assume that you and the rest of their community of readers have certain criteria, or standards, which you expect positions to meet. If a position fails to meet these commonly held criteria, you have grounds for rejecting it.

COMMONLY HELD CRITERIA

- *Accuracy:* A position should be accurate; it ought to portray the facts of the matter truthfully.
- *Comprehensiveness:* A position should be comprehensive; it ought to cover all the relevant circumstances.
- *Feasibility:* A position should be feasible; it ought to be something that can be done.
- *Consistency:* A position should be consistent; it ought not to contradict itself.
- *Effectiveness:* A position should be effective; it ought to work.
- *Fairness:* A position ought to be fair; it ought to apply equally to all those involved.

Authors may also offer more specialized reasons for rejecting a position, such as failure to achieve reliability of .80 or higher, or failure to cut the national debt by a targeted percentage. If your issue is a specialized one, you may have to familiarize yourself with such specialized criteria. In any case, you need to notice and understand the criteria the author is offering or assuming as grounds for rejecting alternative faulty positions.

For Class 3.3

Listed below are eight topic clusters of points we noted when reading Nash's essay "The Irony of Victory." Decide whether each of our points lies on a main, faulty, or return path in Nash's argument.

1. The problem of increasing demand
   a. "The growth of appreciation for the wilderness in the American mind inevitably resulted in an increasing demand for actual contact with wild country" (par. 1). _____
   b. "American hunger for experiencing wilderness had come of age" (par. 1). _____
   c. "Ironically, the very increase in appreciation of wilderness threatened to prove its undoing. Having made extraordinary gains in the public's estimation in the last century, wilderness could well be loved out of existence in the next" (par. 1). _____
   d. "The problem is that dams, mines, and roads are not the basic threat to the wilderness quality of an environment. People are, and

whether they come with economic or recreational motives is, in a sense, beside the point" (par. 2).

   e. "Even appropriate kinds of recreational use detract from and, in sufficient quantity, destroy wilderness (par. 2).

2. Parks are for people—Julber

   a. "The fact that recreational use, even by innumerable people, does not consume the environmental resource in the same way as lumbering or mining has confused recent American discussion of preserving wilderness (par. 3).

   b. "Wildernesses should be 'opened up' for the general public" (par. 3).

   c. " 'If Americans were permitted access to Wilderness areas in the manner I have suggested, we would soon create a generation of avid nature lovers' " (par. 4).

   d. "Julber's confusion lay in equating 'nature,' 'scenery,' and 'beauty' with 'wilderness' " (par. 4).

3. National parks and Centennial report

   a. "Preservation, not recreation, should be the focus of park management" (par. 6).

   b. "The national parks, in their opinion, were already doing an excellent job of preserving wilderness" (par. 7).

   c. " 'Parks,' he and other Congressional leaders made clear, 'are for people' " (par. 7).

   d. Indiscriminate application of the parks-are-for-people principle doomed wilderness, at least as it was traditionally defined in the American context" (par. 8).

   e. "Wilderness, in particular, required more specificity in both definition and management than other kinds of outdoor recreation resources" (par. 8).

4. Carrying capacity

   a. "When a region's carrying capacity is exceeded it is no longer wild. And recreational use can tax the carrying capacity of wild country just as severely as economic exploitation does" (par. 9).

   b. "Carrying capacity may be thought of as having three dimensions" (par. 10).

   c. "When such synthetic objects are felt by the visitor to dominate the scene, its physical carrying capacity is exceeded" (par. 10).

   d. "When an area's natural complement of plants and animals is substantially altered, biological carrying capacity is exceeded" (par. 11).

   e. "Most visitors to the wilderness seem able to accept the presence of others up to a saturation point. After this, this quality of their experience deteriorates rapidly" (par. 12).

5. The Sierra wilderness

   a. "In California's backbone of mountain wilderness, called the Sierra, recent years have seen wilderness recreation use rise at a much sharper rate than the national 12 percent" (par. 13).

   b. "Old Sierra hands already say the mountains are no longer wild" (par. 14).

   c. "Certainly the advent of improved equipment, particularly lightweight freeze-dried food, has contributed to the crowding of the mountains" (par. 14).

6. The Boundary Waters Canoe Area
   a. "Further east, in the Boundary Waters Canoe Area (also known as the Quetico-Superior) of northern Minnesota, the carrying capacity of the wilderness is also being approached" (par. 15).   _____
   b. "People, however, are still a problem" (par. 15).   _____
   c. "For many visitors such events completely destroy the sense of wildness" (par. 15).   _____

7. The Grand Canyon
   a. "These figures tell the story of the transformation of the Grand Canyon river-run from the category of a high-risk expedition into unknown country to that of a family vacation" (par. 17).   _____
   b. "The impact of the increase of visitation on the wilderness of the inner Grand Canyon is heightened by seasonal and physical concentration" (par. 18).   _____
   c. "In many minds the Grand Canyon is on the verge of being disqualified as wilderness, and the blame, ironically, rests on those who love it" (par. 18).   _____

8. Quotas
   a. "The most obvious and direct remedy for problems of carrying-capacity violation such as exist in the Sierra, the Boundary Waters Canoe Area, and the Grand Canyon is restriction of visitors. Quotas based on the carrying-capacity concept could do much toward preserving wilderness" (par. 19).   _____
   b. "The acceptance of such quotas is based on respect for the quality of the experience" (par. 20).   _____
   c. "Respect for the quality of the wilderness experience argues for the acceptance of regulated use" (par. 21).   _____
   d. "The idea of the intense control that quota systems entail is difficult to square with the meaning of wilderness" (par. 22).   _____
   e. "Considering both the gains in appreciation for the wilderness and the losses in the amount of wild country left to appreciate, it is increasingly evident that the future of the American wilderness depends on American civilization's deliberately keeping it wild" (par. 22).   _____

Annotate the Points

As the final step in completing your second reading of an argumentative text, add an annotation concerning the contents of each main, faulty, or return path. Place this annotation next to the label you've already put in the right-hand margin.

An annotation is a phrase or short sentence that captures the central idea of a point. The function of this annotation for the contents of main, faulty, and return paths is to remind you of the point made in the text. If you ever forget what the annotation means, you can always go back to reread the text itself. To annotate points Tucker made in his section on the effects of preservation, for example, we inserted the following phrases to remind us of the contents of his main, faulty, and return paths:

The results have been mixed. The wilderness concept appears valid if it is recognized for what it is—an attempt to create what are essentially "ecological museums" in scenic and biologically significant areas of these lands. But "wilderness," in the hands of environmentalists, has become an all-purpose tool for stopping economic activity as well. This is particularly crucial now because of the many mineral and energy resources available on western lands that environmentalists are trying to push through as wilderness designations. The original legislation specified that lands were to be surveyed for valuable mineral resources before they were put into wilderness preservation. Yet with so much land being reviewed at once, these inventories have been sketchy at best. And once land is locked up as wilderness, it becomes illegal even to explore it for mineral or energy resources.

> EFFECTS OF   11
> PRESERVATION
>
> *main:* valid to create ecological museums
>
> *return:* tool for stopping economic activity
>
> *return:* land locked up without adequate resources   12

Thus the situation in western states—where the federal government still owns 68 percent of the land, counting Alaska—has in recent years become a race between mining companies trying to prospect under severely restricted conditions, and environmental groups trying to lock the doors to resource development for good. This kind of permanent preservation—the antithesis of conservation—will probably have enormous effects on our future international trade in energy and mineral resources.

> *return:* negative effects on international trade in energy and minerals

---

At stake in both the national forests and the Bureau of Land Management holdings are what are called the "roadless areas." Environmentalists call these lands "de facto wilderness," and say that because they have not yet been explored or developed for resources they should not be explored and developed in the future. The Forest Service began its Roadless Area Resources Evaluation (RARE) in 1972, while the Bureau of Land Management began four years later in 1976, after Congress brought its 174 million acres under jurisdiction of the 1964 act. The Forest Service is studying 62 million roadless acres, while the BLM is reviewing 24 million.

> ROADLESS   13
> AREAS
> *main:* fight over roadless areas
> *faulty:* de facto wildernesses

In 1974 the Forest Service recommended that 15 million of the 50 million acres then under study be designated as permanent wilderness. Environmental groups, which wanted much more set aside, immediately challenged the decision in court. Naturally, they had no trouble finding flaws in a study intended to cover such a huge amount of land, and in

> 14
>
> *faulty:* challenge to RARE studies

1977 the Carter administration decided to start over with a "RARE II" study, completed in 1979. This has also been challenged by a consortium of environmental groups that include the Sierra Club, the Wilderness Society, the National Wildlife Federation, and the Natural Resources Defense Council. The RARE II report also recommended putting about 15 million acres in permanent wilderness, with 36 million released for development and 11 million held for further study. The Bureau of Land Management is not scheduled to complete the study of its 24 million acres until 1991.

The effects of this campaign against resource development have been powerful. From 1972 to 1980, the price of a Douglas fir in Oregon increased 500 percent, largely due to the delays in timber sales from the national forests because of the battles over wilderness areas. Over the decade, timber production from the national forests declined slightly, putting far more pressure on the timber industry's own lands. The nation has now become an importer of logs, despite the vast resources on federal lands. In 1979, environmentalists succeeded in pressuring Congress into setting aside 750,000 acres in Idaho as the Sawtooth Wilderness and National Recreational Area. A resource survey, which was not completed until *after* the congressional action, showed that the area contained an estimated billion dollars' worth of molybdenum, zinc, silver, and gold. The same tract also contained a potential source of cobalt, an important mineral for which we are now dependent on foreign sources for 97 percent of what we use.

15

return: timber prices increase

—timber imports

—Sawtooth Wilderness set aside

Perhaps most fiercely contested are the energy supplies believed to be lying under the geological strata running through Colorado, Wyoming, and Montana just east of the Rockies, called the Overthrust Belt. Much of this land is still administered by the Bureau of Land Management for multiple usage. But with the prospect of energy development, environmental groups have been rushing to try to have these high-plains areas designated as wilderness areas as well (cattle grazing is still allowed in wilderness tracts). On those lands permanently withdrawn from commercial use, mineral exploration will be allowed to continue until 1983. Any mines begun by then can continue on a very restricted basis. But the exploration in "roadless areas" is severely limited, in that in most cases there can be no roads constructed (and no use of off-roads vehicles) while exploration is going on. Environmentalists have argued that wells can still be drilled and

OVERTHRUST   16
BELT
main: fiercely contested

faulty: designate plains wilderness

—exploration only 'til 1983

— restricted mining

test mines explored using helicopters. But any such exploration is likely to be extraordinarily expensive and ineffective.
Wilderness restrictions are now being drawn so tightly that
people on the site are not allowed to leave their excrement
in the area.

return: too ex-
pensive and in-
efficient

For Class 3.4

Return to the points quoted in "For Class 3.3" and annotate the contents for each one.

For Your Notebook #6

Complete a second reading of the argumentative texts you have selected on your issue.

- In the left-hand margin, label the author's sources.
- Divide the text into sections according to topic and insert a label for each topic in the left-hand margin.
- Finally, classify the points within each topic area as lying on main, faulty, or return paths, and write an annotation concerning the contents of each one.

IS NATURE TOO GOOD FOR US?

William Tucker

It's not much of an environment if you can't get in.

Probably nothing has been more central to the environmental movement   1
than the concept of wilderness. "In wildness is the preservation of the
world," wrote Thoreau, and environmental writers and speakers have intoned his message repeatedly. Wilderness, in the environmental pantheon,
represents a particular kind of sanctuary in which all true values—that is, all
nonhuman values—are reposited. Wildernesses are often described as "temples," "churches," and "sacred ground"—refuges for the proposed "new re-

ligion" based on environmental consciousness. Carrying the religious metaphor to the extreme, one of the most famous essays of the environmental era
holds the Judeo-Christian religion responsible for "ecological crisis."

The wilderness issue also has a political edge. Since 1964, long-standing 2
preservation groups like the Wilderness Society and the Sierra Club have
been pressuring conservation agencies like the National Forest Service and
the Bureau of Land Management to put large tracts of their holdings into
permanent "wilderness designations," countering the "multiple use" concept
that was one of the cornerstones of the Conservation Era of the early 1900s.

Preservation and conservation groups have been at odds since the end of 3
the last century, and the rift between them has been a major controversy of
environmentalism. The leaders of the Conservation Movement—most notably Theodore Roosevelt, Gifford Pinchot, and John Wesley Powell—called
for rational, efficient development of land and other natural resources: multiple use, or reconciling competing uses of land, and also "highest use," or
forfeiting more immediate profits from land development for more lasting
gains. Preservationsts, on the other hand, the followers of California woodsman John Muir, have advocated protecting land in its natural state, setting
aside tracts and keeping them inviolate. "Wilderness area" battles have become one of the hottest political issues of the day, especially in western
states—the current "Sage-brush Revolt" comes to mind—where large quantities of potentially commercially usable land are at stake.

The term "wilderness" generally connotes mountains, trees, clear 4
streams, rushing waterfalls, grasslands, or parched deserts, but the concept
has been institutionalized and has a careful legal definition as well. The one
given by the 1964 Wilderness Act, and that most environmentalists favor, is
that wilderness is an area "where man is a visitor but does not remain."
People do not "leave footprints there," wilderness exponents often say. Wildernesses are, most importantly, areas in which *evidence of human activity is
excluded;* they need not have any particular scenic, aesthetic, or recreational
value. The values, as environmentalists usually say, are "ecological"—which
means, roughly translated, that natural systems are allowed to operate as free
from human interference as possible.

The concept of excluding human activity is not to be taken lightly. One 5
of the major issues in wilderness areas has been whether or not federal agencies should fight forest fires. The general decision has been that they should
not, except in cases where other lands are threatened. The federal agencies
also do not fight the fires with motorized vehicles, which are prohibited in
wilderness areas except in extreme emergencies. Thus in recent years both
the National Forest Service and the National Park Service have taken to letting forest fires burn unchecked, to the frequent alarm of tourists. The defense is that many forests require periodic leveling by fire in order to make
room for new growth. There are some pine trees, for instance, whose cones
will break open and scatter their seeds only when burned. This theoretical
justification has won some converts, but very few in the timber companies,

which bridle at watching millions of board-feet go up in smoke when their own "harvesting" of mature forests has the same effect in clearing the way for new growth and does less damage to forest soils.

The effort to set aside permanent wilderness areas on federal lands began 6 with the National Forest Service in the 1920s. The first permanent reservation was in the Gila National Forest in New Mexico. It was set aside by a young Forest Service officer named Aldo Leopold, who was later to write *A Sand County Almanac,* which has become one of the bibles of the wilderness movement. Robert Marshall, another Forest Service officer, continued the program, and by the 1950s nearly 14 million of the National Forest System's 186 million acres had been administratively designated wilderness preserves.

Leopold and Marshall had been disillusioned by one of the first great 7 efforts at "game management" under the National Forest Service, carried out in the Kaibab Plateau, just north of the Grand Canyon. As early as 1906 federal officials began a program of "predator control" to increase the deer population in the area. Mountain lions, wolves, coyotes, and bobcats were systematically hunted and trapped by game officials. By 1920, the program appeared to be spectacularly successful. The deer population, formerly numbering 4,000, had grown to almost 100,000. But it was realized too late that it was the range's limited food resources that would threaten the deer's existence. During two severe winters, in 1924–26, 60 percent of the herd died, and by 1939 the population had shrunk to only 10,000. Deer populations (unlike human populations) were found to have no way of putting limits on their own reproduction. The case is still cited as the classic example of the "boom and bust" disequilibrium that comes from thoughtless intervention in an ecological system.

The idea of setting aside as wilderness areas larger and larger segments 8 of federally controlled lands began to gain more support from the old preservation groups. In part, this came from preservationists' growing realization, during the 1950s, that they had not won the battle during the Conservation Era, and that the national forests were not parks that would be protected forever from commercial activity.

Pinchot's plan for practicing "conservation" in the western forests was 9 to encourage a partnership between the government and large industry. In order to discourage overcutting and destructive competition, he formulated a plan that would promote conservation activities among the larger timber companies while placing large segments of the western forests under federal control. It was a classic case of "market restriction," carried out by the joint efforts of larger businesses and government. Only the larger companies, Pinchot reasoned, could generate the profits that would allow them to cut their forest holdings *slowly* so that the trees would have time to grow back. In order to ensure these profit margins, the National Forest Service would hold most of its timber lands out of the market for some time. This would hold up the price of timber and prevent a rampage through the forests by smaller companies trying to beat small profit margins by cutting everything in sight.

Then, in later years, the federal lands would gradually be worked into the "sustained yield" cycles, and timber rights put up for sale. It was when the national forests finally came up for cutting in the 1950s that the old preservation groups began to react.

The battle was fought in Congress. The 1960 Multiple Use and Sustained 10 Yield Act tried to reaffirm the principles of the Conservation Movement. But the wilderness groups had their day in 1964 with the passing of the Wilderness Act. The law required all the federal land-management agencies— the National Forest Service, the National Park Service, and the Fish and Wildlife Service—to review all their holdings, keeping in mind that "wilderness" now constituted a valid alternative in the "multiple use" concept—even though the concept of wilderness is essentially a rejection of the idea of multiple use. The Forest Service, with 190 million acres, and the Park Service and Fish and Wildlife Service, each with about 35 million acres, were all given twenty years to start designating wilderness areas. At the time, only 14.5 million acres of National Forest System land were in wilderness designations.

The results have been mixed. The wilderness concept appears valid if it 11 is recognized for what it is—an attempt to create what are essentially "ecological museums" in scenic and biologically significant areas of these lands. But "wilderness," in the hands of environmentalists, has become an all-purpose tool for stopping economic activity as well. This is particularly crucial now because of the many mineral and energy resources available on western lands that environmentalists are trying to push through as wilderness designations. The original legislation specified that lands were to be surveyed for valuable mineral resources before they were put into wilderness preservation. Yet with so much land being reviewed at once, these inventories have been sketchy at best. And once land is locked up as wilderness, it becomes illegal even to explore it for mineral or energy resources.

Thus the situation in western states—where the federal government still 12 owns 68 percent of the land, counting Alaska—has in recent years become a race between mining companies trying to prospect under severely restricted conditions, and environmental groups trying to lock the doors to resource development for good. This kind of permanent preservation—the antithesis of conservation—will probably have enormous effects on our future international trade in energy and mineral resources.

At stake in both the national forests and the Bureau of Land Management 13 holdings are what are called the "roadless areas." Environmentalists call these lands "de facto wilderness," and say that because they have not yet been explored or developed for resources they should not be explored and developed in the future. The Forest Service began its Roadless Area Resources Evaluation (RARE) in 1972, while the Bureau of Land Management began four years later in 1976, after Congress brought its 174 million acres under jurisdiction of the 1964 act. The Forest Service is studying 62 million roadless acres, while the BLM is reviewing 24 million.

In 1974 the Forest Service recommended that 15 million of the 50 million   14
acres then under study be designated as permanent wilderness. Environmental groups, which wanted much more set aside, immediately challenged the
decision in court. Naturally, they had no trouble finding flaws in a study
intended to cover such a huge amount of land, and in 1977 the Carter administration decided to start over with a "RARE II" study, completed in 1979.
This has also been challenged by a consortium of environmental groups that
include the Sierra Club, the Wilderness Society, the National Wildlife Federation, and the Natural Resources Defense Council. The RARE II report also
recommended putting about 15 million acres in permanent wilderness, with
36 million released for development and 11 million held for further study.
The Bureau of Land Management is not scheduled to complete the study of
its 24 million acres until 1991.

The effects of this campaign against resource development have been   15
powerful. From 1972 to 1980, the price of a Douglas fir in Oregon increased
500 percent, largely due to the delays in timber sales from the national forests
because of the battles over wilderness areas. Over the decade, timber production from the national forests declined slightly, putting far more pressure
on the timber industry's own lands. The nation has now become an importer
of logs, despite the vast resources on federal lands. In 1979, environmentalists
succeeded in pressuring Congress into setting aside 750,000 acres in Idaho as
the Sawtooth Wilderness and National Recreational Area. A resource survey,
which was not completed until *after* the congressional action, showed that
the area contained an estimated billion dollars' worth of molybdenum, zinc,
silver, and gold. The same tract also contained a potential source of cobalt,
an important mineral for which we are now dependent on foreign sources
for 97 percent of what we use.

Perhaps most fiercely contested are the energy supplies believed to be   16
lying under the geological strata running through Colorado, Wyoming, and
Montana just east of the Rockies, called the Overthrust Belt. Much of this
land is still administered by the Bureau of Land Management for multiple
usage. But with the prospect of energy development, environmental groups
have been rushing to try to have these high-plains areas designated as wilderness areas as well (cattle grazing is still allowed in wilderness tracts). On
those lands permanently withdrawn from commercial use, mineral exploration will be allowed to continue until 1983. Any mines begun by then can
continue on a very restricted basis. But the exploration in "roadless areas"
is severely limited, in that in most cases there can be no roads constructed
(and no use of off-roads vehicles) while exploration is going on. Environmentalists have argued that wells can still be drilled and test mines explored using helicopters. But any such exploration is likely to be extraordinarily expensive and ineffective. Wilderness restrictions are now being drawn
so tightly that people on the site are not allowed to leave their excrement in
the area.

IMPOSSIBLE PARADISES

What is the purpose of all this? The standard environmental argument is 17
that we have to "preserve these last few wild places before they all disappear." Yet it is obvious that something more is at stake. What is being purv-
eyed is a view of the world in which human activity is defined as "bad" and
natural conditions are defined as "good." What is being preserved is evi-
dently much more than "ecosystems." What is being preserved is an *image*
of wilderness as a semisacred place beyond humanity's intrusion.

It is instructive to consider how environmentalists themselves define the 18
wilderness. David Brower, former director of the Sierra Club, wrote in his
introduction to Paul Ehrlich's *The Population Bomb* (1968):

> Whatever resources the wilderness still held would not sustain [man] in his
> old habits of growing and reaching without limits. Wilderness could, however,
> provide answers for questions he had not yet learned how to ask. He could pre-
> dict that the day of creation was not over, that there would be wiser men, and
> they would thank him for leaving the source of those answers. Wilderness would
> remain part of his geography of hope, as Wallace Stegner put it, and could,
> merely because wilderness endured on the planet, prevent man's world from
> becoming a cage.

The wilderness, he suggested, is a source of peace and freedom. Yet 19
setting wilderness aside for the purpose of solitude doesn't always work very
well. Environmentalists have discovered this over and over again, much to
their chagrin. Every time a new "untouched paradise" is discovered, the first
thing everyone wants to do is visit it. By their united enthusiasm to find
these "sanctuaries," people bring the "cage" of society 'with them. Very
quickly it becomes necessary to erect bars to keep people *out*—which is exactly what most of the "wilderness" legislation has been all about.

In 1964, for example, the Sierra Club published a book on the relatively 20
"undiscovered" paradise of Kauai; the second most westerly island in the
Hawaiian chain. It wasn't long before the island had been overrun with tourists. When *Time* magazine ran a feature on Kauai in 1979, one unhappy island
resident wrote in to convey this telling sentiment: "We're hoping the short-
ages of jet fuel will stay around and keep people away from here." The age
of environmentalism has also been marked by the near overrunning of popular national parks like Yosemite (which now has a full-time jail), intense
pressure on woodland recreational areas, full bookings two and three years
in advance for raft trips through the Grand Canyon, and dozens of other
spectacles of people crowding into isolated areas to get away from it all.
Environmentalists are often critical of these inundations, but they must recognize that they have at least contributed to them.

I am not arguing against wild things, scenic beauty, pristine landscapes, 21
and scenic preservation. What I am questioning is the argument that wilder-

ness is a value against which every other human activity must be judged, and that human beings are somehow unworthy of the landscape. The wilderness has been equated with freedom, but there are many different ideas about what constitutes freedom. In the Middle Ages, the saying was that "city air makes a man free," meaning that the harsh social burdens of medieval feudalism vanished once a person escaped into the heady anonymity of a metropolitan community. When city planner Jane Jacobs, author of *The Death and Life of Great American Cities,* was asked by an interviewer if "overpopulation" and "crowding into large cities" weren't making social prisoners of us all, her simple reply was: "Have you ever lived in a small town?"

It may seem unfair to itemize the personal idiosyncrasies of people who 22 feel comfortable only in wilderness, but it must be remembered that the environmental movement has been shaped by many people who literally spent years of their lives living in isolation. John Muir, the founder of the National Parks movement and the Sierra Club, spent almost ten years living alone in the Sierra Mountains while learning to be a trail guide. David Brower, who headed the Sierra Club for over a decade and later broke with it to found the Friends of the Earth, also spent years as a mountaineer. Gary Snyder, the poet laureate of the environmental movement, has lived much of his life in wilderness isolation and has also spent several years in a Zen monastery. All these people far outdid Thoreau in their desire to get a little perspective on the world. There is nothing reprehensible in this, and the literature and philosophy that emerge from such experiences are often admirable. But it seems questionable to me that the ethic that comes out of this wilderness isolation—and the sense of ownership of natural landscapes that inevitably follows—can serve as the basis for a useful national philosophy.

THAT FRONTIER SPIRIT

The American frontier is generally agreed to have closed down physi- 23 cally in 1890, the year the last Indian Territory of Oklahoma was opened for settlement. After that, the Conservation Movement arose quickly to protect the remaining resources and wilderness from heedless stripping and development. Along with this came a significant psychological change in the national character, as the "frontier spirit" diminished and social issues attracted greater attention. The Progressive Movement, the Social Gospel among religious groups, Populism, and Conservation all arose in quick succession immediately after the "closing of the frontier." It seems fair to say that it was only after the frontier had been settled and the sense of endless possibilities that came with open spaces had been constricted in the national consciousness that the country started "growing up."

Does this mean the new environmental consciousness has arisen because 24 we are once again "running out of space"? I doubt it. Anyone taking an airplane across almost any part of the country is inevitably struck by how much greenery and open territory remain, and how little room our towns and cities really occupy. The amount of standing forest in the country, for example, has not diminished appreciably over the last fifty years, and is 75 percent of what it was in 1620. In addition, as environmentalists constantly remind us, trees are "renewable resources." If they continue to be handled intelligently, the forests will always grow back. As farming has moved out to the Great Plains of the Middle West, many eastern areas that were once farmed have reverted back to trees. Though mining operations can permanently scar hillsides and plains, they are usually very limited in scope (and as often as not, it is the roads leading to these mines that environmentalists find most objectionable).

It seems to me that the wilderness ethic has actually represented an at- 25 tempt psychologically to reopen the American frontier. We have been desperate to maintain belief in unlimited, uncharted vistas within our borders, a preoccupation that has eclipsed the permanent shrinking of the rest of the world outside. Why else would it be so necessary to preserve such huge tracts of "roadless territory" simply because they are now roadless, regardless of their scenic, recreational, or aesthetic values? The environmental movement, among other things, has been a rather backward-looking effort to recapture America's lost innocence.

The central figure in this effort has been the backpacker. The backpacker 26 is a young, unprepossessing person (inevitably white and upper middle class) who journeys into the wilderness as a passive observer. He or she brings his or her own food, treads softly, leaves no litter, and has no need to make use of any of the resources at hand. Backpackers bring all the necessary accouterments of civilization with them. All their needs have been met by the society from which they seek temporary release. The backpacker is freed from the need to support himself in order to enjoy the aesthetic and spiritual values that are made available by this temporary *removal* from the demands of nature. Many dangers—raging rivers or precipitous cliffs, for instance— become sought-out adventures.

Yet once the backpacker runs out of supplies and starts using resources 27 around him—cutting trees for firewood, putting up a shelter against the rain—he is violating some aspect of the federal Wilderness Act. For example, one of the issues fought in the national forests revolves around tying one's horse to a tree. Purists claim the practice should be forbidden, since it may leave a trodden ring around the tree. They say horses should be hobbled and allowed to graze instead. In recent years, the National Forest Service has come under pressure from environmental groups to enforce this restriction.

Wildernesses, then, are essentially parks for the upper middle class. They 28 are vacation reserves for people who want to rough it—with the assurance that few other people will have the time, energy, or means to follow them into the solitude. This is dramatically highlighted in one Sierra Club book that shows a picture of a professorial sort of individual backpacking off into the woods. The ironic caption is a quote from Julius Viancour, an official of the Western Council of Lumber and Sawmill Workers: "The inaccessible wilderness and primitive areas are off limits to most laboring people. We must have access. . . ." The implication for Sierra Club readers is: "What do these beer-drinking, gun-toting, working people want to do in *our* woods?"

This class-oriented vision of wilderness as an upper-middle-class preserve 29 is further illustrated by the fact that most of the opposition to wilderness designations comes not from industry but from owners of off-road vehicles. In most northern rural areas, snowmobiles are now regarded as the greatest invention since the automobile, and people are ready to fight rather than stay cooped up all winter in their houses. It seems ludicrous to them that snow-mobiles (which can't be said even to endanger the ground) should be re-stricted from vast tracts of land so that the occasional city visitor can have solitude while hiking past on snowshoes.

The recent Boundary Waters Canoe Area controversy in northern Min- 30 nesota is an excellent example of the conflict. When the tract was first des-ignated as wilderness in 1964, Congress included a special provision that al-lowed motorboats into the entire area. By the mid-1970s, outboards and inboards were roaming all over the wilderness, and environmental groups began asking that certain portions of the million-acre preserve be set aside exclusively for canoes. Local residents protested vigorously, arguing that fishing expeditions, via motorboats, contributed to their own recreation. Nevertheless, Congress eventually excluded motorboats from 670,000 acres to the north.

A more even split would seem fairer. It should certainly be possible to 31 accommodate both forms of recreation in the area, and there is as much to be said for canoeing in solitude as there is for making rapid expeditions by powerboat. The natural landscape is not likely to suffer very much from either form of recreation. It is not absolute "ecological" values that are really at stake, but simply different tastes in recreation.

NOT ENTIRELY NATURE

At bottom, then, the mystique of the wilderness has been little more 32 than a revival of Rousseau's Romanticism about the "state of nature." The notion that "only in wilderness are human beings truly free," a credo of environmentalists, is merely a variation on Rousseau's dictum that "man is born free, and everywhere he is in chains." According to Rousseau, only society could enslave people, and only in the "state of nature" was the "noble savage"—the preoccupation of so many early explorers—a fulfilled human being.

The "noble savage" and other indigenous peoples, however, have been 33 carefully excised from the environmentalists' vision. Where environmental efforts have encountered primitive peoples, these indigenous residents have often proved one of the biggest problems. One of the most bitter issues in Alaska is the efforts by environmental groups to restrict Indians in their hunting practices.

At the same time, few modern wilderness enthusiasts could imagine, for 34 example, the experience of the nineteenth-century artist J. Ross Browne, who wrote in *Harper's New Monthly Magazine* after visiting the Arizona territories in 1864:

> Sketching in Arizona is . . . rather a ticklish pursuit. . . . I never before traveled through a country in which I was compelled to pursue the fine arts with a revolver strapped around my body, a double-barreled shot-gun lying across my knees, and half a dozen soldiers armed with Sharpe's carbines keeping guard in the distance. Even with all the safeguards . . . I am free to admit that on occasions of this kind I frequently looked behind to see how the country appeared in its rear aspect. An artist with an arrow in his back may be a very picturesque object . . . but I would rather draw him on paper than sit for the portrait myself.

Wilderness today means the land *after* the Indians have been cleared away but *before* the settlers have arrived. It represents an attempt to hold that particular moment forever frozen in time, that moment when the visionary American settler looked out on the land and imagined it as an empty paradise, waiting to be molded to our vision.

In the absence of the noble savage, the environmentalist substitutes him- 35 self. The wilderness, while free of human dangers, becomes a kind of basic-training ground for upper-middle-class values. Hence the rise of "survival" groups, where college kids are taken out into the woods for a week or two and let loose to prove their survival instincts. No risks are spared on these expeditions. Several people have died on them, and a string of lawsuits has already been launched by parents and survivors who didn't realize how seriously these survival courses were being taken.

The ultimate aim of these efforts is to test upper-middle-class values 36 against the natural environment. "Survival" candidates cannot hunt, kill, or use much of the natural resources available. The true test is whether their zero-degree sleeping bags and dried-food kits prove equal to the hazards of the tasks. What happens is not necessarily related to nature. One could as easily test survival skills by turning a person loose without money or means in New York City for three days.

I do not mean to imply that these efforts do not require enormous 37 amounts of courage and daring—"survival skills." I am only suggesting that what the backpacker or survival hiker encounters is not entirely "nature," and that the effort to go "back to nature" is one that is carefully circumscribed by the most intensely civilized artifacts. Irving Babbitt, the early twentieth-century critic of Rousseau's Romanticism, is particularly vigorous in his dissent from the idea of civilized people going "back to nature." This type, he says, is actually "the least primitive of all beings":

> We have seen that the special form of unreality encouraged by the aesthetic romanticism of Rousseau is the dream of the simple life, the return to a nature that never existed, and that this dream made its special appeal to an age that was suffering from an excess of artificiality and conventionalism.

Babbitt notes shrewdly that our concept of the "state of nature" is actually one of the most sophisticated productions of civilization. Most primitive peoples, who live much closer to the soil than we do, are repelled by wilderness. The American colonists, when they first encountered the unspoiled landscape, saw nothing but a horrible desert, filled with savages.

What we really encounter when we talk about "wilderness," then, is one 38 of the highest products of civilization. It is a reserve set up to keep people *out,* rather than a "state of nature" in which the inhabitants are "truly free." The only thing that makes people "free" in such a reservation is that they can leave so much behind when they enter. Those who try to stay too long find out how spurious this "freedom" is. After spending a year in a cabin in the north Canadian woods, Elizabeth Arthur wrote in *Island Sojourn:* "I never felt so completely tied to *objects,* resources, and the tools to shape them with."

What we are witnessing in the environmental movement's obsession 39 with purified wilderness is what has often been called the "pastoral impulse." The image of nature as unspoiled, unspotted wilderness where we can go to learn the lessons of ecology is both a product of a complex, technological society and an escape from it. It is this undeniable paradox that forms the real problem of setting up "wildernesses." Only when we have created a society that gives us the leisure to appreciate it can we go out and experience what we imagine to be untrammeled nature. Yet if we lock up too much of our land in these reserves, we are cutting into our resources and endangering the very leisure that allows us to enjoy nature.

The answer is, of course, that we cannot simply let nature "take over" 40 and assume that because we have kept roads and people out of huge tracts of land, then we have absolved ourselves of a national guilt. The concept of stewardship means taking responsibility, not simply letting nature take its course. Where tracts can be set aside from commercialism at no great cost, they should be. Where primitive hiking and recreation areas are appealing, they should be maintained. But if we think we are somehow appeasing the gods by *not* developing resources where they exist, then we are being very shortsighted. Conservation, not preservation, is once again the best guiding principle.

The cult of wilderness leads inevitably in the direction of religion. Once 41 again, Irving Babbitt anticipated this fully:

> When pushed to a certain point the nature cult always tends toward sham spirituality. . . . Those to whom I may seem to be treating the nature cult with undue severity should remember that I am treating it only in its pseudo-religious aspect. . . . My quarrel is only with the aesthete who assumes an apocalyptic pose and gives forth as a profound philosophy what is at best only a holiday or weekend view of existence. . . .

It is often said that environmentalism could or should serve as the basis 42 of a new religious consciousness, or a religious "reawakening." This religious trend is usually given an Oriental aura. E. F. Schumacher has a chapter on Buddhist economics in his classic *Small Is Beautiful*. Primitive animisms are also frequently cited as attitudes toward nature that are more "environmentally sound." One book on the environment states baldly that "the American Indian lived in almost perfect harmony with nature." Anthropologist Marvin Harris has even put forth the novel view that primitive man is an environmentalist, and that many cultural habits are unconscious efforts to reduce population and conserve the environment. He says that the Hindu prohibition against eating cows and the Jewish tradition of not eating pork were both efforts to avoid the ecological destruction that would come with raising these grazing animals intensively. The implication in these arguments is usually that science and modern technology have somehow dulled our instinctive "environmental" impulses, and that Western "nonspiritual" technocracy puts us out of harmony with the "balance of nature."

Perhaps the most daring challenge to the environmental soundness of 43 current religious tradition came early in the environmental movement, in a much quoted paper by Lynn White, professor of the history of science at UCLA. Writing in *Science* magazine in 1967, White traced "the historical roots of our ecologic crisis" directly to the Western Judeo-Christian tradition in which "man and nature are two things, and man is master." "By destroying pagan animism," he wrote, "Christianity made it possible to exploit nature in a mood of indifference to the feelings of natural objects." He continued:

> Especially in its Western form, Christianity is the most anthropocentric religion the world has seen. . . . Christianity, in absolute contrast to ancient paganism and Asia's religions (except, perhaps, Zoroastrianism), not only established a dualism of man and nature but also insisted that it is God's will that man exploit nature for his proper ends. . . . In antiquity every tree, every spring, every stream, every hill had its own genius loci, its guardian spirit. . . . Before one cut a tree, mined a mountain, or dammed a brook, it was important to placate the spirit in charge of that particular situation, and keep it placated.

But the question here is not whether the Judeo-Christian tradition is 44 worth saving in and of itself. It would be more than disappointing if we canceled the accomplishments of Judeo-Christian thought only to find that our treatment of nature had not changed a bit.

There can be no question that White is onto a favorite environmental 45 theme here. What he calls the "Judeo-Christian tradition" is what other writers often term "Western civilization." It is easy to go through environmental books and find long outbursts about the evils that "civilization and progress" have brought us. The long list of Western achievements and advances, the scientific men of genius, are brought to task for creating our "environmental crisis." Sometimes the condemnation is of our brains, pure and simple. Here, for example, is the opening statement from a book about pesticides, written by the late Robert van den Bosch, an outstanding environmental advocate:

Our problem is that we are too smart for our own good, and for that matter, the good of the biosphere. The basic problem is that our brain enables us to evaluate, plan, and execute. Thus, while all other creatures are programmed by nature and subject to her whims, we have our own gray computer to motivate, for good or evil, our chemical engine. . . . Among living species, we are the only one possessed of arrogance, deliberate stupidity, greed, hate, jealousy, treachery, and the impulse to revenge, all of which may erupt spontaneously or be turned on at will.

At this rate, it can be seen that we don't even need religion to lead us astray. We are doomed from the start because we are not creatures of *instinct,* programmed from the start "by nature."

This type of primitivism has been a very strong, stable undercurrent in 46 the environmental movement. It runs from the kind of fatalistic gibberish quoted above to the Romanticism that names primitive tribes "instinctive environmentalists," from the pessimistic predictions that human beings cannot learn to control their own numbers to the notion that only by remaining innocent children of nature, untouched by progress, can the rural populations of the world hope to feed themselves. At bottom, as many commentators have pointed out, environmentalism is reminiscent of the German Romanticism of the nineteenth century, which sought to shed Christian (and Roman) traditions and revive the Teutonic gods because they were "more in touch with nature."

But are progress, reason, Western civilization, science, and the cerebral 47 cortex really at the root of the "environmental crisis?" Perhaps the best answer comes from an environmentalist himself, Dr. René Dubos, a world-renowned microbiologist, author of several prize-winning books on conservation and a founding member of the Natural Resources Defense Council. Dr. Dubos takes exception to the notion that Western Christianity has produced a uniquely exploitative attitude toward nature:

> Erosion of the land, destruction of animal and plant species, excessive exploitation of natural resources, and ecological disasters are not peculiar to the Judeo-Christian tradition and to scientific technology. At all times, and all over the world, man's thoughtless interventions into nature have had a variety of disastrous consequences or at least have changed profoundly the complexity of nature.

Dr. Dubos has catalogued the non-Western or non-Christian cultures that have done environmental damage. Plato observed, for instance, that the hills in Greece had been heedlessly stripped of wood, and erosion had been the result; the ancient Egyptians and Assyrians exterminated large numbers of wild animal species; Indian hunters presumably caused the extinction of many large paleolithic species in North America; Buddhist monks building temples in Asia contributed largely to deforestation. Dubos notes:

All over the globe and at all times . . . men have pillaged nature and disturbed the ecological equilibrium . . . nor did they have a real choice of alternatives. If men are more destructive now . . . it is because they have at their command more powerful means of destruction, not because they have been influenced by the Bible. In fact, the Judeo-Christian peoples were probably the first to develop on a large scale a pervasive concern for land management and an ethic of nature.

The concern that Dr. Dubos cites is the same one we have rescued out 48 of the perception of environmentalism as a movement based on aristocratic conservatism. That is the legitimate doctrine of *stewardship* of the land. In order to take this responsibility, however, we must recognize the part we play in nature—that "the land is ours." It will not do simply to worship nature, to create a cult of wilderness in which humanity is an eternal intruder and where human activity can only destroy.

"True conservation," writes Dubos, "means not only protecting nature 49 against human misbehavior but also developing human activities which favor a creative, harmonious relationship between man and nature." This is a legitimate goal for the environmental movement.

THE IRONY OF VICTORY
Roderick Nash

*During the 1970 season, 106,000 people, about 44 per cent
more than the preceding year, came into [the] Desolation
[Wilderness] and very nearly loved the place to death.*

Ezra Bowen, 1972

*The woods are overrun and sons of bitches like me are half
the problem.*

Colin Fletcher, 1971

1 The growth of appreciation for the wilderness in the American mind inev- 1
itably resulted in an increasing demand for actual contact with wild country. By the 1970s a wilderness recreation boom of unprecedented proportions was in full stride. It was most apparent, of course, in the nation's remaining backcountry, where visitation leapt upward at a conservatively estimated 12 percent annually, doubling in a decade and, according to pro-

Roderick Nash, "The Irony of Victory," epilogue to *Wilderness and the American Mind*, rev. ed. (New Haven: Yale University Press, 1973). Reprinted by permission of the publisher.

jections, expected to increase ten times by the year 2000.[1] <u>Another</u> index was the emergence of a wilderness equipment business, catering to back-packers and growing industry-wide at a rate of 25 percent annually. The nation's largest manufacturer, Camp Trails of Phoenix, Arizona, reported a gain in sales of 500 percent since 1966.[2] Responding to the new demand, organizations offering guided wilderness trips proliferated. In the 1972 season at least fifteen different operations included "wilderness" in their titles, including Wilderness Encounters, Wilderness Expeditions, American Wilderness Experience, Wilderness Waterways, and Way of the Wilderness.[3] Older wilderness-oriented outing programs, such as those of the Sierra Club, the Wilderness Society, and Outward Bound, <u>also</u> flourished. It was a sellers' market. American hunger for experiencing wilderness had come of age. The hopes of Thoreau and Marshall and Leopold seemed fulfilled. Confirming Muir's forecast, "thousands of tired, nerve-shaken, over-civilized people" *had* come to the wilderness and discovered that "wildness is a necessity." <u>Indeed</u> two million had—every season. Wilderness recreation had never been so popular, and a strong base of political support for wilderness preservation seemed assured. <u>But</u> even as preservationists were celebrating their apparent victory, the more perceptive among them saw a disturbing new threat to wilderness in their own enthusiasm. Ironically, the very increase in appreciation of wilderness threatened to prove its undoing. Having made extraordinary gains in the public's estimation in the last century, wilderness could well be loved out of existence in the next.

2   The problem is that dams, mines, and roads are not the basic threat to the wilderness quality of an environment. People are, and whether they come with economic or recreational motives is, in a sense, beside the point. For the devotee of wilderness, <u>in other words</u>, a campground full of Boy Scouts, or even of people like himself, is just as destructive of the essence of wilderness as a highway. Any definition of wilderness implies an absence of civilization, and wilderness values are so fragile that even appropriate kinds of recreational use detract from and, in sufficient quantity, destroy wilderness. As ecologist Stanley A. Cain has remarked, "innumerable people cannot enjoy solitude together."[4]

3   The fact that recreational use, even by innumerable people, does not II consume the environmental resource in the same way as lumbering or mining has confused recent American discussion of preserving wilderness. Los Angeles attorney Eric Julber, <u>for instance</u>, told the Senate Subcom-

1. Due to the current lack of control over access to wilderness, precise figures are hard to establish. The best available are in Wildland Research Center, *Wilderness and Recreation,* pp. 203–54, especially 236–37. See also Ezra Bowen, *The High Sierra* (New York, 1972), p. 156.

2. Susan Sands, "Backpacking: 'I Go to the Wilderness to Kick the Man-World Out of Me,'" New York *Times,* May 9, 1917, p. 1.

3. *Adventure Trip Guide,* ed. Pat Dickman (New York, 1972).

4. As quoted in Ann and Myron Sutton, *The Wilderness World of the Grand Canyon* (Philadelphia, 1971), p. 204. Cain has amplified his idea in conversations with the author on numerous occasions.

mittee on Parks and Recreation in 1972 that the United States wildernesses should be "opened up" for the general public. Pointing to Switzerland as a case in point, Julber argued that breathtaking mountain scenery could be readily accessible by mechanical means. "Where the automobile cannot go, railroads take you; and when the going gets too steep for cogwheel trains, you catch an aerial tramway." At the top of the Swiss mountain a restaurant patio affords a sweeping panorama of natural beauty. For Julber this is entirely acceptable. Neither does he see a violation of wilderness in the idea of installing a tramway to the bottom of the Grand Canyon or building a hotel and cable-car complex on top of Half Dome in Yosemite National Park.[5]

4   In defense of Eric Julber and those who share his opinions, his " 'access' philosophy" is not aimed at minimizing the value of wilderness in American civilization. On the contrary, he declared it is his "firm belief that if Americans were permitted access to Wilderness areas in the manner I have suggested, we would soon create a generation of avid nature lovers."[6] The difficulty here is that, according to most definitions, the wilderness quality of the area would vanish when the tramways and hotels arrived. Julber's confusion lay in equating "nature," "scenery," and "beauty" with "wilderness."

5   A similar confusion in definition and terminology embroiled the III American public on the occasion of the National Parks Centennial celebration in 1972. The citizen task forces organized by the Conservation Foundation to draft a report addressed themselves to the essential ambiguity in national park policy. Since the establishment of Yellowstone National Park in 1872, and certainly since the National Park Service Act of 1916, the parks had labored awkwardly under the dual charge of preserving nature and advancing public recreation. In the larger parks, like Yellowstone, time clarified the dilemma as one involving a choice between wilderness values and those of civilization.

6   The Centennial Task Force recommended that this dilemma could be resolved if the meaning of the nation in creating national parks was construed to be preservation for the enjoyment of the people *in* the wilderness being preserved. This meant that park visitors would be expected to take their pleasure from experiencing unmodified nature. The corollary was that the parks could be fully enjoyed only if they were preserved unimpaired, and that preservation, not recreation, should be the focus of park management. It followed that anyone desiring to use a park for recreation must do so on the wilderness's terms (backpacking, bicycling, canoeing, camping) rather than on civilization's (roads, cars, trailers, motels, and hotels).[7]

5. Eric Julber, "Let's Open Up Our Wilderness Areas," *Reader's Digest, 100* (1972), 125–28 and "The Wilderness: Just How Wild Should It Be?" *Trends, 9* (1972), 15–18.
6. Julber, "Let's Open Up Our Wilderness Areas," p. 128.
7. Conservation Foundation. *National Parks for the Future: An Appraisal of the National Parks as They Begin Their Second Century in a Changing America* (Washington, D.C., 1972), pp. 9–39.

7   National reaction to the 254-page Centennial Report indicated the existence on a public level of the <u>same</u> misconceptions that plagued Eric
Julber. Although a considerable segment of the articles and editorials concerning the report supported its recommendations, a number of journalists
and government officials, right up to Secretary of the Interior Rogers C.
B. Morton, expressed strong disagreement. The national parks, in their
opinion, were already doing an excellent job of preserving wilderness.
<u>And</u>, they asked, wasn't the point to bring people in contact with wild
country? The recommendations of the Centennial Task Force to phase out
motorized access 'discriminate," in Secretary Morton's words, against the
elderly, the infirm, and families with young children. "Parks," he and
other Congressional leaders made clear, "are for people."[8]

8   Wilderness advocates retorted that the critics of the Centennial Report
did not have a clear conception of the meaning of wilderness. Indiscriminate application of the parks-are-for-people principle doomed wilderness,
at least as it was traditionally defined in the American context. Sometimes
it might be necessary to resolve a wilderness versus people issue *against*
people. A case in point was the recommendation against roads and hotels.
Difficult access was the price paid for the existence of wilderness. Preservationists, <u>in sum</u>, believed the Centennial Report was correct in its feeling that parks could not be all things to all people. Wilderness, <u>in partic-
ular</u>, required more specificity in both definition and management than
other kinds of outdoor recreation resources.

9   Public discussion in the 1970s of the problem of loving wilderness to IV
death made frequent use of an old rangeland and livestock term, "carrying
capacity." The simplified meaning of this concept as applied to wilderness
is the ability of an environment to absorb human influence and still retain
its wildness. When a region's carrying capacity is exceeded it is no longer
wild. <u>And</u> recreational use can tax the carrying capacity of wild country
just as severely as economic exploitation does.[9]

10   In the case of wilderness, carrying capacity may be thought of as hav-

8. New York *Times*, Sept. 25, 1972.
9. MacKaye, "The Gregarious and the Solitary," vol. 7, and "A Wilderness Philosophy," vol.
2; Arthur H. Carhart, *Planning for America's Wildlands* (Harrisburg, Pa., 1961); Wildland
Research Center, *Wilderness and Recreation,* pp. 117 ff., 298 ff.; Gilligan, "Forest Service
Primitive and Wilderness Areas," pp. 227 ff.; Robert C. Lucas, "The Quetico-Superior Area:
Recreational Use in Relation to Capacity" (unpublished Ph.D. dissertation, University of
Minnesota, 1962), Lucas, "Wilderness Perception and Use: The Example of the Boundary
Waters Canoe Area," *Natural Resources Journal, 3* (1964), 394–411, which also appears in
Readings in Resource Management and Conservation, eds. Ian Burton and Robert W. Kates
(Chicago, 1965), pp. 363–74, and Lucas, "The Recreational Capacity of the Quetico-Superior
Area," *United States Forest Service Research Paper* LS–15 (St. Paul, Minn., 1965); John Alan
Wagar, "The Carrying Capacity of Wild Lands for Recreation" (unpublished Ph.D.
dissertation, University of Michigan, 1961); Gorman Gilbert, "The Use of Markov Renewal
Theory in Planning Analysis: An Application to the Boundary Waters Canoe Area"
(unpublished Ph.D. dissertation, Northwestern University, 1972).

ing three dimensions. *Physical carrying capacity* refers to the effect of human visitation on the nonliving environment. The ability of a particular terrain to resist trail erosion is one factor. So is a region's capacity to "absorb" constructed trails, bridges, roads, signs, and other man-made features without a significant effect on its wild qualities. When such synthetic objects are felt by the visitor to dominate the scene, its physical carrying capacity is exceeded. The availability of firewood and space for camping (many very large wildernesses have extremely limited camping areas) are additional components.

11   By *biological carrying capacity* planners have in mind the impact of visitation on the living things that occupy the wilderness and on wilderness ecosystems. When an area's natural complement of plants and animals is substantially altered, biological carrying capacity is exceeded and the preservation function aborted. An instance is when the pressure of man causes a particular bird or animal to vacate its usual habitat or behave abnormally. The rash of grizzly bear attacks, notably in Glacier National Park in the late 1960s, comes to mind in this regard. The "fishing out" of a lake or stream is another illustration, and so is the destruction of a mountain meadow by the grazing and trampling of pack animals.

12   *Psychological carrying capacity* is the most subtle, but in many ways the most important, component of the carrying capacity idea. It relates to the effect of other people's presence on the experience of a visitor to the wilderness. The basic assumption here is that wilderness implies the absence of man, and any human evidence—even that of fellow campers—is disruptive to a degree. Levels of tolerance for other people vary, of course. At one extreme are those for whom the sight, sound, and even the knowledge that another camper or camping party is in the vicinity spoils the wilderness experience completely. At the other extreme are people whose chief delight in a wilderness comes from association with other visitors. For them an empty campground would not only be disappointing but positively frightening. The conclusions of recreational psychologists are still highly tentative, but most visitors to the wilderness seem able to accept the presence of others up to a saturation point. After this, this quality of their experience deteriorates rapidly. The region is no longer perceived as wilderness; it has been loved to death.

---

13   This tripartite definition of carrying capacity acquires more meaning v when specific cases are brought to light. In California's backbone of mountain wilderness, called the Sierra, recent years have seen wilderness recreation use rise at a much sharper rate than the national 12 percent. Such estimates, of course, must be tentative because until 1971, when the Forest Service began requiring permits, visits were unrecorded. And it is still the case that at most of the Sierra trailheads a person simply parks his car and starts walking. As he climbs, the increase in visitation is readily apparent. In meadows and on marshy ground, trails worn by innumerable

boots and hooves are often as deep as they are wide. Frequently a badly eroded trail is abandoned and new ruts cut alongside in the manner of a multi-lane freeway. At the more popular lakes the detergent that campers use for dishes and laundry is turning up in the water in traceable amounts. Streams flowing from such bodies of water produce telltale suds. Fire-wood has been scoured for as much as a mile around popular camps. Most fishing is maintained by periodic stocking. People pollution is <u>also</u> present. As many as 450 have camped at relatively small Shadow Lake in the Min-arets Wilderness *at one time.* Three hundred people climb Mt. Whitney, the Sierra's tallest peak, on the average summer weekend, and most of them stay overnight at Mirror Lake, converting it into a tube-tent city. The figure reaches 1,500 on the Labor Day holiday. The problem exists on a <u>lesser</u> scale almost everywhere in the Sierra. In the summer months one seldom camps alone anymore. Thefts of packs and equipment have become a standard occurrence in many areas.[10]

14   Old Sierra hands already say the mountains are no longer wild. Many of them knew the country when first ascents were possible and maps were excitingly vague. Then it was the horseman's domain. Backpacking in the high country before 1940 was rare, confined to a few John Muirs and David Browers. But today the proportions are reversed. The professional guide with his string of pack animals is finding it difficult to make ends meet, while do-it-yourself backpacking thrives. <u>Certainly</u> the advent of improved equipment, particularly light-weight freeze-dried food, has con-tributed to the crowding of the mountains. <u>So</u> have detailed trail maps and guidebooks.[11] Equipped with these equivalents of the motorists' tour guide, backpackers confidently penetrate the far corners of the wilderness. In some minds this marks a welcome maturation of love for the American wilderness; to others the publication of the guidebooks was the worst crime ever committed against the wildness of the Sierra. Jealously, they guard knowledge of the few places that are off the beaten track for fear that they might have standing-room only next season.

15   Further east, in the Boundary Waters Canoe Area (also known as the VI Quetico-Superior) of northern Minnesota, the carrying capacity of the wilderness is <u>also</u> being approached. <u>In fact</u>, the BWCA is generally con-ceded to be the nation's most intensively used wilderness recreation area.

10. Bowen, *High Sierra,* pp. 156–69. The Sierra Club has long been concerned with the problem of overuse to which, of course, it makes a notable contribution. See Brower, ed., *Wildlands in Our Civilization,* pp. 130–38, 144–53, and H. T. Harvey, R. J. Hartesveldt, and J. T. Stanley, *Wilderness Impact Study Report: An Interim Report to the Sierra Club Outing Committee on the Effects of Human Recreational Activities on Wilderness Ecosystems* (San Francisco, 1972).

11. The best-known examples are Walter A. Starr, Jr.'s *Starr's Guide to the John Muir Trail and the High Sierra Region* (San Francisco, 1964), which is now in its ninth edition, and Karl Schwenke and Thomas Winnett's *Sierra South* and *Sierra North* (Berkeley, 1968), which outline two hundred backcountry trips.

Forest Service regulations, such as those prohibiting cans and bottles (food must be carried in burnable containers) and barring outboard motors from some lakes, have helped to maintain wildness. People, <u>however</u>, are still a problem. <u>Even</u> on remote, interior lakes, securing one of the infrequent campsites along the heavily forested shoreline often becomes the subject of competition and canoe races among several parties. For many visitors <u>such</u> events completely destroy the sense of wildness. The trip may still be "fun," and furnish good fishing, <u>but</u> it is not a wilderness experience.[12]

16   The most intensely supervised wilderness in the United States is the VII Grand Canyon in Arizona. Close control by national park officers is facilitated by topography. Access is limited to a few easily patrolled trails and the Colorado River, which can be reached by vehicles at only one point. The Grand Canyon, <u>moreover</u>, is far more difficult country for the average wilderness-user than either the Sierra or the Boundary Waters Canoe Area. Smart backpackers who venture off the established trails take special pains to notify park authorities of their whereabouts. The river route through Grand Canyon is particularly susceptible to control because of the necessity of launching boats for the 280-mile float trip at the ranger-managed Lee's Ferry landing. <u>And</u> prior to national park administration, Grand Canyon river trips were so rare and so newsworthy as to be fully known. <u>Consequently</u>, an exceptionally complete set of visitor data for one portion of the American wilderness does exist. (See table on page 70.)

17   These figures tell the story of the transformation of the Grand Canyon river-run from the category of a high-risk expedition into unknown country to that of a family vacation. The cause of the change is both technological and intellectual. The development of inflatable rubberized rafts, as long as 33 feet and possessing remarkable buoyancy and flexibility, has made the trip safe even for the disabled and the blind. When steered by powerful outboard motors, these rafts reduce the risk of running some of the largest rapids in the world approximately to the level of flying in a commercial airplane. <u>But</u> the improved technology would have had little impact on the amount of visitation without a simultaneous growth in appreciation of wilderness. Just as in the case of backpacking, equipment and ideas have combined to bring the pressure of popularity to bear on the Grand Canyon.

18   The impact of the increase of visitation on the wilderness of the inner Grand Canyon is heightened by seasonal and physical concentration. Nearly all the annual visitors make the river-run in June, July, and Au-

12. Lucas, "The Quetico-Superior Area"; Lucas, "Wilderness Perception and Use"; Lucas, "The Recreational Capacity of the Quetico-Superior"; Gilbert, "The Use of Markov Renewal Theory"; Richard D. James, "The Call of the Wild: Many Americans, Tired of Crowds and Cities, Vacation in Wilderness," *Wall Street Journal*, Aug. 8, 1969.

Travel on the Colorado River Through Grand Canyon

Year or Years	Number of People	Year or Years	Number of People
1869–1940	44	1956	55
1941	4	1957	135
1942	8	1958	80
1943	0	1959	120
1944	0	1960	205
1945	0	1961	255
1946	0	1962	372
1947	4	1963–64★	44
1948	6	1965	547
1949	12	1966	1,067
1950	7	1967	2,099
1951	29	1968	3,609
1952	19	1969	6,019
1953	31	1970	9,935
1954	21	1971	10,942
1955	70	1972	16,428

Note: Data is compiled from records of individual expeditions and, after 1941, from the records of the Superintendent, Grand Canyon National Park. Penetration of the inner wilderness of the Grand Canyon began in 1869 with the pioneering descent of John Wesley Powell's expedition. Statistics from 1869 through 1955 are not exact (for example, repeat river-runners are not included for 1941–54), but the margin of error is very small.

★Travel on the Colorado River in these years was affected by the completion of Glen Canyon Dam and the resulting disruption of flow.

gust. There is extremely little river travel between October and April. Moreover, the nature of river trips is such that everyone funnels through the same narrow course. This means that visitors tend to concentrate in certain places. As many as five hundred gather at the Lee's Ferry roadhead for departure on the same day. Downstream the rafts accumulate at the major rapids, at points of special interest, and at the limited number of campsites afforded by the generally steep-walled gorge. Physical and biological deterioration, much of it stemming from human excrement, inevitably results. But the major threat is to the Grand Canyon's psychological carrying capacity. In many minds the Grand Canyon is on the verge of being disqualified as wilderness, and the blame, ironically, rests on those who love it. Having been saved from the dam builders, the canyon's wildness is now threatened by the saviors themselves.[13]

19   The most obvious and direct remedy for problems of carrying-capacity VIII

---

13. Peter Cowgill, "Too Many People on the Colorado River," *National Parks and Conservation Magazine,* 45 (1971), 10–14; Roderick Nash, "Rivers and Americans: A Century of Conflicting Priorities" in *Environmental Quality and Water Development,* ed. Charles R. Goldman (San Francisco, 1972), Chapter 4.

violation such as exist in the Sierra, the Boundary Waters Canoe Area, and the Grand Canyon is restriction of visitors. Quotas based on the carrying-capacity concept could do much toward preserving wilderness. In fact, the Forest Service and the National Park Service are already experimenting with rationing systems in selected areas as a prelude to more general application later in the 1970s. In the Grand Canyon the number of commercial outfitters authorized to conduct river trips has been frozen, and each outfitter has been assigned a maximum number of user-days per season. Grand Canyon backpackers are also issued permits based on the space available in the various backcountry campgrounds. Those who arrive without reservations are turned away by the ranger in charge. Similarly, on the Forest Service-managed Middlefork of the Salmon River in Idaho, boating parties are required to make campground reservations for an entire trip and to keep their schedule so as not to violate another party's assignment. Formerly, it was enough to let wilderness alone in order to implement a preservation policy; the price of popularity is intense management.

20   Man in a state of civilization readily accepts quota-type restrictions on many of his activities. Admission to airplanes, apartments, and colleges is normally based on the rationing concept. People buy tickets for the theater, or if the performance is sold out, they wait for the next show or even the next season; they don't insist on sitting on each other's laps. Ultimately, the acceptance of such quotas is based on respect for the quality of the experience. One hundred people might be physically able to squeeze onto a tennis court, but the game they then played would not be tennis. So they wait their turn, placing the integrity of the game ahead of personal considerations. They realize, of course, that when they do get a chance to play, they will be accorded the same respect.

21   The same logic could be used in support of wilderness quotas. Wilderness is also a "game" that, by definition, cannot be played at any one time and place by more than a few people. Respect for the quality of the wilderness experience argues for the acceptance of regulated use. Inconvenience and disappointment for some individuals is the inevitable concomitant, but otherwise no one will experience real wilderness. With quotas, when one's turn arrives, the wilderness is at least there to enjoy.[14]

22   Still, the idea of the intense control that quota systems entail is difficult to square with the meaning of wilderness. Essentially, a man-managed wilderness is a contradiction because wilderness necessitates an *absence* of civilization's ordering influence. The quality of freedom so

---

14. For brief discussions of quotas and other management policy options for wilderness, see William C. Everhart, *The National Park Service* (New York, 1972), pp. 87 ff., and Stephen F. Arno, "They're Putting 'Wild' Back in Wilderness," *National Parks and Conservation Magazine,* 45 (1971), 10–14, and Garrett Hardin, "We Must Earn Again For Ourselves What We Have Inherited" in *Wilderness: The Edge of Knowledge,* ed. Maxine E. McCloskey (San Francisco, 1970), pp. 260–66.

frequently associated with wilderness is diminished, if not destroyed, by regulation. Campgrounds become sleeping-bag motels with defined capacities and checkout times. The point is underscored by the fact that wilderness, in the final analysis, is a state of mind. It is a resource, <u>in other words</u>, that is defined by human perception. Simply to know that one visits a wilderness by the grace of and under conditions established by governmental agencies could break the spell for many people. <u>Yet</u>, considering both the gains in appreciation for the wilderness and the losses in the amount of wild country left to appreciate, it is increasingly evident that the future of the American wilderness depends on American civilization's deliberately keeping it wild.

⊞ 4 VISUALIZE THE LINE OF ARGUMENT

By reading and marking an argumentative text, you have followed an author point by point along a line of argument. But to understand this argument completely, you must get a sense of the whole journey the author wants you to make. In most cases, this journey can be understood as a movement through three **milestones** of argument, as shown in the sketch below. That is, the line of argument should move you *from* what the author sees as the issue *toward* what the author considers an appropriate resolution.

In this chapter, you will learn to paraphrase an author's points, place them at the milestones of argument, and visualize the full line of argument from problem to solution. These steps will help you take an author's line of argument apart, examine how one part leads to another, and anticipate its twists and turns. By the end of this chapter, then, you should understand more clearly how authors contribute to a community's effort to resolve an issue.

PARAPHRASE THE POINTS

Thus far, your attention to an author's points have been limited to marking in the margins of the text. To visualize the whole line of argument, however, you will need a format you can more easily manipulate. This format is usually a set of *notes*—paraphrases of an author's points, often written on 3 × 5 notecards, in which you elaborate on your marginal notations, topic area by topic area. Generally speaking, you should try to create one notecard per topic area and, within that area, paraphrase each of the points lying on main, faulty, and return paths:

SAMPLE NOTECARD ON TUCKER

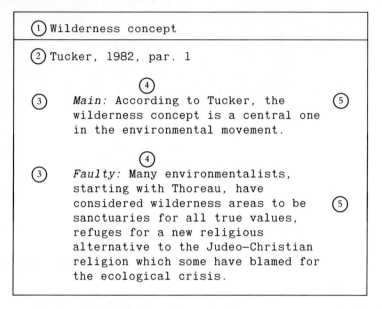

As the circled numbers above indicate, your notecards should contain five types of information:

INFORMATION TO INCLUDE IN YOUR NOTES

1. the *topic area,* listed in the top left-hand corner of the notecard
2. the *citation,* including author's name, date, and page number, listed on the top line of the notecard
3. the *function* of each of the points (main, faulty, or return)
4. the *source* of each point. If the point is not attributed to someone else, list the author as the source
5. a *paraphrase* of each point

You can transfer the first four of these items directly from your marginal notations. To create the fifth item, the paraphrase, you need to examine the text for several types of information, which we discuss in the following sections.

Look for Support

Support is any information offered to make a point more credible or believable. Authors almost always provide support for major points along their line of argument. In addition to increasing your belief, support can also help you to understand a point more completely. That is, a point that seems unclear or obscure in the abstract can come down to earth and make sense when examined in light of its support.

In paraphrasing a point, you must decide whether or not to include its support. How important is the support to your understanding and belief? Do you anticipate using it later in constructing your own position? If so, your paraphrase should include a brief reference to the support. When we wrote the following note on Tucker's discussion of Leopold and Marshall, for instance, we decided to include a reference to Tucker's support, the experience on the Kaibab Plateau:

A PARAPHRASE INCLUDING SUPPORT

Leopold and Marshall
Tucker, 1982, par. 6–7

point	*Main:* The preservationist effort, according to Tucker, was begun by Aldo Leopold, a Forest Service officer working in the Gila National Forest in the 1920s. It was continued by Robert Marshall until 14 million acres of national forest had been set aside by the 1950s.
point	*Faulty:* Both Leopold and Marshall worked to preserve wilderness areas because of their experience in the Kaibab Plateau. There the
support	Service systematically eradicated predators in an effort to increase the deer population. The program worked until 60 percent of the herd died from starvation in two severe winters. Leopold and Marshall felt that this case showed that humans cannot intervene in natural ecosystems without doing damage, no matter how good the intentions are.

As you read, notice that authors use one of three kinds of support: the support of experience, the support of statistics, and the support of authority.

The *support of experience* includes specific cases an author offers as evidence for a point. These cases may be referred to briefly or, as Tucker does, by more extended descriptions of situations:

TUCKER'S USE OF THE SUPPORT OF EXPERIENCE

The concept of excluding human activity is not to be taken lightly. One of the major issues in wilderness areas has been whether or not federal agencies should fight forest fires. The general decision has been that they should not, except in cases where other lands are threatened. The federal agencies also do not fight the fires with motorized vehicles, which are prohibited in wilderness areas except in extreme emergencies. Thus in recent years both the National Forest Service and the National Park Service have taken to letting forest fires burn unchecked, to the frequent alarm of tourists (par. 5).

Another kind of support authors often use is the *support of statistics*, which includes descriptions of the frequency or quantity of a certain type of experience. Rather than specific cases, statistics give you a sense of the general trends among cases. Tucker, for example, offers several statistics in support of his point that preserving wilderness has negative effects:

TUCKER'S USE OF THE SUPPORT OF STATISTICS

The effects of this campaign against resource development have been powerful. From 1972 to 1980, the price of a Douglas fir in Oregon increased 500 percent, largely due to the delays in timber sales from the national forests because of the battles over wilderness areas. Over the decade, timber production from the national forests declined slightly, putting far more pressure on the timber industry's own lands. The nation has now become an importer of logs, despite the vast resources on federal lands (par. 15).

One final kind of support you can expect authors to use is that of authority. The *support of authority* includes citations to other people who have provided information or points that lend credibility to an author's own points. By citing authorities on an issue, authors hope to show you that other people in the community share their beliefs. Tucker, for example, cites René Dubos as an authority to support his contention that Western civilization is not the cause of the ecological crisis:

TUCKER'S USE OF THE SUPPORT OF AUTHORITY

But are progress, reason, Western civilization, science, and the cerebral cortex really at the root of the "environmental crisis"? Perhaps the best answer comes from an environmentalist himself, Dr. René Dubos, a world-renowned microbiologist, author of several prize-winning books on conservation and a founding member of the National Resources Defense Council. Dr. Dubos takes exception to the notion that Western Christianity has produced a uniquely exploitative attitude toward nature (par. 47).

Look for Amplifications

While many authors make their points concisely in a single sentence, you will often find the opposite to be true: they stretch out their point over a number of amplifying statements. *Amplifications* are statements that extend and refine a previous point; they go further in explaining an author's meaning. Unlike support, amplifications are not optional information for your notes. They are central to understanding an author's complete meaning. When you paraphrase, then, you must be sure to include any amplifications to an original point.

In presenting the environmentalist's definition of wilderness, for example, Tucker stretches out his point over several amplifying statements:

TUCKER'S USE OF AMPLIFICATION

The term "wilderness" generally connotes mountains, trees, clear streams, rushing waterfalls, grasslands, or parched deserts, but the concept has been institutionalized and has a careful legal definition as well. ① The one given by the 1964 Wilderness Act, and that most environmentalists favor, is that wilderness is an area "where man is a visitor but ② does not remain." People do not "leave footprints there," wilderness ③ exponents often say. Wildernesses are, most importantly, areas in which ④ *evidence of human activity is excluded;* they need not have any partic- ⑤ ular scenic, aesthetic, or recreational value. The values, as environmentalists usually say, are "ecological"—which means, roughly translated, ⑥ that natural systems are allowed to operate as free from human interference as possible (par. 4).

In this paragraph, Tucker uses six statements to amplify the environmentalists' definition of wilderness. When we paraphrase his point, though, we must sort out and condense them into a single statement:

OUR PARAPHRASE OF TUCKER'S AMPLIFICATION

Definition of wilderness
Tucker, 1982, par. 4
Faulty: According to Tucker, the definition of wilderness used by environmentalists and given in the Wilderness Act of 1964 is an area in which evidence of human activity is excluded for ecological, rather than scenic or recreational, purposes.

Look for Qualifications

Another kind of information authors often include in their texts is qualification. *Qualifications* modify the scope of a point by limiting its possible interpretation. Taken alone, you might take a point in a more absolute sense than the author intends, or you might draw conclusions the author does not want.

Authors who are taking an unusual position often find the need to qualify against inappropriate interpretations. For example, when Tucker argues against the preservationist stand, readers could easily conclude that he was indifferent to the beauty of wilderness. Because Tucker was aware of this possible misinterpretation, however, he included the following qualification:

TUCKER'S USE OF QUALIFICATION

> I am not arguing against wild things, scenic beauty, pristine landscapes, and scenic preservation. What I am questioning is the argument that wilderness is a value against which every other human activity must be judged, and that human beings are somehow unworthy of the landscape. The wilderness has been equated with freedom, but there are many different ideas about what constitutes freedom.

When you are paraphrasing a point that an author has qualified, you may or may not want to include the qualification in your paraphrase. Qualifications don't change a point; they only cut off misinterpretations. Therefore, you should include a qualification only if you find yourself tempted by the misinterpretation. Otherwise, it is probably not crucial to following an author's line of argument.

For Class 4.1

The points listed in the columns below are quoted from Roderick Nash's essay, "The Irony of Victory."

a. Match each point in the left-hand column to the support, amplification, or qualification in the right-hand column. Follow the hints given in parentheses.
b. Write a paraphrase of each point in the right-hand column. Decide whether or not to include the additional information supplied by the right-hand column.

In class, discuss your strategies for paraphrasing and your reasons for including or excluding the information in the left-hand column.

1. The growth of appreciation for the wilderness experience in the American mind inevitably resulted in an increasing demand for actual wild country. (support)

A. In defense of Eric Julber and those who share his opinion, his "'access'" philosophy is not aimed at minimizing the value of wilderness in American civilization.

2. The hopes of Thoreau and Marshall and Leopold seemed fulfilled. (amplification)

3. Any definition of wilderness implies an absence of civilization, and wilderness values are so fragile that even appropriate kinds of recreational use detract from and, in sufficient quantity, destroy wilderness. (support)

4. Julber's confusion lay in equating "nature," "scenery," and "beauty" with "wilderness." (qualification)

5. Since the establishment of Yellowstone National Park in 1872, and certainly since the National Park Service Act of 1916, the parks had labored awkwardly under the dual charge of preserving nature and advancing public recreation. (amplification)

6. Sometimes it might be necessary to resolve a wilderness versus people issue *against* people. (support)

7. Public discussion in the 1970s of the problem of loving wilderness to death made frequent use of an old rangeland and livestock term, "carrying capacity." (amplification)

8. The basic assumption here is that wilderness implies the absence of man, and any human evidence—even that of fellow campers—is disruptive to a degree. (qualification)

9. In California's backbone of mountain wilderness, called the Sierra, recent years have seen wilderness recreation use rise at a much sharper rate than the national 12 percent. (qualification)

10. As he climbs, the increase in visitation is readily apparent. (support)

11. Access is limited to a few easy patrolled areas and the Colorado River, which can be reached by vehicles at only one point. (amplification)

12. Quotas based on the carrying-capacity concept could do much toward preserving wilderness. (support)

13. Man in a state of civilization readily

B. Yet considering both the gains in appreciation for the wilderness and the losses in the amount of wild country left to be appreciated, it is increasingly evident that the future of the American wilderness depends on American civilization's deliberately keeping it wild.

C. A case in point was the recommendation against roads and hotels.

D. Confirming Muir's forecast, "thousands of tired, nerve-shaken, over-civilized people" *had* come to the wilderness.

E. The simplified meaning of this concept as applied to wilderness is the ability of an environment to absorb human influence and still retain its wildness.

F. At the more popular lakes the detergent that campers use for dishes and laundry is turning up in the water in traceable amounts.

G. Still, the idea of intense control that quota systems entail is difficult to square with the meaning of wilderness.

H. Another index was the emergence of a wilderness equipment business.

I. Levels of tolerance for people vary, of course.

J. And it is still the case that at most of the Sierra trailheads a person simply parks his car and starts walking.

K. Ultimately, the acceptance of such quotas is based on respect for the quality of the experience.

L. As ecologist Stanley A. Cain has remarked, "innumerable people cannot enjoy solitude together."

M. The Grand Canyon, moreover, is far more difficult country for the average wilderness-user than either the Sierra or Boundary Waters Canoe Area.

N. In fact, the Forest Service and the National Park Service are already experimenting with rationing systems as a prelude to more general application later in the 1970s.

O. In larger parks, like Yellowstone, time clarified the dilemma as one involving a accepts quota-type restrictions of many of his activities. (amplification)

14. Respect for the quality of the wilderness experience argues for the acceptance of regulated use. (qualification)

15. The quality of freedom so frequently associated with wilderness is diminished, if not destroyed, by regulation. (qualification)

choice between wilderness values and those of civilization.

For Your Notebook #7

Create a set of notes to paraphrase the points made in each of the argumentative texts you have gathered.

- Review your marginal notations, topic area by topic area, and transfer this information to 3 × 5 notecards.
- Paraphrase each of the main points, deciding whether to include references to the support, amplification, and qualifications the author gives.

DIVIDE YOUR NOTES BY MILESTONE

As we have already discussed, authors create argumentative texts in order to help a community resolve a set of problem cases. A successful line of argument will generally achieve this purpose by moving a community of readers through three milestones, or stages, of argument: "seeing the issue," "defining the problem," and "choosing a solution." Each of these three milestones brings the readers closer to the desired resolution. The next step in visualizing an author's line of argument, then, is to divide your notes according to the milestone they address.

Generally speaking, you will find that a notecard on a single topic can be placed within a single milestone. Place the name of the milestone in the upper right-hand corner. You will also find that once you have placed one notecard at a particular milestone, you should place the ones you took after it similarly. That's because authors tend to cluster their points. And finally, you can expect to begin with arguments for seeing the issue, work through arguments for defining the problem, and end with arguments for choosing a solution. Authors often depart from this normal order, of course, but when they do, you will probably sense that the author is backtracking to "fill in" arguments.

In the sections below, we describe the kinds of arguments you should expect to find on the main path at each of the milestones. Remember, however, that a milestone should also include any faulty positions that lead away from this main path and return paths to lead you back. Thus, for example, you would classify an author's characterization and dismissal of an inappropriate problem definition as an argument for "defining the problem" just as much as you would an author's own problem definition.

"Seeing the Issue"

At the first milestone of argument, **"seeing the issue,"** authors try to convince readers to care enough about the issue to want it resolved. If they succeed, their readers will have a stake in following the rest of the argument. If they fail, their readers won't care much about whatever else they have to say. Thus, authors often place their arguments for "seeing the issue" at the beginning of their texts as a way to convince readers to go on.

One way authors make arguments for seeing the issue is by describing typical, recurring, or provocative problem cases. If authors can convince you to see the importance of their cases, they will create a common cause with you in eliminating the underlying problem. For example, Tucker tries to get us concerned in his essay "Is Nature Too Good for Us?" by reciting a litany of problem cases that he says have resulted from the preservation effort. Here are our notes from these sections. Notice that we have put the phrase "seeing the issue" in the upper right-hand corner of each.

TUCKER ON SEEING THE ISSUE THROUGH PROBLEM CASES

Effects	Seeing the issue
Tucker, 1982, par. 11–12 *Main:* According to Tucker, the wilderness concept is valid for creating ecological museums in scenic and biologically significant areas. But the result of the preservation effort has more often been to lock up mineral and energy resources in western states without adequate resource reviews, causing serious harm to our international trade.	western states

---

Roadless areas   Seeing the issue

Tucker, par. 13–15

Main: According to Tucker, the main fight involves roadless areas.

Faulty: Preservationists argue that these areas are *de facto* wildernesses and have fought the two RARE studies that recommended their release.

Main: This fight, according to Tucker, has increased timber prices, made the U.S. an importer of timber, and caused the hurried set–aside of the mineral–rich Sawtooth Wilderness.

roadless
areas

Overthrust Belt   Seeing the issue

Tucker, 1982, par. 16

Main: According to Tucker, the Overthrust Belt is one of the most hotly contested areas.

Faulty: Environmentalists want these areas designated as wildernesses and have allowed mineral exploration under restricted conditions only until 1982.

Main: According to Tucker, these restricted conditions make exploration expensive and ineffective.

Overthrust Belt

Another way authors make readers see the issue is through a historical account of the controversy. If an author can convince you that an issue has caused a great deal of controversy in your community, you may well continue listening out of a desire to see peace return. Tucker uses this strategy when he gives a historical account of the preservationist policy. Again, we have labeled our notes in the upper right-hand corner:

TUCKER ON SEEING THE ISSUE THROUGH A HISTORICAL ACCOUNT

Leopold and Marshall   Seeing the issue

Tucker, 1982, par. 6–7

Main: The preservationist effort, according to Tucker, was begun by Aldo Leopold, a Forest Service officer working in the Gila National Forest in the 1920s. It was continued by Robert Marshall until in the 1950s 14 million acres of National Forest had been set aside.

Faulty: Both Leopold and Marshall worked to preserve wilderness areas, according to Tucker, because of their experience in the Kaibab Plateau. There the Service systematically eradicated predators in an effort to increase the deer population. The program worked until 60 percent of the herd died from starvation in two severe winters. Leopold and Marshall felt that this case showed that humans cannot intervene in natural ecosystems without doing damage, no matter how good the intentions are.

the
effort
begins

Pinchot and National Forests   Seeing the issue

Tucker, 1982, par. 8–9

Main: The preservation effort expanded in the 1950s in a fight over the National Forests.

Faulty: Many environmentalists believed that the National Forests would be preserved forever.

Main: Pinchot had originally withheld them from timber cutting in order to keep prices high enough to allow ''sustained yield'' cutting. When they came due for release in the 1950s the preservationists reacted.

the
effort
expands

Congressional battle	Seeing the issue

Tucker, 1982, par. 10

Main: According to Tucker, the conservationists originally won the battle with the Multiple Use and Sustained Yield Act of 1960. But then the wilderness advocates won the day with the passage of the Wilderness Act of 1964, which allowed ''wilderness'' as an alternative to multiple use.

the
effort
prevails

Historical accounts of controversy like the one used here are an effective means of persuading us to see the issue because they show us that the tension is ongoing and unresolved. Historical accounts also show us that others before us have been seriously concerned with the issue, thus encouraging us to become involved ourselves.

"Defining the Problem"

Authors make arguments for **"defining the problem"** in order to explain or define the source of the tension in the issue. The purpose of this second milestone of argument is to give readers the terms they need to understand the heart of the problem.

For Tucker, understanding the real problem of wilderness means understanding its definition. While many environmentalists claim that wilderness is "primitive," Tucker argues that it is actually the product of a civilized society. Here are our notes:

TUCKER ON DEFINING THE PROBLEM THROUGH SPECIALIZED TERMS

Closed frontier	Defining the problem

Tucker, 1982, par. 23–25

Main: After the frontier closed in 1890, the U.S. grew up——one sign, according to Tucker, was the conservation movement.

Faulty: Many preservationists act as if we are now running out of space

Return: Tucker believes that the preservation effort is really an immature effort to reopen the American frontier.

```
┌─────────────────────────────────────────────────┐
│  State of nature          Defining the problem   │
├─────────────────────────────────────────────────┤
│  Tucker, 1982, par. 37-40                         │
│  Faulty: Many preservationists argue that         │
│  the backpacker has a unique contact with         │
│  primitive nature.                                │
│  Return: Actual primitive people are              │
│  repelled by wilderness.                          │
│  Main: Tucker believes, quoting Babbitt,          │
│  that the wilderness ideal is actually the        │
│  product of a very civilized society.             │
└─────────────────────────────────────────────────┘
```

```
┌─────────────────────────────────────────────────┐
│  Civilized concept        Defining the problem   │
├─────────────────────────────────────────────────┤
│  Tucker, 1982, par. 37-40                         │
│  Main: According to Tucker, wilderness is         │
│  the product of a complex technological           │
│  society that has created economic leisure.       │
│  Main: According to Tucker, the preservation      │
│  impulse endangers this economic leisure          │
│  because it ties up needed resources.             │
└─────────────────────────────────────────────────┘
```

By introducing a new definition of the concept of wilderness, Tucker is able, as our notes indicate, to explain what is at issue. As we noted in an earlier chapter, this tension is, for Tucker, the "undeniable paradox" lying at the heart of the wilderness issue. To pinpoint the paradox, Tucker must use the terms "nature" and "leisure" in new ways.

"Choosing a Solution"

At the third and final milestone of authors' lines of argument, they must convince readers to accept and act on their recommendations for the future. These recommendations for **"choosing a solution"** usually try to persuade readers to adopt a specific action or belief. Such actions or beliefs, authors argue, are what the community needs to eliminate the original set of problem cases.

You can recognize a "choosing a solution" argument if you find an author talking about what should be done beyond the scope of the actual essay. Whereas arguments for seeing the issue often deal with the past, and arguments for defining the problem often deal with the present, arguments for choosing a solution are arguments for the future.

Authors may be more or less specific in their recommendations at this final milestone of argument. Tucker, for example, spends very little time in making recommendations; he is more concerned with stopping current preservationist policy than with describing his preferred policy. Nevertheless he makes it clear that he would like to see a different policy adopted. Here are our notes:

TUCKER ON CHOOSING A SOLUTION

Religious impulse   Choosing a solution

Tucker, 1982, par. 41–45

Faulty: Many environmentalists such as E. F. Schumacher and Marvin Harris have argued that wilderness preservation should serve as the basis of a new religion with a more environmentally sound perspective.

Faulty: According to Lynn White, the Western Judeo–Christian religion is the source of the environmental crisis because it assumes man is the master of nature.

Return: Tucker, however, is not convinced that doing away with the Judeo–Christian tradition would change the way we treat nature.

Primitivism   Choosing a solution

Tucker, 1982, par. 46–47

Faulty: According to romantic notions often argued by environmentalists, primitive people were more environmentally sound.

Return: According to Tucker, quoting René Dubos, many primitive cultures caused extensive ecological damage.

> Stewardship   Choosing a solution
>
> ---
>
> Tucker, 1982, par. 48–49
>
> *Main:* According to Tucker, we must adopt a
> conservative policy of stewardship toward
> the land, recognizing the part we play in
> nature. He quotes Dubos as saying that we
> must develop creative and harmonious ways
> to live with nature. This, according to
> Tucker, should be the goal of the
> environmental movement.

For Class 4.2

The following are our notes on Roderick Nash's essay, "The Irony of Victory" (Chapter 3). Reread the essay, if necessary, then divide these notes according to the three milestones of argument. Be prepared to justify your division in class discussion.

A.

> Increased appreciation
>
> ---
>
> Nash, 1978, par. 1
>
> *Main:* According to Nash, Americans'
> increasing appreciation of the wilderness
> has increased the demand for access and may
> paradoxically end up destroying wilderness.
> Threat to wilderness may come from
> recreational as well as economic uses—it
> doesn't matter which.

B.

Julber
Nash, 1978, par. 3–4 *Faulty:* Los Angeles lawyer Eric Julber has argued that wilderness ought to be opened up for the general public as in Switzerland in order to increase Americans' love of nature. *Return:* According to Nash, Julber has confused wilderness with scenic beauty. Wilderness, according to Nash, would disappear with the kind of access Julber imagines.

C.

Centennial report
Nash, 1978, par. 5–8 *Main:* The Centennial Task Force argued in 1972 that the major purpose of the National Parks should be the preservation of the wilderness, not the increase of recreational access. *Faulty:* Critics of the report such as Interior Secretary Morton argued that the National Parks were already doing a good job of preservation and ought to be doing more for recreation. *Return:* According to wilderness advocates, this parks–are–for–people concept would end up destroying wilderness. Wilderness requires special definition and management to survive.

D.

Carrying capacity

Nash, 1978, par. 9–12, #1 of 2

Main: According to Nash, ''When a region's carrying capacity is exceeded it is no longer wild,'' no matter whether that excess is recreational use or economic exploitation.

Main: Carrying capacity has three dimensions: physical, biological, and psychological.

Main: The physical carrying capacity of an area includes the presence of synthetic objects produced by human visitation, e.g., trail erosion, trails, bridges, roads, signs, firewood, camping space.

E.

Carrying capacity

Nash, 1978, par. 9–12, #2 of 2

Main: The biological carrying capacity, including a region's plants and animals, can be exceeded when substantially altered, e.g., grizzly bear attacks, fishing out a lake, trampling a meadow.

Main: A region's psychological carrying capacity includes the effects of other people's presence on a visitor's experience.

F.

The Sierra

Nash, 1978, par. 13–14

Main: According to Nash, the Sierra Mountains are an example of a wilderness region whose carrying capacity has been exceeded, e.g., scavenged firewood, regular stocking of fish, excess concentration of campers, worn trails, detergent in water, efforts to keep trails a secret.

G.

BWCA

Nash, 1972, par. 15

Main: According to Nash, the Boundary
Waters Canoe Area is now approaching its
carrying capacity despite tough
restrictions on use.

H.

Grand Canyon

Nash, 1972, par. 16–18

Main: The Grand Canyon is also nearing its
carrying capacity despite naturally limited
access. The cause: inflatable rubber rafts
have made the trip safe.

I.

Quotas

Nash, 1972, par. 19–22

Main: According to Nash, the only way to
remedy carrying–capacity violations is
through the acceptance of visitation quotas
based on respect for the experience.

Faulty: Some people will feel that quotas
diminish or destroy the idea of wilderness
by imposing human regulation.

Return: According to Nash, however, the
increased appreciation they produce and the
destruction they decrease make quotas the
only acceptable solution to wilderness
destruction.

SKETCH EACH MILESTONE OF THE ARGUMENT

Once you have divided your notes according to milestone, your next step
is to make a sketch of each milestone. To make these sketches, you need to
work out the relationships among the author's points. That is, within each mile-

stone, you must look for connections among the author's main, faulty, and return paths.

Begin this effort with the main path. Ideally, you should come up with one overarching point along the main path of each milestone—for a total of three main points along the entire line of argument. This usually requires you to review a number of different notes you have labeled as "main," discarding some and consolidating others. For instance, our notes on Tucker's points at "defining the problem" included four points marked "main":

TUCKER'S POINTS ON THE MAIN PATH AT "DEFINING THE PROBLEM"

1. *Main:* After the frontier closed in 1890, the U.S. grew up—one sign, according to Tucker, was the conservation movement (par. 23-25).
2. *Main:* Tucker believes, quoting Babbitt, that the wilderness ideal is actually the product of a very civilized society (par. 37-40).
3. *Main:* According to Tucker, wilderness is the product of a complex technological society that has created economic leisure (par. 37-40).
4. *Main:* According to Tucker, the preservation impulse endangers this economic leisure because it ties up needed resources (par. 37-40).

To create an overarching main point, we needed to consider how to consolidate these four into Tucker's overall position. To do this, we discarded the first point concerning the maturity of the conservation movement and consolidated the remaining three points:

TUCKER'S OVERARCHING MAIN POINT

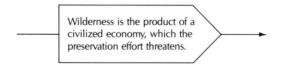
Wilderness is the product of a civilized economy, which the preservation effort threatens.

The next step in sketching a milestone of argument is to establish relationships between the overarching main point and the points lying on faulty and return paths. You should understand how each point on a faulty path leads away from the point you've just placed on the main path and how each point lying on a return path leads back again. Furthermore, you should be able to see the relationships among all of the faulty path/return path combinations.

Begin with your notes on faulty paths. Sometimes authors bring up and dismiss few or no faulty positions in the course of their argument at a particular milestone. Occasionally, however, they will make quite complicated arguments and you will have a number of points marked "faulty" in your notes. In this case, your sketch will be considerably simplified if you can see some of the points as elaborations of others. For instance, when we reviewed our notes on faulty paths in the Tucker essay, we found eight such notes:

TUCKER'S POINTS ON FAULTY PATHS

1. *Faulty:* According to many preservationists, the set-aside effort is necessary to save the few remaining wild places (par. 17).
2. *Faulty:* According to Tucker, one of the most common arguments for preservation is the claim that wilderness is a source of peace and freedom (par. 18-21).
3. *Faulty:* Many of the early founders of the preservation movement preferred to live long periods in the wilderness isolation (par. 22).
4. *Faulty:* Many preservationists act as if we are now running out of space (par. 23-25).
5. *Faulty:* The preservationist ideal, according to Tucker, is the backpacker who goes into the wilderness as a passive observer, bringing all his supplies with him (par. 26-27).
6. *Faulty:* Environmentalists want to restrict access to wilderness to backpackers and canoers (par. 28-31).
7. *Faulty:* According to Tucker, the preservationists' effort is a revival of the romanticism of Rousseau who argued that man was free in nature and enslaved by civilization (par. 32-34).
8. *Faulty:* Many environmentalists believe in testing middle-class values through survival clubs (par. 35-36).

When we examined these faulty paths carefully, however, we felt that Tucker characterized the environmentalists as making three basic arguments: that we have few wild places left (points 1 and 4); that wilderness is a source of peace and freedom (points 2, 3, 5, and 6); and that primitive is better (points 7 and 8). We added this set of three faulty paths to our sketch as follows:

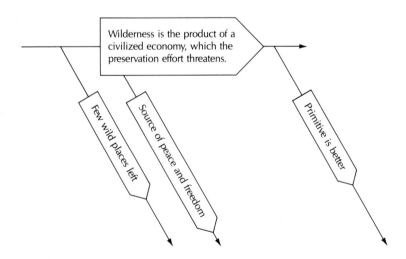

The final step in constructing a sketch of a milestone of argument is adding the return paths. Each faulty path in your sketch must have at least one return path. Some may have several. Usually, you will find the return path to an argument directly next to the faulty path in your notes, but occasionally, you will need to look more widely or think more deeply.

Tucker gave the second faulty position in our sketch a great deal of attention. He counters the environmentalists' argument that wilderness is a source of peace and freedom with six different points on return paths:

TUCKER'S POINTS ON RETURN PATHS

1. *Return:* People overrun an area as soon as they hear that it is a wilderness.
2. *Return:* People have many different senses of freedom.
3. *Return:* According to Tucker, an ethic based on wilderness isolation cannot serve as the basis for a useful national philosophy.
4. *Return:* Tucker believes that the preservationist effort is really an immature effort to reopen the American frontier.
5. *Return:* The problem with the backpacking ideal, according to Tucker, is that if the backpacker actually had to live off the wilderness, he would violate the Wilderness Act.
6. *Return:* According to Tucker, wildernesses are just parks for upper middle-class tastes in recreation.

Obviously, Tucker has more than one argument to convince us not to accept the preservationist's position. But again, we try to consolidate across these points to get a smaller number of paths. In this case, we decide there are three distinctive return paths for this single faulty path: overrun by people (point 1); isolationist and middle-class taste (points 2, 3, and 6); and impractical frontier myth (points 4 and 5). Now our sketch looks like the one on the next page.

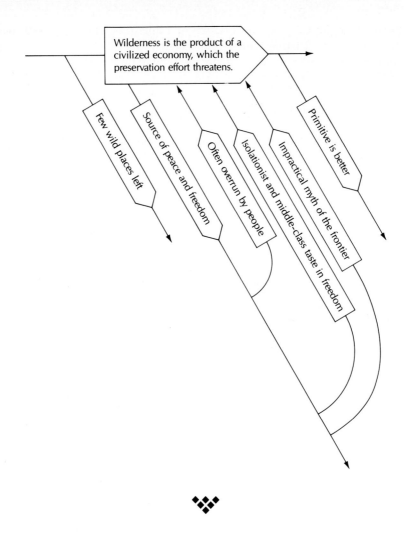

Wilderness is the product of a civilized economy, which the preservation effort threatens.

Few wild places left

Source of peace and freedom

Often overrun by people

Isolationist and middle-class taste in freedom

Impractical myth of the frontier

Primitive is better

❖❖❖

For Class 4.3

1. From the following points marked "return" in our notes, construct one or more return paths from the faulty path "Primitive is better." Where would you insert these paths in the proceeding sketch of Tucker's second milestone?

   a. *Return:* According to Tucker, environmentalists actually do not approve of many primitive practices, such as those used by Alaskan natives, and try to restrict them (par. 32-34).

   b. *Return:* Also, according to Tucker, environmentalists usually underestimate the dangerousness of actual wilderness (par. 32-34).

   c. *Return:* According to Tucker, the preservationists actually want a mythical place frozen in time: after the Indians leave, before the settlers arrive (par. 32-34).

    d. *Return:* According to Tucker, a stay in New York City would be just as much of a test of middle-class values as the survival clubs (par. 35-36).

    e. *Return:* Actual primitive people are repelled by wilderness (par. 37-40).

    f. *Return:* Actual survival in the wilderness binds us more closely to things rather than setting us free (par. 37-40).

2. Return to the notes on Nash's essay given in "For Class 4.2" (page 87) and sketch each of Nash's three milestones of argument.

REVIEW THE FULL LINE OF THE ARGUMENT

In an ideal argument, each of the milestones you have sketched in the previous section should flow from one to the next in an uninterrupted journey from problem to solution. As a final check on your understanding of the full line of argument, you should review the relationships formed when you put your three milestones side by side.

Begin with the second milestone ("defining the problem") and work backward to "seeing the issue." Do the problem cases given at "seeing the issue" exhibit the tension you have located at "defining the problem"? Can you describe these cases using the specialized terms you have attributed to the author? If not, can you reword the problem definition or the problem cases to bring them more in line?

Now work forward to the third milestone ("choosing a solution"). Can you see how the solution you have identified there eliminates the tension you have placed at "defining the problem"? Further, will this solution eliminate the problem cases you have described at "seeing the issue"? If not, can you recharacterize the solution to bring it more in line?

In making this review, keep in mind that you are walking a fine line between staying true to an author's points and making sense of the author's argument. Often, you will find that a slight rethinking of an author's points will make the line of argument clear to you. In this case, you should not hesitate to modify your initial reading.

Occasionally, you will find that your efforts to make sense of the argument actually do require some slight departure from what the author actually seemed to say. In this case, obey the rules of charity and recognize that you are making sense of what the author *probably* meant rather than what the author actually said. And finally, if you find that you can only make sense of the full line of argument by making substantial alterations in what the author actually says, you should note the author's inconsistency and consider your sketch *your* best interpretation of what he or she might have been aiming at. In all these cases, however, the key is to distinguish what the author actually says from your interpretation of what the author intended to say.

For Your Notebook #8

Review the set of notecards you have created for each of the argumentative texts on your issue:

- Divide these notes according to the three milestones of argument.
- Sketch each milestone with its main, faulty, and return paths. Consolidate points if necessary.
- Review the full line of argument to see how each milestone leads to the next. Make any adjustments required to make sense of the line of argument, but keep in mind the difference between your interpretation and what the author actually says.

▢▢▢ 5 DRAFT THE
SUMMARY

Thus far, you have used your notes and sketches to make other authors' lines of argument clear for yourself alone. Before you go on, however, you will find it useful to put this knowledge to work in prose for other readers. By writing for others, you move beyond a world of private meaning to refine your ideas in language and earn public credit for your work. In doing so, you will both draw on the work you have done in previous chapters and set the stage for work you will do in forthcoming chapters. There's an important lesson to be learned from this progression: in a cycle of reading and writing, what enables you to read well is also what will enable you to write well. Thus, at every stage in your work, you can capitalize on your thinking to write something for others. Drafting a summary is the first of these opportunities.

For our purposes, a *summary* is an attempt to tell others about your understanding of the line of argument constructed by another author. In a summary, you strive to give readers a fair characterization of that line of argument and place it in the context of the appropriate issue. You have now worked through the twists and turns of many authors' arguments, so you are well suited to this task. Readers will turn to your work for a quick but valid impression of what a single author says. Further, they may also use a set of your summaries as an annotated bibliography to quickly survey an entire issue. In this chapter, you will move through the activities of outlining, drafting, and revising to produce a set of these summaries for your issue.

OUTLINE THE BODY

Readers turn to a summary for a quick overview of an author's argument. Thus, summaries are generally short—from a half page to two pages—depending on the length of the work to be summarized. Such short drafts generally don't require an elaborate outline, but you will find it useful to jot down the points you want to cover. This list will then serve you as an outline for the body of your text.

To decide what points to include in your outline, work directly from the sketches you produced in Chapter 4. Those sketches include all the information you need for your summary: the author's milestones of argument, and the author's points on main, faulty, and return paths within each milestone.

In outlining, your first decision concerns the order in which to list the milestones of argument. If the author's text has ordered the three milestones straightforwardly from "seeing the issue" to "choosing a solution," you can simply follow this order in your outline. If, on the other hand, the author has presented the arguments in a different order, you have a choice. You may either follow the author's order or use the ordering from problem to solution. Either strategy will produce an adequate summary. Your instructor may specify one or the other; if not, use the one you prefer.

In outlining the body of our summary for Tucker, for example, we noted that he proceeds directly from "seeing the issue" to "choosing a solution." Thus, we easily decided to follow that order in our outline:

OUR ORDERING OF TUCKER'S MILESTONES

I. The issue
II. The problem
III. The solution

Your next decision in outlining concerns the order of points on main, faulty, and return paths. Within each milestone, the order of your discussion should reflect the author's emphasis. If an author emphasizes faulty paths, list these first in your outline. If the emphasis is on points on the main path, list them first instead.

In filling in major points at Tucker's milestones of argument, for example, we worked through the points at each milestone, one at a time. At "seeing the issue," we had few decisions to make since our sketch indicated only one main point:

OUR OUTLINE OF TUCKER AT "SEEING THE ISSUE"

I. The issue
   Main: The continuing battle between preservationists and conservationists now threatens U.S. international trade.

At "defining the problem," our sketch was more complicated, showing faulty paths and numerous return paths. Tucker's emphasis is clearly on characterizing and refuting these opposing positions. Thus, in our outline we place the faulty paths first:

OUR OUTLINE OF TUCKER AT "DEFINING THE PROBLEM"

II. The problem
   A. *Faulty:* running out of space

Return: plenty of room left
Return: something more at stake

B. *Faulty:* source of peace and freedom
Return: often overrun by people
Return: limited tastes in freedom
Return: impractical return to the frontier

C. *Faulty:* primitive is better
Return: disapprove of primitative practices
Return: underestimate danger
Return: mythical place frozen in time
Return: primitive people repelled

D. *Main:* Wilderness is a product of an economically advanced civilization, but preservation threatens this economic well-being.

Our sketch at "choosing a solution," though less complicated, revealed the same emphasis:

OUR OUTLINE OF TUCKER AT "CHOOSING A SOLUTION"

III. The solution
Faulty: new religious alternative to Western J-C
Return: Western J-C not unique in exploitation
Main: doctrine of stewardship

DRAFT THE INTRODUCTION

With a rough outline of points in hand, you begin drafting with the introduction. An introduction serves to orient readers to the text you're summarizing, to the issue, and to your summary. It usually runs about two sentences and should include the following information:

INFORMATION TO INCLUDE IN THE INTRODUCTION

- The *citation* for the text to be summarized (includes author and publication)
- The *issue* addressed by the author
- The *overall claim* made by the author.

Here's our introduction to the summary of Tucker's essay:

INTRODUCTION TO A SUMMARY OF TUCKER

citation   Writing in *Harper's* in March 1982, William Tucker addresses
issue   the issue of wilderness preservation in an essay entitled "Is Na-
                  ture Too Good for Us?" There Tucker argues that the preserva-

overall claim   tion effort is driven by fundamental misconceptions concerning the relationship between man and nature.

The general rule in composing your sentences is that your subject or topic—the thing you're talking about—should always be the author. In our introduction, for example, the topic of both of our sentences is Tucker:

THE AUTHOR AS TOPIC

<u>Tucker</u> addresses the issue of wilderness preservation. . . . <u>Tucker</u> argues that the preservation effort . . .

If the text you are summarizing is unsigned, you should substitute a phrase describing the author for the author's actual name. For example, if Tucker's article had been published unsigned, we would write, "The editor argues" or even "The author argues" in place of "Tucker argues." Never, however, take the title of the text as your topic. That is, never write, " 'Is Nature Too Good for Us?' argues that . . ." People argue, not texts.

For Class 5.1

Using the following information, draft an introduction to a summary for the following argumentative texts:

1. *Citation:*   Nash, Roderick, "The Irony of Victory," from *Wilderness and the American Mind* (New Haven: Yale University Press, 1979)
   Issue: Access to wilderness
   Claim: Wilderness requires special definition and handling.

2. *Citation:*   Swain, Edward B., "Wilderness and the Maintenance of Freedom," *The Humanist,* May-April, 1983
   Issue: Wilderness preservation
   Claim: We must preserve wilderness as a way of maintaining our freedom.

3. *Citation:*   Julber, Eric, "Let's Open Up Our Wilderness Areas," *Reader's Digest,* May, 1972
   Issue: Wilderness access
   Claim: We must open up wilderness areas to all Americans.

4. *Citation:*   Ehrlich, Paul, and Anne Ehrlich, "Should We Mourn the Dinosaurs?" from *Extinction: The Causes and Consequences of The Disappearance of Species* (New York: Random House, 1981)
   Issue: Endangered species
   Claim: We must recognize our dependency on the world's intricate ecosystem.

5. *Citation:*   Jackson, Senator Henry M. "Should Congress Enact the Wilderness Protection Act of 1982?" *The Congressional Digest,* December, 1982.

Issue: Wilderness protection
Claim: Congress should pass the Wilderness Protection Act to prevent unnecessary leasing of wilderness areas.

DRAFT THE BODY

In the body of your summary, you describe the author's points for "seeing the issue," "defining the problem," and "choosing a solution," following the order in your preliminary outline. In the interests of brevity, however, you may combine points in various ways not indicated by the outline. For example, when we drafted the paragraph for "defining the problem" for Tucker's essay, we combined all of his characterizations of faulty positions in one sentence and all his points on return paths in the following sentence:

COMBINING POINTS IN THE BODY

faulty   The preservationist effort is fueled, according to Tucker, by a number of misconceptions: that we are running out of wilderness, that wilderness provides a necessary source of peace and freedom, and that primitive practices are generally better than more civilized practices.

return   Tucker argues that, in point of fact, the United States has plenty of open space and that the search for peace and freedom is just a middle-class attempt to retreat from the responsibilities of modern life.

In drafting the body, you must also remember to remind your readers that you are talking about the author's points, not making points of your own. This means inserting author attributions at appropriate intervals throughout the summary:

USING AUTHOR ATTRIBUTIONS

The preservationist effort is fueled, according to Tucker, by a number of misconceptions: that we are running out of wilderness, that wilderness provides a necessary source of peace and freedom, and that primitive practices are generally better than more civilized practices. Tucker argues that in point of fact the U.S. has plenty of open space and that the search for peace and freedom is just a middle-class attempt to retreat from the responsibilities of modern life. The real danger in this effort, he argues, is that by locking up needed natural resources we may actually jeopardize the economic well-being that has allowed us to enjoy such respites from the daily need to support ourselves.

The alternative <u>for Tucker</u> is clear. We do not need to search for a new religious consciousness based in more primitive or less Western civilizations. They, after all, do no better than we at ecology. What we need is to return to the conservationists' doctrine of stewardship of the land. That is, we must seek to develop a creative and harmonious relationship with nature rather than setting ourselves apart from it.

By using author attributions like these, you help your readers separate your voice from the voice of the author you're talking about. As someone trying to establish your own authorship, this is an important accomplishment. Your readers should always know when you are talking and when you are paraphrasing claims made by someone else.

Finally, in drafting, you may give a full paragraph or just a sentence to each milestone of argument depending on the length of the original text and the needs of your readers. For our completed summary of Tucker, we combined our introduction with the arguments for "seeing the issue" and gave each of the succeeding milestones one paragraph each:

DRAFT OF A SUMMARY OF TUCKER

introduction

"seeing
the issue"

Writing in *Harper's* in March of 1982, William Tucker addresses the issue of wilderness preservation in an essay entitled "Is Nature Too Good for Us?" There Tucker argues that the preservation effort is driven by fundamental misconceptions concerning the relationship between man and nature. Although the preservationist philosophy has long been opposed by conservationists, it was not until the passage of the Wilderness Act of 1964 that the preservationists held the upper hand. Now, Tucker argues, preservationist efforts in the western states are threatening future U.S. international trade.

"defining
the problem"

The preservationist effort is fueled, according to Tucker, by a number of misconceptions: that we are running out of wilderness, that wilderness provides a necessary source of peace and freedom, and that primitive practices are generally better than more civilized practices. Tucker argues that, in point of fact, the United States has plenty of open space and that the search for peace and freedom is just a middle-class attempt to retreat from the responsibilities of modern life. The real danger in this effort, he argues, is that by locking up needed natural resources we may actually jeopardize the economic well-being that has allowed us to enjoy such respites from the daily need to support ourselves.

"choosing
a solution"   The alternative for Tucker is clear. We do not need to
search for a new religious consciousness based in more primitive or less Western civilizations. They, after all, do no better
than we at ecology. What we need is to return to the conservationists' doctrine of stewardship of the land. That is, we must
seek to develop a creative and harmonious relationship with
nature rather than setting ourselves apart from it.

For Class 5.2

Rewrite the following summary of Nash's "The Irony of Victory" to include
enough author attributions to clearly distinguish the summarizer's voice from Nash's
voice.

Recent increases in the national appreciation for wilderness have created a new
danger for wilderness preservation: overuse through recreational exploitation. Many
people who argue that wildernesses must be opened up for recreational use confuse
simple natural beauty with wilderness. Wildernesses are special areas that can be
destroyed if their physical, biological, or psychological carrying capacities are exceeded. Changes in wilderness equipment have recently caused the carrying capacities of the Sierra Mountains, the Boundary Waters Canoe Area, and the Grand Canyon to be met or exceeded through recreational use. The only way to protect
wilderness from these excesses is to impose quotas on visitation. While these quotas
may diminish some people's sense of freedom in wilderness, they are the price we
have to pay to ensure that wilderness remains to be enjoyed by future generations.

For Your Notebook #9

For each of the texts you've collected on your issue, draft a one-page summary.
Make sure to:

- Include the text, the issue, and the author's major claim in your introduction.
- Cover the author's major points as shown in your sketch of the line of argument.
- Focus on the author as topic.
- Use author attributions to distinguish the author's voice from your own.

REVISE FOR YOUR READERS

The final step in drafting a summary is to revise to meet the needs of your
readers. This revision should take into account differences between your readers
and those for whom the author wrote. By adding detail and transitions, you
can help your readers follow an author's line of argument more closely.

Adding *detail* to your summary makes an author's claims more understandable and credible. Detail helps readers standing outside of an issue to understand what it involves and what an author's claims mean. Choosing detail can also help you to better understand the relationship between the major points and the supporting evidence. In revising our original paragraph for "seeing the issue," for example, we added the underlined detail to explain the two competing philosophies toward the environment:

REVISED SUMMARY WITH ADDED DETAIL

The preservationist philosophy of setting aside extensive tracts of land in wilderness preserves has long been opposed by conservationists who favor policies of multiple use and highest use. But it was not until passage of the Wilderness Act of 1964 that the preservationists held the upper hand. Now preservationist efforts in the western states are threatening U.S. international trade for years to come by locking up scarce energy and mineral resources in permanent preserves.

In addition to adding detail to your summary, you should make sure you have included enough *transitions* to allow your reader to follow the structure of the argument. In our final draft of a summary of Tucker, for example, we included the following underlined transitions to make sure that Tucker's argument was clear:

REVISED SUMMARY WITH ADDED TRANSITIONS

Writing in *Harper's* in March of 1982, William Tucker addresses the issue of wilderness preservation in an essay entitled "Is Nature Too Good for Us?" There Tucker argues that the preservation effort is driven by fundamental misconceptions concerning the relationship between man and nature. Although the preservationist philosophy of setting aside extensive tracts of land in wilderness preserves has *long* been opposed by conservationists who favor policies of multiple use and highest use, it was not until passage of the Wilderness Act of 1964 that the preservationists held the upper hand. Now, Tucker argues, preservationist efforts in the western states are threatening U.S. international trade for years to come by locking up scarce energy and mineral resources in permanent preserves.

The preservationist effort is fueled, according to Tucker, by a number of misconceptions: that we are running out of wilderness, that wilderness provides a necessary source of peace and freedom, and that primitive practices are generally better than more civilized practices. Tucker argues that, in point of fact, the United States has plenty of open space and that the search for peace and freedom is just a middle-class attempt to retreat from the responsibilities of modern life. The real danger in this effort, he argues, is that by locking up needed natural resources we may <u>actually</u> jeopardize the economic well-being that has allowed us to enjoy such respites from the daily need to support ourselves.

    <u>The alternative for Tucker is clear</u>. We do not need to search for a new religious consciousness based in more primitive or less Western civilizations. They, <u>after all</u>, do no better than we at ecology. What we need is to return to the conservationists' doctrine of stewardship of the land. <u>That is</u>, we must seek to develop a creative and harmonious relationship with nature rather than setting ourselves apart from it.

    As a final stage in revising your summary, you'll ask a friend or classmate to use the following revision checklist while reading through your summary, and you'll use the responses to guide your revision.

REVISION CHECKLIST FOR SUMMARIES

    Read through the summary and then answer the following questions to help the author revise:

- Do you know who wrote the text being summarized?
- What issue is addressed by this author?
- What is the main point made by the author?
- Would you be able to locate the text in the library? Where would you look?
- Can you clearly separate the points made by the author of the summary and the points made by the author of the text being summarized? Mark any points about which you're unsure.
- How does the author of the text being summarized see the issue?
- What does the author being summarized feel is the real problem?
- What solution does the author of the text being summarized recommend?
- Judging from this summary, what did the author of the text being summarized emphasize: beliefs or actions we should accept or beliefs or actions we should reject?
- Are there any terms used in this summary that you don't understand? Underline them.
- Are there any points in the summary that made you wonder, "Why did the author say that?" Mark them.

For Your Notebook #10

    Ask a friend or classmate to use the revision checklist to review the drafts of your summaries. Review your reader's answers to see if you have any questions. Then use the results to revise.

ADDITIONAL ARGUMENTATIVE ESSAYS ON WILDERNESS

SHOULD WE MOURN
THE DINOSAURS?

Paul Ehrlich and Anne Ehrlich

*The worst thing that can happen—will happen [in the
1980s]—is not energy depletion, economic collapse, limited
nuclear war, or conquest by a totalitarian government. As
terrible as these catastrophes would be for us, they can be
repaired within a few generations. The one process ongoing
in the 1980s that will take millions of years to correct is the
loss of genetic and species diversity by the destruction of
natural habitats. This is the folly our descendants are least
likely to forgive us.*

—E. O. Wilson, *Harvard Magazine*, January-February 1980

In a hillside clearing in the riverine forest sloping down to Lake Tangan- 1
yika, Flo is grooming her daughter Fifi. Seated with them are Fifi's son Freud
and Flo's youngest son Flint. Freud, still a baby, is in his mother's arms.
Flint, half grown, is grooming his sister. The small group of Chimpanzees
seems oblivious to the idyllic setting, the lake sparkling through gaps in the
foliage, the flight of metallic-colored *Naja* butterflies, the calls of birds. They
also seem oblivious to our presence and that of two young women from
Stanford University who are making careful notes on their behavior.

Suddenly a roaring breaks the spell. The chimps scatter, scrambling up 2
trees, as Figan—a young male soon to become the dominant individual of
his troop—plunges into the clearing, running on all fours with hair erect. In
an apparent fit of rage, he dashes about and flings a five-pound rock forty
feet as easily as a man might do with a tennis ball. We all stand stock-still
while Figan picks up a dead palm frond and thrashes first one of the students
and then the other. He then runs at us—we're next in line. Figan pulls up
short in front of Paul, raises the frond, and then hesitates as they stare at each
other. Then Figan drops his arm and saunters off, his "anger" apparently
spent. No one is injured—indeed, no human being has ever been hurt by a
chimp here, but our adrenaline has flowed. The researchers tell us that the

chimps seem to sense the difference between men and women and are less likely to act aggressively toward men—even though an adult male chimp could easily demolish the strongest man.

This incident occurred in the early 1970s at the Gombe Stream Reserve, 3 established by the British behaviorist Jane Goodall a decade before as a base for studying chimp behavior. We were starting long-term work on the population biology of some of the forest butterflies, hoping that the presence of the famous chimps would guarantee protection of the site. Finding places to do long-term research in tropical forests had become increasingly difficult because those forests were (and still are) under escalating assault by the rapidly growing populations of poor tropical countries and by the commercial interests of rich temperate-zone nations. Most preserves in Africa are maintained to protect large savannah animals such as lions, elephants, giraffes, and antelopes. Having already been forced to abandon one tropical forest research site in South America, we had chosen Gombe, in Tanzania, for a second try.

Even if one is working fourteen hours a day marking numbers on but- 4 terflies, releasing them, seeing where they are recaptured, writing field notes and tabulating data, it is impossible to ignore the chimps (to say nothing of the baboons!). Before arriving at Gombe, we had forsworn imputing human characters to these animals, being determined to look at them through the "dispassionate" eyes of scientists. Our resolution lasted about ten minutes. It disappeared the first time that a frightened young chimp jumped into its mother's arms and was comforted with precisely the kinds of pats and strokes that a human mother would use in similar circumstances.

It is Jane Goodall's hope that by observing these seductively humanlike 5 animals, light will be shed on the behavior of *Homo sapiens*. Whether that hope is fulfilled or not, the behavior of the chimps is so fascinating that most would agree that the existence of wild Chimpanzees enriches the human environment. Indeed, we found watching them irresistible, to the occasional detriment of our own research.

One incident observed by researchers while we were at Gombe made an 6 especially deep impression on us. A strange female carrying a young infant wandered into the territory of the local Chimpanzee troop. She was attacked by local males, beaten to the ground, and then stomped on. The baby was caught beneath its mother and was badly injured. The males took the infant, killed it, and then passed it around and ate small parts of it. Then, according to the watchers, the males "seemed to know they were doing something wrong." One took the infant's body, carried it two miles through the forest, and deposited it on the front doorstep of Jane Goodall's laboratory!

Did the chimps realize they were being studied? Could the concept of 7 "being studied" possibly pass through the mind of a chimp? Did they feel "guilty"? Did they think that Jane and her associates were some sort of gods? Was it all pure coincidence or a response to some undetected cue given by the researchers? We'll leave the interpretation of this disquieting incident to you.

What is indisputable is that chimps are among our closest living relations 8 and have some intellectual abilities that exceed similar abilities in many human beings. Some chimps can perform better than many people on some tests of intelligence. One chimp has solved problems involving five levels of ambiguity, while many children and some adult human beings are stumped by tests presenting only three levels. (As an example, a test in which a reward was under either a square or round cover on a red or blue tray—under square if the tray is red, under round if it is blue—presents two levels of ambiguity.) If there is any species the *Homo sapiens* should have natural empathy for, it should be *Pan troglodites,* the Chimpanzee. And yet we are wiping them out.

Jane Goodall first traveled to Gombe in 1960 to start what to many 9 seemed a hopeless task—gaining the confidence of Chimpanzees in order to study them. When she arrived, the forest habitat of the chimps stretched unbroken for sixty miles eastward from the shores of Lake Tanganyika. Ten years later Jane had become world-famous because of her success with the Chimpanzees. In the same period the exploding human population of Tanzania cleared the forest and established farms over almost all of those sixty miles, narrowing the chimp habitat to the patrolled reserve area, a slender strip along the lake, extending inland to the first ridge line less than two miles from the shore.

Africa's potential for explosive population growth is enormous. Unlike 10 most other poor areas of the world, tropical Africa has not yet felt the full impact of Western medical technology. As a result, death rates are still relatively high, around eighteen deaths per thousand people in the population per year in East Africa, in contrast with rates of around thirteen per thousand in Southeast Asia and nine in tropical South America. If modern death-control methods take hold in Africa as they have elsewhere, there will be a substantial increase in the rate of population growth from the present level of about 3 percent per year to almost 4 percent per year—unless there is a counterbalancing decline in birthrates.

Under such great human population pressure, it is extremely unlikely 11 that the Chimpanzees will long survive in nature; extinction is their almost certain fate. They most likely will not disappear because of deliberate hunting by human beings, but, as at Gombe, because of destruction of the ecosystem of which they are living components. They will doubtless survive in zoos and laboratories, at least for a while. But natural groups of chimps will no longer exist. Then all that is left will be movies and reports of them caring for each other, being tolerant of their rambunctious young, using twigs as tools to dig food out of narrow holes, battling over territories, helping their own wounded,[1] and behaving in many other ways that are reminiscent of their much more abundant human relatives.

---

1. Jane Goodall, "Life and death at Gombe," *National Geographic* 155:592–620, May 1979.

WHY SAVE ENDANGERED SPECIES?

Most sensitive human beings will care, will mourn the loss. But only a 12 relative few will realize that the coming disappearance of this prominent endangered species[2] is not just a single tragedy but symptomatic of a planetary catastrophe that is bearing down upon all of us. For along with the chimp will go the other living elements of the chimp's ecosystem—components all of Earth's crucial life-support systems.

There are four prime arguments for the preservation of our fellow trav- 13 elers on Spaceship Earth. One is that simple compassion demands their preservation. This argument is based on the notion that other products of evolution also have a right to existence, that the needs and desires of human beings are not the only basis for ethical decisions.

A second argument is that other species should be preserved because of 14 their beauty, symbolic value, or intrinsic interest: the argument from esthetics. Chimpanzees, elephants, multihued reef fishes, iridescent blue *Morpho* butterflies, and plants with beautiful flowers or bizarre shapes seem automatically to appeal to most members of Western culture, if not most human beings. And many people, especially biologists, find beauty in such unlikely places as the fine scaling on the wings of a malaria-carrying mosquito, the iridescent patches on the back of an African tick, or the delicate sculpturing of the "shell" of a microscopic single-celled diatom.

The third argument is basically economic: preserve the whales because X 15 dollars can be made annually through harvesting them on a sustained-yield basis; save the Amazon jungle because of the immense value of the as-yet-undiscovered foods and drugs that could be extracted from Amazonian plants. In short, other species provide *direct* benefits to *Homo sapiens* and should be preserved for that reason.

The first three arguments for the preservation of other species are easily 16 understandable, even by those who do not find them persuasive. The fourth argument is rarely heard and even less frequently understood, because it involves *indirect* benefits to humanity. This argument is that other species are living components of vital ecological systems (ecosystems) which provide humanity with indispensable free services—services whose substantial disruption would lead inevitably to a collapse of civilization. By deliberately or unknowingly forcing species to extinction, *Homo sapiens* is attacking *itself*: it is certainly endangering society and possibly even threatening our own species with extermination. This is the most important of all the arguments . . . .

---

2. A basic source on endangered animal species are the volumes of the *Red Data Book,* published in looseleaf form and continually updated by the International Union for the Conservation of Nature and Natural Resources (IUCN): Volume 1, *Mammalia*; Volume 2, *Aves*; Volume 3, *Amphibia and Reptilia*; and Volume 4, *Pisces*. For plants, there is the bound 1978 volume, *The IUCN Plant Red Data Book*, complied by Gren Lucas and Hugh Synge. All are published at Morges, Switzerland.

There Have Always Been Extinctions

There are, of course, counterarguments raised by those who see nothing 17
wrong with humanity helping to usher other species off the stage. Perhaps
the commonest is that extinction is a perfectly natural evolutionary process,
one that has gone on for millions of years with or without human participa-
tion. Why worry if we're just helping nature take her course?

When people think of evolution, they tend to think of new kinds of life 18
being produced from old—of one species (kind) changing through time into
another, or of two or more species evolving where previously there was only
one. When Charles Darwin put forth his theory of evolution and the evidence supporting it in 1859, he not only came up with natural selection as
the driving force of the evolutionary process but also recognized the inevi-
tability of extinctions: ". . . as new forms are continually and slowly being
produced, unless we believe that the number of specific forms goes on per-
petually and almost indefinitely increasing, numbers inevitably must become
extinct."[3]

Before Darwin, the idea of extinction had been toyed with by various 19
naturalists and geologists, but it was a shocking concept to most people in
the mid-nineteenth century. Living things were thought to have been designed by God in a sequence of increasing complexity. Species had been created once and for all, and extinction was explicitly ruled out in the "creation-
ist" view of the origin of species. But now things seem to have come full
circle. Not only is extinction no longer a shocking idea, but Darwin's name
is even taken in vain by people who want to justify the extermination of
other species of *Homo sapiens.*

For example, one Sam Witchell, a financial and corporate public relations 20
consultant, published an op ed piece in the *New York Times* (May 3, 1974)
entitled "Give Me the Old-Time Darwin." The message of Witchell's article
was that, since Darwin showed the extinction of species to be part and parcel
of the evolutionary process, there is no reason to be concerned about the
disappearance of species: "The Darwin people tell us that species come and
go, that this is nature's way of experimenting with life. The successful experiments survive for a time; the failures disappear to no one's detriment."

There is, of course, one thing that people who make this kind of argu- 21
ment overlook: that humanity has already raised the *rate* of species extinction
far above the historic rates of species formation. Species now are disappearing much more rapidly than they are appearing, and the rate of disappearance
promises to continue accelerating rapidly. The statement above reminds one
of a man who, observing water spurting through ever-widening cracks in
the face of a huge dam, says to the people downstream, "Not to worry—
after all, water has always come over the spillway anyway."

---

3. *Origin of Species*, 1st ed., p. 109. A good brief introduction to evolution for laypeople is
Frank H. T. Rhodes, *Evolution*, Golden Press, New York, 1974. A great deal of information is
presented simply and accurately.

The rate of extinction of bird and mammal species between 1600 and   22
1975 has been estimated to be between five and fifty times higher than it was
through most of the eons of our evolutionary past. Furthermore, in the last
decades of the twentieth century, that rate is projected to rise to some forty
to four hundred times "normal."[4] To understand the significance of these
estimates, one should know something about what species are, how they
have come into being, and how they have disappeared . . . .

Who Misses the Dinosaurs?

One possible response to the news that extinction is rapidly outpacing   23
species formation is so what? After all, the dinosaurs went extinct, and humanity has not suffered any loss—or so the litany goes. Indeed, when the
talk turns to extinction, it often also turns to dinosaurs. An economist once
said to us that anything can be had for a price. He challenged us to tell him
something that couldn't be produced if one were willing to pay enough. We
answered, "Produce a living *Tyrannosaurus rex*." After claiming (incorrectly)
that, given enough time and money, one of the giant carnivorous dinosaurs
could be produced, he fell back on a familiar theme. The dinosaurs, after all,
were nothing of value. They became extinct and he certainly did not miss
them. This argument is sometimes generalized to: the dinosaurs became extinct and nobody misses them; why, then, should we worry about extinction
at all?

We do not find this line of reasoning at all persuasive. First, in a sense,   24
the dinosaurs did not all go extinct. The group that included the dinosaurs,
the "ruling reptiles," has living representatives.[5] Crocodiles and alligators are
members of this group, and they at least supply human beings with some
fancy leather goods as well as spine-chilling stories of man-eating. The roles
of crocodilians in the ecosystems of swamps and estuaries are not well understood; they may be crucially important. Alligators, for example, are vital
elements of the sawgrass marsh ecosystem of the Florida Everglades. With
their tails, alligators scoop out depressions ten to a hundred feet wide. Scarce
water collects in these "alligator holes" in the dry season. This permits a
variety of aquatic and semiaquatic organisms, including plankton, fishes,

---

4. Estimates are from P. R. Ehrlich, A. H. Ehrlich and J. P. Holdren, *Ecoscience: Population,
Resources, Environment*, W. H. Freeman, San Francisco, 1977, p. 142. The estimates are of
course *very* rough.
5. Crocodilians are representatives of archosaurian (ruling) reptiles, of which the dinosaurs
comprised two different groups (Saurischia and Ornithischia) that may be no more closely
related to one another than they are to the crocodilians. Pterosaurs, often popularly considered
dinosaurs, are a third group of archosaurs. Some scientists think, however, that the two
dinosaur groups are closely related and were actually warm-blooded, and that the birds, which
descended from the Saurischia, should be included with the Saurischia and Ornithischia in the
class Dinosauria (R. T. Bakker and P. M. Galton, "Dinosaur monophyly and a new class of
vertebrates," *Nature* 248:165–172, 1974).

frogs, turtles, and the alligators, to survive until the rainy season refloods the Everglades.[6]

It is also quite possible, of course, that the ultimate demise of most cro- [25] codilians would affect only people with a lust for fine shoes and handbags or a feeling of compassion for these interesting, though somewhat dim-witted, reminders of an ancient era. Their concern, however, should be considered, too.

An even more important group of dinosaur relatives is the birds. They [26] are direct descendants of dinosaurs. Indeed, some biologists think they should be considered living dinosaurs. People would surely have missed the birds had their progenitors disappeared without issue, as did most other types of dinosaurs. Colonel Sanders might never have gotten rich, innumerable groups of human beings could never have decorated themselves with feathers, pillows would have been stuffed with straw until somebody invented foam rubber, bird-watching would not amuse millions of people, and poets would have been deprived of much material for describing songs and graceful flight. Indeed, without the bird's example, airplanes might never have been invented. Much more important, insects—by many measures already the most important predators and competitors of *Homo sapiens*—probably would be even more abundant and successful. Indeed, it is conceivable that without the birds, life would have been sufficiently more rigorous for people in an insect-dominated world that the agricultural revolution, and thus the rise of civilization, would have been impossible.[7]

But what about all those dinosaurs that did die out? Should we regret [27] their passage? Well, the answer is yes and no.

From an esthetic standpoint, some of us do regret the disappearance of [28] dinosaurs. What a thrill it would be if in national parks people could see great lumbering brontosauruses weighing forty or fifty tons grazing across the landscape, or herds of ceratopsian dinosaurs roaming like rhinoceri with three gigantic horns! With luck one might even get to watch an attack on a grazer by that mighty predator *Tyrannosaurus*—just as on one occasion we were lucky enough to see a lioness stalk her prey in Africa. Or in Texas a gigantic pterosaur with a forty-foot wingspan—by far the largest animal ever to take to the air—might soar overhead. No human being ever saw these fascinating animals, which died out 50 million years before anything remotely resembling *Homo sapiens* appeared. But people are the poorer for it, nonetheless.

---

6. J. Harte and R. H. Socolow, "The Everglades: Wilderness versus rampant land development in South Florida," in Harte and Socolow, *Patient Earth*. Holt, Rinehart and Winston, New York, 1971.

7. Of course, it is impossible to state exactly the consequences of an entire group not evolving. In the absence of birds, for example, bats might have evolved into day fliers and taken over the ecological roles of insectivorous birds. What *is* certain is that without birds evolutionary history would have been very different, and one could not even state with assurance that humanity would even have appeared on the scene.

Whether anyone misses the dinosaurs is only one question, however, and 29
a relatively minor one. The crucial point is that the dinosaurs became extinct
at a time when evolutionary processes were capable of replacing them with
the mammals. The huge grazing dinosaurs were eventually replaced by such
grazing mammals as deer, antelopes, sheep, goats, buffalo, and cattle—some
of which have been domesticated by humanity. The big carnivorous dinosaurs such as *Tyrannosaurus* were replaced by members of the cat, dog, and
bear families—and by human hunters.

If, on the other hand, the dinosaurs had become extinct and the mam- 30
mals had not evolved to take over the roles that dinosaurs had played, it
would be a very different world indeed. Since we too are mammals, there
would of course be no people; that would be the most important difference
from our point of view! The principal reason, then, that people *don't* miss
the dinosaurs or other groups of long-extinct organisms is because replacements for them have evolved.

Extinctions that are occurring today and that can be expected in the fu- 31
ture are likely to have much more serious consequences than those of the
distant past. First of all, unless action is taken, contemporary extinctions
seem certain to delete a far greater proportion of the world's store of biological diversity than did earlier extinctions. Furthermore, the same human activities that are causing extinctions today are also beginning to shut down
the process by which diversity could be regenerated. Entire new groups of
organisms are unlikely to evolve as replacements for those lost if Earth's flora
and fauna are decimated now.

Would We Miss the Snail Darter?

Okay, you say, everyone should be concerned about the growing imbal- 32
ance between the rate of extinction and the rate of species creation. But does
this mean that our concern should be lavished on *every* species? Was the Snail
Darter, for example, really worth all the fuss by the conservationists? Wasn't
it preposterous to try to stop the Tellico dam, a multimillion-dollar construction project in Tennessee, because it would destroy an insignificant fish, unknown even to most ichthyologists?

It wasn't. Even if the Tellico dam had not been a massive boondoggle 33
(which a distinguished committee of Cabinet members decided it was), even
if it had not threatened other values, it should have been stopped *just because*
it threatened the Snail Darter. We could, and will later, raise the arguments
of compassion and esthetics. We could point out that the Snail Darter is one
more rivet in our spaceship—and that popping *any* rivet in this day and age
is inherently stupid and potentially dangerous. But there is, we think, a still
stronger argument: *the line has to be drawn somewhere.*

If the value of each endangered species or population must be compared 34
one on one with the value of the particular development scheme that would
exterminate it, we can kiss goodbye to most of Earth's plants, animals, and
microorganisms. After all, dam X will be able to supply power to illuminate

fifty thousand homes; freeway Y will make it possible to cut twenty minutes from the drive between Jonesville and Smith City; Sunny Acres Apartments will provide decent housing for two thousand people now condemned to existence in a slum; mine Z will create two hundred and fifty badly needed jobs. How can any organism win in the face of such arguments?

In an overdeveloped society such as the United States, questions and 35 alternatives can be posed with respect to all such projects, however worthy they may appear. For instance, how critical is the twenty minutes' commuting time between Smith City and Jonesville? Couldn't the same result or nearly the same result be achieved by improving an existing highway—and at lower cost? Couldn't the new apartments be provided by redevelopment right on the slum site? Might there not be some less destructive way to provide jobs than by opening a new mine? Can't the ore be produced from existing mines? Is the electricity from the dam really needed in a nation that wastes enormous amounts of energy, as the United States does?

A great many development projects yield short-term benefits for a few 36 and pass on long-term costs to society, as studies of their environmental consequences often make abundantly clear. "Development" in the United States has until recently been considered entirely beneficial. In the last decade or so, however, as conflicts over land use, water rights, and environmental values have proliferated, this view increasingly has been questioned. And the need for preserving endangered species has lately become one of the conflicting values. In our view, it may be the most crucial value; the rate at which populations and species are being eradicated has reached the point where a society like the United States would be better off doing without even the most "necessary" projects if they cannot be carried out without causing further extinctions.

The choices will be very tough ones, as you will see. Indeed, they often 37 will be difficult to pose. In many cases, species and populations are endangered by activities far from their habitats. A new coal-burning power plant in central Indiana, for instance, may add to the acid rain that is exterminating trout populations in Maine. Against the value system of a growth-oriented Western society, defending endangered organisms on a one-by-one, place-by-place basis will be difficult even when the connections are clear. In the long run, it is a losing game. A Tellico dam will eventually be found for every population and species of nonhuman organism, and there will always be developers, politicians, and just plain people to argue that short-range economic values must take precedence over other values. For they do not understand that *their own fates* are intertwined with the Snail Darters of our planet. They are unaware of how much they would indeed miss those little fishes.

Are There Any Organisms We Would Not Miss?

Of course, not all killing of members of other species in the past or in 38 the present is automatically bad, even if one takes a view of the world that is not centered on *Homo sapiens*. Since the time of Darwin, biologists have recognized that the success of some species is normally paid for by the reduction in population size or extinction of others. It is, for example, perfectly natural for human beings to attempt to control, or even force to extinction, populations or species that prey upon people or threaten their resources.

If, for example, some magic way were found to exterminate just the   39 *Anopheles* mosquitoes that transmit the most important of all human diseases, malaria, it would be a tempting thing to do. But ecologists would caution that doing so would entail some small chance that the inevitable consequent changes in Earth's ecosystems would make the world less hospitable for humanity, causing worse suffering than that previously inflicted by malaria. And some demographers might warn that the sudden decline in human death rates in some developing countries could cause an acceleration in population growth that would exacerbate their already serious social and economic problems. Life is full of chances, though, and we personally would be sorely tempted to kiss the *Anopheles* goodbye and attempt to deal with the other problems if and when they arose.

But of course it is never that simple, since magic devices do not exist for   40 selectively deleting a single species—especially an insect pest—from Earth's living complement, and since most of the techniques we use for dealing with our predators and competitors have turned out to be two-edged swords.

Even when things appear superficially simple, close investigation usually   41 reveals unhappy complexities. In some parts of Africa, elephants have become dangerous pests—destroying the fields of poor, hungry, hard-working Africans and sometimes killing them. At the moment, either the elephants are being killed or the temporary compromise solution of moving them to other places is being attempted. But Africa is fast running out of both elephants and places to move them to.

Wiping out the massive beasts would be relatively simple—indeed, that   42 is one of the reasons elephants are endangered. But, even from the point of view of the Africans, that is not necessarily the "right" answer. It can be argued that the future economic prosperity of large areas of Africa would not be maximized by converting all usable land to subsistence agriculture. Future African generations would almost certainly be better served by maintaining some of those areas as potential tourist meccas, with elephants being the top tourist attraction.

The basic conflict, of course, is caused by burgeoning human populations   43 encroaching more and more on the elephants' habitat. In this case, as in so many others, efforts to control the growth and spread of the human population would inevitably be more beneficial to Africans in the long run than efforts to exterminate the elephants. With the elephants out of the way, the people could expand for a few more years, but they would soon run out of more land to convert to agriculture. Then human population growth would be halted by nature anyway. African leaders, though, are locked into a short-term decision-making process just as surely as American politicians are. Of course, from a broader ethical point of view, one could argue that the remaining herds of those gigantic and intelligent beasts should be protected absolutely.

The degree to which a strongly anthropocentric, or human-centered, approach to these problems should be taken is clearly an area on which moral and honorable people will continue to differ. For many millions of years, quite likely up until this century, an anthropocentric viewpoint was the only possible and sensible one for *Homo sapiens*. And for people living in an industrial city today, surrounded by human-made objects and supported by what seems to be an entirely manufactured system, it is very easy to believe that human beings are separate from nature and quite independent of it. Religions have reinforced this arrogant idea by teaching that dominion over Earth and other living things is humanity's God-given right. But now, with our utter domination of the planet, the time has come for a softening of such human chauvinism. 44

Perhaps the best way to erode human chauvinism in industrial nations would be to launch crash programs of education—to familiarize people, especially children, with our traveling companions on Spaceship Earth, and teach people not only to appreciate them for their beauty or intrinsic interest, but to understand that *we need them* as much as they need our protection to survive. Television shows on the living world have accomplished a great deal in this regard, but they are no substitute for personal experience. It is too bad that everyone can't have a guided tour, for instance, of some of the world's great coral reefs. Reefs could provide an ideal introduction to the beauty and fascination of relatively unfamiliar organisms, the intricacy of their relationships with one another, and their importance to humanity. And such appreciation of the reef ecosystem might lead to real concern about the ongoing destruction of Earth's biological resources. 45

THE CORAL REEF SYSTEM

An introduction to coral reefs might be given at the outer edge of the Australian Great Barrier Reef, perhaps at a spot where we have dived several times near Lizard Island at the northern end of the reef. There a fantastic coral garden marks the seaward side of an area that contains literally thousands of different reef fish species. Squadrons of larger parrot fishes swim gracefully over the outer slope, scraping coral heads with their beaklike teeth, digesting out the living parts, and excreting clouds of white limestone remains. They move over the reef like mowing machines, leaving behind them pure white sand. Schools of large jacks float by over the abyss, and gazing down the slope toward the miles-deep Coral Sea, one might occasionally glimpse the shape of a great oceanic shark. Both jacks and sharks are carnivorous; they eat smaller fish. 46

But it is over the shallower reefs that one can best enjoy the diversity of living things and observe their relationships. In this area we have been able 47 to study twenty-five species of butterfly fishes, among the most beautiful denizens of the reefs. They are flattened from side to side, like the angelfishes often found in aquariums, and brightly colored with white, black, gold, blue, orange, or yellow.[8]

The butterfly fishes do not all feed on the same things. Some species are 48 specialists in eating certain kinds of corals; other search for small invertebrates on the corals or in the sand. In more recent work around Lizard Island, we and our colleagues have seen the orderly way in which species with similar lifestyles—potential competitors—replace each other in different locations. For example, three species feeding on hard corals in the clear waters near the outer Barrier are replaced by two other hard-coral feeders in the murky waters over the reefs near the Queensland shore.[9] Not only is the unfamiliar living world of the reef beautiful and diverse, but it has a complex organization not immediately apparent to an untrained visitor to the underwater "classroom." Lesson: even though they are very similar, two species usually function differently in ecosystems. If one goes extinct, the other may be unable to take over its role.

Even to a trained biologist, the fish fauna of an area like Lizard Island 49 presents a daily series of lessons in ecology. The entire surface of the reef is occupied by small damselfishes, each defending a little territory and feeding mostly on plants growing there. Above the reef hang other damselfishes feeding in the constant flow of plankton—tiny plants and animals floating in the water—that drifts over the reefs. Each of the two related groups has specialized in different food sources.

In tubes in the reef live saber-toothed blennies, roughly the shape of your 50 forefinger and almost twice as long. These are "dash-and-grab" predators. When a large sluggish fish comes by, if you are lucky, you may see a blenny spring from its tube like a crossbow bolt, grab a bite from a passing fish, and vanish back into its hole so quickly that the entire motion is a blur. The larger fish just twitches and moves on. The abundance of these blennies is determined by the abundance of suitable holes. Lesson: a shortage of resources (holes) can limit population size. Question: why are there no dash-and-grab predators that live on land? It is a nice puzzle to which ecologists can give no real answer. We can just be thankful, since if they did exist, Sunday strolls could be a lot less pleasant!

At certain places on the reef, brilliantly colored four-inch-long "cleaner" 51 wrasses have set up their stations, and one can observe the various other fishes of the reef lined up like motorists at the gas pump waiting to be groomed. When its turn comes, each customer assumes a characteristic

8. For the results of work we did on the significance of the colors of these fishes, see P. R. Ehrlich, T. H. Talbot, B. C. Russell, and G. R. V. Anderson, "The behaviour of chaetodontid fishes with special reference to Lorenz's 'poster colouration' hypothesis," *Journal of Zoology, London* 183:213–228, 1977.
9. G. Anderson, A. Ehrlich, P. Ehrlich, J. Roughgarden, B. Russel and F. Talbot, "The community structure of coral reef fishes," in press, *American Naturalist.*

"cleanee" pose and hangs in an apparently stunned state as the cleaner wrasse goes over it, meticulously removing parasites from the skin, gills, and inside of the mouth. It is one of the wonders of nature to see these little fishes enter the mouth of a large predator and in perfect safety pick parasites from between its daggerlike teeth! Lesson: evolution can produce some very unexpected associations and patterns of behavior.

And if you were really lucky, you might even observe the activities of 52 the flimflam man of the reef—a cleaner mimic. Blennies, relatives of the dash-and-grab predator, have evolved a color pattern virtually identical to that of the cleaner wrasse and a behavior pattern that matches also. They advertise cleaning, but when a naïve fish comes along and goes into its cleanee pose, the mimics simply bite off a piece and proceed to chew it with extreme brazenness. The victim seems incapable of bringing itself to attack a fish in cleaner garb. Lesson: things are not always what they seem in the natural world either. And, like human victims of confidence games, even fishes find it difficult to admit they've been conned!

Fascinating and diverse as the fish fauna of the coral reef is, it is only 53 part of the story of the living reef. The structure of the reef itself is the result of the activities of tiny coral animals, which have within their bodies symbiotic algae that, like other green plants, photosynthesize. The gigantic reefs—far larger than any human-made structures—are the product of the activities of these tiny colonial animals and the algae, being made up of their limestone skeletons deposited over untold millennia. Lesson: tiny organisms, given enough time, can produce very large geological features.

The rest of the animals of the reef, including myriad crustacea, worms, 54 snails, and other invertebrate animals, are in many ways as fascinating as the fish fauna—although not always as obviously beautiful to behold. And there are lessons to learn from all of them, if we care to look in the right way.

The economic values supplied to *Homo sapiens* by the reef are also man- 55 ifold. Reef fishes provide an important protein supplement to the diets of many peoples in tropical areas; on some islands they are a major source of food. In addition, the reef ecosystem is an esthetic resource that is important to the tourist industries of many tropical countries and to the burgeoning recreational industry of scuba diving. The entire reef complex is a focus of high productivity in the otherwise relatively unproductive ecosystems of tropical seas. Their destruction would inevitably have cascading effects on fish species throughout tropical oceans, as well as threatening the shores and harbors they now physically protect from erosion and wave action. It also has been suggested that the reefs are involved in the crucial task of regulating the salt content of the oceans. In essence, the reefs create vast evaporation lagoons between themselves and tropical shores.[10] Lesson: things that are beautiful and educational can also be economically valuable.

---

10. J. E. Lovelock, *Gaia: A New Look at Life on Earth*, Oxford University Press, New York, 1978, pp. 97–98.

Homo sapiens, unfortunately, is threatening the destruction of the world's 56
coral reefs—indeed, in a few places that destruction is already far advanced.
If the destruction of coral reefs is carried to completion, many human beings
will almost certainly be hungrier and will surely have lost important biological resources. All of us would lose as well an esthetic resource that could
delight our descendants for countless generations. The loss of the reef system
and the species that comprise it could be a much more severe one than the
loss of the giant dinosaurs, for it is quite possible that nothing would evolve
to replace the reef ecosystem. Certainly nothing could replace it on a time
scale of any interest to humanity.

WILDERNESS AND
THE MAINTENANCE
OF FREEDOM

Edward B. Swain

The motivation to preserve wilderness has its basis in a
fundamental human need.

It has not been clear *why* people argue for the preservation of wilderness. 1
The stated reasons have usually taken one of two courses: arguing that wilderness areas and rare species have either *utilitarian* value or *intrinsic* value.
Under the first value system, wilderness areas should be preserved because
they are useful to humans, and, under the second, they should be preserved
because they simply have the right to exist. In this essay, I argue that these
reasons for preservation are merely manifestations of an ultimate reason—
simply that people greatly value the *knowledge* that wilderness exists. In addition, I argue that it is important for our future quality of life to recognize
why so many persons value wilderness.

In his book, *The Arrogance of Humanism*, zoologist David Ehrenfeld 2
makes the perceptive observation that most of the utilitarian arguments are
contrived. Apparently preservationists using the arguments are primarily
motivated by some inner drive to preserve, and only secondarily do they
clutch at any number of diverse reasons why that preservation would be
good. Ehrenfeld identified nine categories of utilitarian arguments that have
been put forward, and they include undiscovered medical or agricultural uses
for rare species, stabilization of ecosystems (ultimately preserving the human

Edward B. Swain, "Wilderness and the Maintenance of Freedom." This article first appeared
in *The Humanist* issue of March/April 1983 and is reprinted by permission.

environment), and aesthetic value. One by one, Ehrenfeld shows that these arguments are not adequate to protect most wilderness areas and rare species.

UTILITARIAN VS. INTRINSIC

It was not difficult for Ehrenfeld to demonstrate the weakness of these 3 arguments. Many are not politically realistic; others are simply not true or are exaggerations or distortions of scientific knowledge—the evidence that preservation is necessary for human survival has often been overstated. For instance, there is scant evidence that ecosystems with fewer species are inherently less stable. Just as in the case of the boy who cried "Wolf" too many times, the public is becoming accustomed to the warnings of the ecological catastrophe that never occurs. Many of the utilitarian arguments have merit, but the claims have been made so immoderately that there is an understandable tendency to dismiss all of them in a wholesale fashion.

It appears that contrivances to preserve wilderness areas have the poten- 4 tial of causing a public backlash and are therefore probably not the best way for preservationists to succeed. Certainly the utilitarian arguments do not actually provide any universally valid reason to preserve all wilderness and all rare species.

Ehrenfeld, convinced that preservation cannot be ensured by contriving 5 and assigning utilitarian, or anthropocentric, values to wilderness areas, goes on to seek a better value system. He feels, as others such as Lynn White have before him, that the condensation and superiority implied by such a materialistic (he says "humanistic") world view led us into our current environmental situation and that Western cultures need to completely change their environmental value system. He argues that the best criterion of value is the "religious" one: that natural areas and species should be preserved simply because they exist. In short, he rejects utilitarian values as secondary and embraces an ultimate reason that cannot be debated. He leaves the problem of how to implement such a value system to others.

Other preservationists have also reached the conclusion that we need a 6 new value system, often ascribing, as Ehrenfeld does, a religious dimension to nature and to its ecological workings. But not all preservationists who espouse the intrinsic right of existence for the nonhuman world depend on the view that nature is sacred. Both C. D. Stone and L. H. Tribe have promoted the idea that species and landscapes have the intrinsic right of existence and therefore should have legal rights. These views are essentially a reaction against anthropocentrism; Tribe finishes one article by asking, "Who can fail to admit that the logic of self-interest leads finally not to human satisfaction but to the loss of humanity itself?" But Ehrenfeld, Tribe, and Stone have all chosen to see only the greedy side of anthropocentrism and to view falsely humanism as mere materialism.

I agree with others who take the contrary stand that an expanded concept 7 of anthropocentrism is actually the *solution* to our environmental problems.

We certainly do not need to adopt new value and legal systems. It is reasonable to dismiss the "intrinsic right of existence" value system as unnecessary and unworkable and, instead, to broaden the concept of anthropocentrism to include a human need for a quality environment.

A HUMAN NEED

Philosopher John Passmore is one who argues strongly that a new value system is not needed to provide adequate preservation of wilderness areas. He notes that the cry "for a new morality, as a new religion, which would transform man's attitude to nature, which would lead him to believe that it is *intrinsically* wrong to destroy a species, cut down a tree, clear a wilderness . . ." is loudest by those who have realized that utilitarian values cannot ensure preservation. "What it needs, for the most part, is not so much a new ethic as a more general adherence to a perfectly familiar ethic. For the major sources of our ecological disasters—apart from ignorance—are greed and shortsightedness." As biologist W. H. Murdy has suggested, we need to recognize that each "individual's well-being depends on the well-being of both its social group and ecological support system." This is simply a utilitarian value system that recognizes that there are nonmateralistic but nevertheless very important human values. [8]

I feel that we may have missed an important, perhaps the most important, utilitarian value of wilderness. Ehrenfeld alluded to it when he observed that the contrived utilitarian values are developed in response to "a deeply conservative distrust of irreversible change." The thing that we have glossed over is that people simply have a gut-level desire to preserve the irreplaceable wilderness areas. And that is why these people have the motivation to contrive, albeit unconsciously, other utilitarian values; simple *wanting* to preserve hasn't seemed a good enough reason. I suggest that the desire to preserve wilderness has its basis in a fundamental human need. [9]

This human need is not to preserve wilderness *per se* but to preserve personal freedom. The desire to preserve wilderness can be understood as a manifestation of the universal human reaction to restricting personal freedom. This phenomenon has been formalized by psychologist Jack Brehm and his coworkers as the "theory of psychological reactance." The theory is familiar to most people as the reverse psychology that one employs with children: tell children that they cannot do something, and they will assert their sense of personal freedom by promptly doing just that thing. The theory has been developed beyond that level of understanding and predicts people's behavior whenever their freedoms are threatened or lost. In general, the theory predicts that people will be motivated to restore and maintain that freedom. [10]

In reference to the threatened loss of wilderness areas, the theory predicts that people will act to preserve the *potential* freedom to see these irreplaceable entities. People can feel acute frustration and anxiety simply if they *perceive* that a basic freedom has been threatened or lost. Similarly, if people *perceive* [11] that they have freedom of choice, they tend to feel more satisfied and happy with life; it is not necessary they actually exercise that freedom of choice. Perhaps this is why people contribute money to preservationist organizations such as the Sierra Club and the Nature Conservancy without having the expectation of actually going to the areas they help to preserve. People apparently feel better just *knowing* that those wilderness areas and race species are still there and that they could, if they really wanted to, exercise their choice to see them.

Psychologists have also found that the degree of reactance to a given 12 threat to a freedom is proportional to how basic that freedom is perceived. For people in North America, wilderness is part of the cultural heritage, and there is an expectation that wilderness areas and the their species will be available. The threat is heightened because wilderness and rare species can never be reconstituted once they are gone. True, forests can be planted on land once cleared and look perfectly natural, but simply the *knowledge* that the area is not truly wilderness is enough to reduce the perception of freedom of choice.

While protecting one's freedom is a fundamental human trait, the percep- 13 tion of wilderness and rare species as being something desirable to protect is not. Until this century, most people felt that wilderness was a dangerous place that needed to be tamed. As wilderness and its species both became rare, the perception of their value grew, at least partially just because of that rareness. The theory of psychological reactance predicts that people will desire rare things simply because circumstances threaten to limit one's freedom of access to those rare things. The simplest reaction is to protect one's freedom by preserving the rare. Certainly, however, people actually visit natural areas for reasons other than just to affirm their freedom to choose.

PLASTIC TREES

This way of viewing the basic drive to preserve wilderness areas was 14 anticipated somewhat by Martin Krieger, in a perceptive yet sometimes appalling essay entitled "What's Wrong with Plastic Trees?" He notes that in the United States people began to value natural environments more as the environments became rare and that this sense of value is not fixed. But instead of regarding this value system as valid and proposing changes in our societal structure that would enable individuals to fulfill themselves, he proposes that we manipulate our concept of what kind of environments are "natural," and therefore desirable, so that there are more areas near cities that will satisfy people: "The advertising that created rare environments can also create plentiful substitutes." Such an advertising effort, if attempted, might be frustrated by the tendency of people to react against attempts to manipulate their preferences—a tendency consistent with the theory of psychological reactance. True wilderness could end up as an even more desired thing than before his manipulation effort.

However, if "truly" natural environments *are* ever completely eliminated 15 from North America, people may adjust over time to the situation. For instance, because this has happened in Europe, the concept of "natural" is much different there. The drive Americans presently have to preserve wilderness would be transferred to a desire to preserve recreational areas. If this happens, people could undoubtedly be happy; we are very adaptable to new environments—that is part of being human. But to many there is tragedy in losing the earth that humans haven't manipulated. As ecologist Daniel Goodman notes, "The despair and fury of the hard-core environmentalists is caused by their sensing that people *will* enjoy the artificial lake—the artificial grass and artificial trees and artificial anything else." Perhaps the *real* tragedy is that we will have lost the base line from which to measure the extent of human manipulation of our environment.

Krieger makes me feel the need for the continued preservation of true 16 wilderness by taking the potential for human manipulation of our environment to its logical extreme:

> . . . We may want to create proxy environments by means of substitution and simulation. In order to create substitutes, we must endow new objects with significance by means of advertising the social practice. . . . We may simulate the environment by means of photographs, recordings, models, and perhaps even manipulations in the brain. . . . What's wrong with plastic trees? My guess is that there is very little wrong with them. Much more can be done with plastic trees and the like to give most people the feeling that they are experiencing nature.

Aside from the moral repugnance of manipulating people's values in a 17 way reminiscent of Orwell's *1984,* Krieger has a basic misconception about personal freedom. That misconception is summarized in his statement, "If the forgery provides us with the same kind of experience we might have had with the original, except that we know it is a forgery, then we are snobbish to demand the original." Krieger clearly discounts the importance of the *knowledge* that we have been denied the freedom to experience the original. And, as the theory of psychological reactance predicts, denial of freedom inevitably produces a reaction, which he interprets as snobbery. To be denied a valued choice produces the very human reactions of frustration and unhappiness. If our goal is to foster human happiness and fulfillment, then we must make an effort to provide the freedom that is necessary. We may be able to manipulate our values consciously so that we are happy with substitutes, but individuals will not be happy unless they feel that they made that choice for themselves.

A RENEWABLE ECONOMY

I believe that the utilitarian arguments that have been used up to now to 18 preserve wilderness areas have in most cases been misleading and, ultimately, counterproductive. These arguments tend to overstate the material importance of wilderness areas by suggesting that human survival may depend on their preservation. Humans won't have any problem *surviving* in an environment with no wilderness and relatively few species, but our choice of environments will be limited to those created by ourselves. Humans will have eliminated any natural models with which to compare their creations, and the majority of people won't feel any sense of loss.

In North America, wilderness areas are presently being destroyed 19 through the consumption of nonrenewable resources in an effort to maintain our standard of living. Inevitably we will be forced to create a "renewable" economy based on recycling and the use of renewable energy sources. As we wait to organize a renewable economy, ever-larger quantities of low-grade ores and fossil fuels will be consumed, utilizing correspondingly larger areas of previously underdeveloped land. We essentially face a choice in the near future: to create a renewable economy *before* we eliminate wilderness, or to wait to do so until *after*. If we realize the human importance of maintaining wilderness, we can provide the potential of an enhanced quality of life in the future by providing the perception of choice.

If it were generally recognized that the desire to preserve wilderness is 20 valid in itself, this value would gradually permeate our legal system. We could consciously choose to pay the price of not developing mineral resources, for instance, just to preserve the knowledge that that land is wilderness.

As we do have to tighten our belts and reduce our material consumption 21 while the future era of a renewable economy inevitably approaches, many people will perceive that their personal freedom has been reduced—and they will be correct. If this happens simultaneously with the elimination of wilderness, the combination of the dual withdrawal of freedoms may be quite oppressive.

On the other hand, if we as a group voluntarily shift to a renewable 22 economy *before* it is imposed on us, the act of choosing to do so could allow us to feel quite positive about the whole experience—and our valued wilderness areas would be maintained as potential choices, enhancing people's perception of freedom. It would be intelligent of us to try to minimize the impact that transition to a renewable economy will have on our sense of individual freedom, an impact that Harrison Brown predicted in 1954:

> It seems clear that the first major penalty man will have to pay for his rapid consumption of the earth's nonrenewable resources will be that of having to live in a world where his thoughts and actions are ever more strongly limited, where social organization has become all-pervasive, complex, and inflexible, and where the state completely dominates the actions of the individual.

A conscious effort to shift to that renewable economy *before* we eliminate 23 wilderness and rare species could enhance our sense of personal freedom in two ways: first, we *choose* to change consumption patterns, and, second, we preserve the valued option of seeing wilderness and all its inhabitants.

THE DAMNATION
OF A CANYON
Edward Abbey

There was a time when, in my search for essences, I concluded that the 1
canyonland country has no heart. I was wrong. The canyonlands did have a
heart, a living heart, and that heart was Glen Canyon and the golden, flowing Colorado River.

In the summer of 1959 a friend and I made a float trip in little rubber 2
rafts down through the length of Glen Canyon, starting at Hite and getting
off the river near Gunsight Butte—The Crossing of the Fathers. In this voyage of some 150 miles and ten days our only motive power, and all that we
needed, was the current of the Colorado River.

In the summer and fall of 1967 I worked as a seasonal park ranger at the 3
new Glen Canyon National Recreation Area. During my five-month tour of
duty I worked at the main marina and headquarters area called Wahweap, at
Bullfrog Basin toward the upper end of the reservoir, and finally at Lee's
Ferry downriver from Glen Canyon Dam. In a number of powerboat tours
I was privileged to see almost all of our nation's newest, biggest and most
impressive "recreational facility."

Having thus seen Glen Canyon both before and after what we may fairly 4
call its damnation, I feel that I am in a position to evaluate the transformation
of the region caused by construction of the dam. I have had the unique opportunity to observe first-hand some of the differences between the environment of a free river and a power-plant reservoir.

One should admit at the outset to a certain bias. Indeed I am a "butterfly 5
chaser, googly eyed bleeding heart and wild conservative." I take a dim view
of dams; I find it hard to learn to love cement; I am poorly impressed by
concrete aggregates and statistics in the cubic tons. But in this weakness I am
not alone, for I belong to that ever-growing number of Americans, probably
a good majority now, who have become aware that a fully industrialized,
thoroughly urbanized, elegantly computerized social system is not suitable
for human habitation. Great for machines, yes. But unfit for people.

Lake Powell, formed by Glen Canyon Dam, is not a lake. It is a reser- 6 voir, with a constantly fluctuating water level—more like a bathtub that is never drained than a true lake. As at Hoover (or Boulder) Dam, the sole practical function of this impounded water is to drive the turbines that generate electricity in the powerhouse at the base of the dam. Recreational benefits were of secondary importance in the minds of those who conceived and built this dam. As a result the volume of water in the reservoir is continually being increased or decreased according to the requirements of the Basin States Compact and the power-grid system of which Glen Canyon Dam is a component.

The rising and falling water level entails various consequences. One of 7 the most obvious, well known to all who have seen Lake Mead, is the "bathtub ring" left on the canyon walls after each drawdown of water, or what rangers at Glen Canyon call the Bathtub Formation. This phenomenon is perhaps of no more than aesthetic importance; yet it is sufficient to dispel any illusion one might have, in contemplating the scene, that you are looking upon a natural lake.

Of much more significance is the fact that plant life, because of the un- 8 stable water line, cannot establish itself on the shores of the reservoir. When the water is low, plant life dies of thirst; when high, it is drowned. Much of the shoreline of the reservoir consists of near-perpendicular sandstone bluffs, where very little flora ever did or ever could subsist, but the remainder includes bays, coves, sloping hills and the many side canyons, where the original plant life has been drowned and new plant life cannot get a foothold. And of course where there is little or no plant life there is little or no animal life.

The utter barrenness of the reservoir shoreline recalls by contrast the 9 aspect of things before the dam, when Glen Canyon formed the course of the untamed Colorado. Then we had a wild and flowing river lined by boulder-strewn shores, sandy beaches, thickets of tamarisk and willow, and glades of cottonwoods.

The thickets teemed with songbirds: vireos, warbles, mockingbirds and 10 thrushes. On the open beaches were killdeer, sandpipers, herons, ibises, egrets. Living in grottoes in the canyon walls were swallows, swifts, hawks, wrens and owls. Beaver were common if not abundant: not an evening would pass, in drifting down the river, that we did not see them or at least hear the whack of their flat tails on the water. Above the river shores were the great recessed alcoves where water seeped from the sandstone, nourishing the semitropical hanging gardens of orchid, ivy and columbine, with their associated swarms of insects and birdlife.

Up most of the side canyons, before damnation, there were springs, 11 sometimes flowing streams, waterfalls and plunge pools—the kind of marvels you can now find only in such small-scale remnants of Glen Canyon as the Escalante area. In the rich flora of these laterals the large mammals—mule deer, coyote, bobcat, ring-tailed cat, gray fox, kit fox, skunk, badger and others—found a home. When the river was dammed almost all of these things were lost. Crowded out—or drowned and buried under mud.

The difference between the present reservoir, with its silent sterile shores 12 and debris-choked side canyons, and the original Glen Canyon, is the difference between death and life. Glen Canyon was alive. Lake Powell is a graveyard.

For those who may think I exaggerate the contrast between the former 13 river canyon and the present man-made impoundment, I suggest a trip on Lake Powell followed immediately by another boat trip on the river below the dam. Take a boat from Lee's Ferry up the river to within sight of the dam, then shut off the motor and allow yourself the rare delight of a quiet, effortless drifting down the stream. In that twelve-mile stretch of living green, singing birds, flowing water and untarnished canyon walls—sights and sounds a million years older and infinitely lovelier than the roar of motorboats—you will rediscover a small and imperfect sampling of the kind of experience that was taken away from everybody when the oligarchs and politicians condemned our river for purposes of their own.

The effects of Glen Canyon Dam also extend downstream, causing 14 changes in the character and ecology of Marble Gorge and Grand Canyon. Because the annual spring floods are now a thing of the past, the shores are becoming overgrown with brush, the rapids are getting worse where the river no longer has enough force to carry away the boulders washed down from the lateral canyons, and the beaches are disappearing, losing sand that is not replaced.

Lake Powell, though not a lake, may well be as its defenders assert the 15 most beautiful reservoir in the world. Certainly it has a photographic backdrop of buttes and mesas projecting above the expansive surface of stagnant waters where the speedboats, houseboats and cabin cruisers ply. But it is no longer a wilderness. It is no longer a place of natural life. It is no longer Glen Canyon.

The defenders of the dam argue that the recreational benefits available on 16 the surface of the reservoir outweigh the loss of Indian ruins, historical sites, wildlife and wilderness adventure. Relying on the familiar quantitative logic of business and bureaucracy, they assert that whereas only a few thousand citizens ever ventured down the river through Glen Canyon, now millions can—or will—enjoy the motorized boating and hatchery fishing available on the reservoir. They will also argue that the rising waters behind the dam have made such places as Rainbow Bridge accessible by powerboat. Formerly you could get there only by walking (six miles).

This argument appeals to the wheelchair ethos of the wealthy, upper- 17 middle-class American slob. If Rainbow Bridge is worth seeing at all, then by God it should be easily, readily, immediately available to everybody with the money to buy a big powerboat. Why should a trip to such a place be the privilege only of those who are willing to walk six miles? Or if Pikes Peak is worth getting to, then why not build a highway to the top of it so that anyone can get there? Anytime? Without effort? Or as my old man would say, "By Christ, one man's just as good as another—if not a damn sight better."

Or as ex-Commissioner Floyd Dominy of the U.S. Bureau of Reclama- 18
tion pointed out poetically in his handsomely engraved and illustrated bro-
chure *Lake Powell: Jewel of the Colorado* (produced by the U.S. Government
Printing Office at our expense): "There's something about a lake which
brings us a littler closer to God." In this case, Lake Powell, about five
hundred feet closer. Eh, Floyd?

It is quite true that the flooding of Glen Canyon has opened up to the 19
motorboat explorer parts of side canyons that formerly could be reached only
by people able to walk. But the sum total of terrain visible to the eye and
touchable by hand and foot has been greatly diminished, not increased. Because of the dam the river is gone, the inner canyon is gone, the best parts
of the numerous side canyons are gone—all hidden beneath hundreds of feet
of polluted water, accumulating silt, and mounting tons of trash. This portion of Glen Canyon—and who can estimate how many cubic miles were
lost?—*is no longer accessible to anybody.* (Except scuba divers.) And this, do
not forget, was the most valuable part of Glen Canyon, richest in scenery,
archaeology, history, flora and fauna.

Not only has the heart of Glen Canyon been buried, but many of the 20
side canyons above the fluctuating waterline are now rendered more difficult,
not easier, to get into. This because the debris brought down into them by
desert storms, no longer carried away by the river, must unavoidably build
up in the area where flood meets reservoir. Narrow Canyon, for example, at
the head of the impounded waters, is already beginning to silt up and to
amass huge quantities of driftwood, some of it floating on the surface, some
of it half afloat beneath the surface. Anyone who has tried to pilot a motorboat through a raft of half-sunken logs and bloated dead cows will have his
own thoughts on the accessibility of these waters.

Hite Marina, at the mouth of Narrow Canyon, will probably have to be 21
abandoned within twenty or thirty years. After that it will be the turn of
Bullfrog Marina. And then Rainbow Bridge Marina. And eventually, inevitably, whether it takes ten centuries or only one, Wahweap. Lake Powell,
like Lake Mead, is foredoomed sooner or later to become a solid mass of
mud, and its dam a waterfall. Assuming, of course, that either one stands
that long.

Second, the question of costs. It is often stated that the dam and its res- 22
ervoir have opened up to the many what was formerly restricted to the few,
implying in this case that what was once expensive has now been made
cheap. Exactly the opposite is true.

Before the dam, a float trip down the river through Glen Canyon would 23
cost you a minimum of seven days' time, well within anyone's vacation al-
lotment, and a capital outlay of about forty dollars—the prevailing price of a
two-man rubber boat with oars, available at any army-navy surplus store. A
life jacket might be useful but not required, for there were no dangerous
rapids in the 150 miles of Glen Canyon. As the name implies, this stretch of
the river was in fact so easy and gentle that the trip could be and was made
by all sorts of amateurs: by Boy Scouts, Camp Fire Girls, stenographers,

schoolteachers, students, little old ladies in inner tubes. Guides, professional boatmen, giant pontoons, outboard motors, radios, rescue equipment were not needed. The Glen Canyon float trip was an adventure anyone could enjoy, on his own, for a cost less than that of spending two days and nights in a Page motel. Even food was there, in the water: the channel catfish were easier to catch and a lot better eating than the striped bass and rainbow trout dumped by the ton into the reservoir these days. And one other thing: at the end of the float trip you still owned your boat, usable for many more such casual and carefree expeditions.

What is the situation now? Float trips are no longer possible. The only 24 way left for the exploration of the reservoir and what remains of Glen Canyon demands the use of a powerboat. Here you have three options: (1) buy your own boat and engine, the necessary auxiliary equipment, the fuel to keep it moving, the parts and repairs to keep it running, the permits and license required for legal operation, the trailer to transport it: (2) rent a boat; or (3) go on a commercial excursion boat, packed in with other sightseers, following a preplanned itinerary. This kind of play is only for the affluent.

The inescapable conclusion is that no matter how one attempts to calcu- 25 late the cost in dollars and cents, a float trip down Glen Canyon was much cheaper than a powerboat tour of the reservoir. Being less expensive, as well as safer and easier, the float trip was an adventure open to far more people than will ever be able to afford motorboat excursions in the area now.

What about the "human impact" of motorized use of the Glen Canyon 26 impoundment? We can visualize the floor of the reservoir gradually accumulating not only silt, mud, waterlogged trees and drowned cattle but also the usual debris that is left behind when the urban, industrial style of recreation is carried into the open country. There is also the problem of human wastes. The waters of the wild river were good to drink, but nobody in his senses would drink from Lake Powell. Eventually, as is already sometimes the case at Lake Mead, the stagnant waters will become too foul even for swimming. The trouble is that while some boats have what are called "self-contained" heads, the majority do not, most sewage is disposed of by simply pumping it into the water. It will take a while, but long before it becomes a solid mass of mud Lake Powell ("Jewel of the Colorado") will enjoy a passing fame as the biggest sewage lagoon in the American Southwest. Most tourists will never be able to afford a boat trip on this reservoir, but everybody within fifty miles will be able to smell it.

All of the foregoing would be nothing but a futile exercise in nostalgia 27 (so much water over the dam) if I had nothing constructive and concrete to offer. But I do. As alternate methods of power generation are developed, such as solar, and as the nation establishes a way of life adapted to actual resources and basic needs, so that the demand for electrical power begins to diminish, we can shut down the Glen Canyon power plant, open the diversion tunnels, and drain the reservoir.

This will no doubt expose a drear and hideous scene: immense mud flats 28 and whole plateaus of sodden garbage strewn with dead trees, sunken boats, the skeletons of long-forgotten, decomposing water-skiers. But to those who find the prospect too appalling, I say give nature a little time. In five years, at most in ten, the sun and wind and storms will cleanse and sterilize the repellent mess. The inevitable floods will soon remove all that does not belong within the canyons. Fresh green willow, box elder and redbud will reappear; and the ancient drowned cottonwoods (noble monuments to themselves) will be replaced by young of their own kind. With the renewal of plant life will come the insects, the birds, the lizards and snakes, the mammals. Within a generation—thirty years—I predict the river and canyons will bear a decent resemblance to their former selves. Within the lifetime of our children Glen Canyon and the living river, heart of the canyonlands, will be restored to us. The wilderness will again belong to God, the people and the wild things that call it home.

PART THREE
SYNTHESIZE

□ 6 ESTABLISH COMMON POINTS OF DISCUSSION

Imagine that you have walked into a room where your authors are arguing about a particular issue. Initially, you are confused by the rapid fire of points and counterpoints. But as you listen, you develop some sense of what is going on. To confirm your hunches, you call a halt to the conversation and make a series of claims or statements related to the issue. You then ask each author if he or she agrees or disagrees with each of your statements. As you listen to these responses, you develop a better understanding of where the authors stand on the issue and the differences between them.

In this chapter, you will learn how to put together a scenario like this for your issue. The claims you will make are called "common points of discussion." The authors' responses are the "positions" they take. By developing these common points and positions, you will turn the knowledge you gained in summarizing into a unified picture of the issue.

FORM CLUSTERS OF POINTS

The first step in developing common points of discussion is to cluster the points in your notes around a small set of common topics. Looking over your notes, you try to see what your authors have in common.

The simplest strategy for clustering authors' points relies on *cross-citation*. When authors cite each other, they indicate that they are speaking on the same topic—whether to agree or disagree. When, for example, Roderick Nash cites Eric Julber in his essay "The Irony of Victory," we know that these two authors are making points related to the same topic:

CROSS-CITATION OF CLAIMS IN WILDERNESS

Julber, writing in *Reader's Digest* in 1972:

It is my firm belief that if Americans were permitted access to Wilderness areas in the manner I have suggested, we would soon create a generation of avid nature lovers. Americans would cease to be "alien-ated" from their landscape, and would mend their littering tendencies. If you question any purist or wilderness buff, you will find that what initially "turned him on," in almost every case, was an experience in which he was provided access to natural beauty—be it in Glacier Park, Yellowstone, Grand Canyon, or Yosemite (as in my own case)—by roads, bus or other similar non-purist means. Yet, if purists had had the influence 100 years ago that they have today, there would be no roads or other facilities in Yosemite Valley, and the strong probability is that neither I nor millions of other Americans would ever have seen its beau-ties, except on postcards.

I believe that the purist philosophy is unfair and undemocratic, and that an alternate philosophy, one of enlightened, carefully controlled "access," is more desirable and also ecologically sound. If the Swiss can do it, why can't we?

Nash, responding in his book in 1979:

The fact that recreational use, even by innumerable people, does not consume the environmental resource in the same way as lumbering or mining has confused recent American discussion of preserving wil-derness. Los Angeles attorney Eric Julber, for instance, told the Senate Subcommittee on Parks and Recreation in 1972 that the United States wildernesses should be "opened up" for the general public. Pointing to Switzerland as a case in point, Julber argued that breathtaking mountain scenery could be readily accessible by mechanical means. . . .

In defense of Eric Julber and those who share his opinions, his " 'ac-cess' philosophy" is not aimed at minimizing the value of wilderness in American civilization. On the contrary, he declared it is his "firm belief that if Americans were permitted access to Wilderness areas in the man-ner I have suggested, we would soon create a generation of avid nature lovers." The difficulty here is that, according to most definitions, the wilderness quality of the area would vanish when the tramways and hotels arrived. Julber's confusion lay in equating "nature," "scenery," and "beauty" with "wilderness."

When you encounter cross-citation, you should use it as a clue to look for points other authors may have made on the same topic. If you find more points, you will then have a starting cluster in your issue. Knowing, for example, that both Julber and Nash spoke on the topic of "access," we sorted through the rest of our notes to come up with the following cluster of points:

A CLUSTER OF POINTS ON "ACCESS"

Julber: According to Julber, we should open up our wilderness areas as they have done in Switzerland.

Nash: According to Nash, Julber has confused wilderness with scenic beauty. Wilderness, according to Nash, would disappear with the kind of access Julber imagines.

Tucker: According to Tucker, the environmentalist effort to limit access to wilderness areas to backpackers and canoers is just an effort to impose middle-class tastes in recreation on the whole country.

Ehrlichs: According to the Ehrlichs, closer contact with ecosystems would increase people's understanding of their intrinsic beauty and importance.

Swain: According to Swain, people have a natural desire to preserve their freedom of access to wilderness and rare species, whether or not they actually exercise it.

Abbey: According to Abbey, the damnation of Glen Canyon has led to a decrease in the accessibility of the area, not an increase.

To complete the clustering process, you will usually need to rely on one of two other strategies in addition to cross–citation. In the first, the *systematic review,* you develop clusters by sorting through all of the notes you took in summarizing. As you work, you play with your notes, moving cards around, splitting or combining clusters until you get groupings that make sense to you. As shown in the diagram below, you are trying to impose some order on what can often look like a hodgepodge of unrelated points.

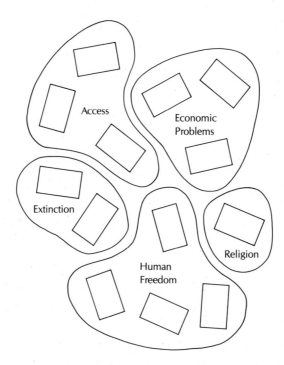

Clusters in a Systematic Review

In the second strategy, you use your notes from a single author to conduct an *anchored review*. To do this successfully, you must choose your anchoring author wisely. He or she should present what you consider to be a comprehensive view of the issue, covering most of the relevant topics. Authors who make unusual points or who respond to a narrow range of topics will not work well. The initial set of clusters they produce will make a poor fit with other authors' points and you will have to make too many adjustments to get a comprehensive sort.

After defining an initial set of clusters to cover your anchoring author's points, you review the rest of your notes, adding them to this anchoring set. If you find that a point doesn't fit into any existing cluster, you either start a new cluster or disregard the point as unimportant. As shown in the diagram below, you continue working in this way, making additions and refinements, until you have a set of clusters that covers all of your authors' important points.

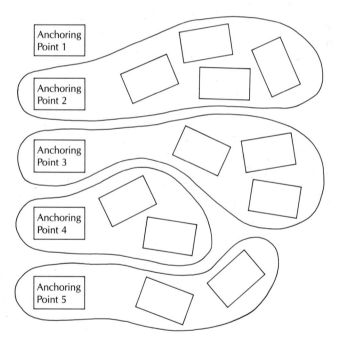

Clusters in an Anchored Review

In deciding whether to pursue a systematic or anchored review, you should consider several factors. To conduct an anchored review, you must be well acquainted with the points your authors make, and you need a suitable anchoring author. Otherwise, you run the risk of discarding important points and producing a lopsided synthesis. With a systematic review, on the other hand, you can refresh your memory if you have been away from your notes for a while. Being systematic does, however, take more time and can seem initially more confusing. Keep in mind, however, that you can always shift from one strategy to the other in mid-course.

For Class 6.1

In groups, use the set of points listed below to complete one of the following activities using the strategy indicated. Then, as a class, compare your results. How do variations in strategy and belief account for differences you find in the way your groups formed clusters?

Group A: Conduct a systematic review.
Group B: Conduct an anchored review using Julber as anchoring author.
Group C: Conduct an anchored review using Nash as anchoring author.
Group D: Conduct an anchored review using Tucker as anchoring author.
Group E: Conduct an anchored review using the Ehrlichs as anchoring authors.
Group F: Conduct an anchored review using Swain as anchoring author.
Group G: Conduct an anchored review using Abbey as anchoring author.

POINTS TO BE CLUSTERED

Nash

1. According to Nash, Americans' increasing appreciation of the wilderness has increased the demand for access and may paradoxically end up destroying wilderness. Threats to wilderness may come from recreational as well as economic uses—it doesn't matter which.

2. Eric Julber has argued that wilderness ought to be opened up for the general public as in Switzerland in order to increase Americans' love of nature. According to Nash, Julber has confused wilderness with scenic beauty. Wilderness, according to Nash, would disappear with the kind of access Julber imagines.

3. The Centennial Task Force argued in 1972 that the major purpose of the National Parks should be the preservation of the wilderness, not the increase of recreational access. Critics of the report like Interior Secretary Morton argued that the National Parks were already doing a good job of preservation and ought to be doing more for recreation. According to wilderness advocates, this parks-are-for-people concept would end up destroying wilderness. Wilderness requires special definition and management to survive.

4. According to Nash, "when a region's carrying capacity is exceeded it is no longer wild," no matter whether that excess is recreational use or economic exploitation. Carrying capacity has three dimensions: physical, biological, and psychological.

5. According to Nash, the Sierra Mountains are an example of a wilderness region whose carrying capacity has been exceeded.

6. According to Nash, the Boundary Waters Canoe Area is now approaching its carrying capacity despite tough restrictions on use.

7. The Grand Canyon is also nearing its carrying capacity despite naturally limited access. The cause: inflatable rubber rafts have made the trip safe.

8. According to Nash, the only way to remedy carrying-capacity violations is through the acceptance of visitation quotas based on respect for the experience. Some people will feel that quotas diminish or destroy the idea of wilderness by imposing human regulation.

Nash *(continued)*

According to Nash, however, the increased appreciation they produce and the destruction they decrease make quotas the only acceptable solution to wilderness destruction.

Julber

1. According to Julber, the dominant philosophy toward wilderness is "purist"—limiting wilderness access to backpackers.
2. According to Julber, the purist philosophy restricts access to less than 1 percent of the population, those with income and professional status.
3. The remaining 99 percent of the country, according to Julber, are stuck with secondary scenic areas.
4. According to Julber, the Swiss have done a good job of making nature accessible to all of Europe through comfortable transportation and accommodations.
5. According to Julber, we should open up our wilderness areas as they have done in Switzerland.
6. If wilderness were opened up, according to Julber, it would turn the nation into a generation of nature lovers.

Tucker

1. According to Tucker, the wilderness concept is a central one in the environmental movement. Many environmentalists, starting with Thoreau, have considered wilderness areas to be sanctuaries for all true values, refuges for a new religious alternative to the Judeo-Christian religion that some have blamed for the ecological crisis.
2. The preservationist effort, according to Tucker, was begun by Aldo Leopold, a Forest Service officer working in the Gila National Forest in the 1920s. It was continued by Robert Marshall until 14 million acres of National Forest had been set aside by the 1950s. Both Leopold and Marshall worked to preserve wilderness areas because of their experience in the Kaibab Plateau. Leopold and Marshall felt that this case showed that humans cannot intervene in natural ecosystems without doing damage, no matter how good the intentions are.
3. According to Tucker, the definition of wilderness used by environmentalists and given in the Wilderness Act of 1964 is an area in which evidence of human activity is excluded for ecological, rather than scenic or recreational, purposes.
4. According to Tucker, the wilderness concept is valid for creating ecological museums in scenic and biologically significant areas. But the result of the preservation effort has more often been to lock up mineral and energy resources in western states without adequate resource reviews, causing serious harm to our international trade.
5. According to Tucker, the main fight involves roadless areas. Preservationists argue that these areas are *de facto* wildernesses and have fought the two RARE studies that recommended their release. This fight, according to Tucker, has increased timber prices, made the United States an importer of timber, and caused the hurried set-aside of the mineral-rich Sawtooth Wilderness.
6. According to Tucker, the Overthrust Belt is one of the most hotly contested areas. Environmentalists want these areas designated as wildernesses and have allowed mineral exploration under restricted conditions only until 1982. According to Tucker, these restricted conditions make exploration expensive and ineffective.
7. According to Tucker, wilderness is the product of a complex technological society that has created economic leisure. The preservation impulse endangers this economic leisure because it ties up needed resources.
8. Many environmentalists such as E. F. Schumacher and Marvin Harris have

Tucker *(continued)*

argued that wilderness preservation should serve as the basis of a new religion with a more environmentally sound perspective. According to Lynn White, the Western Judeo-Christian religion is the source of the environmental crisis because it assumes man is the master of nature. Tucker, however, is not convinced that doing away with the Judeo-Christian tradition would change the way we treat nature.

9. According to romantic notions often argued by environmentalists, primitive people were more environmentally sound. According to Tucker, quoting René Dubos, many primitive cultures caused extensive ecological damage.

10. According to Tucker, we must adopt a conservationist policy of stewardship toward the land, recognizing the part we play in nature. He quotes Dubos as saying that we must develop creative and harmonious ways to live with nature. This, according to Tucker, should be the goal of the environmental movement.

Ehrlichs

1. According to Paul and Anne Ehrlich, population pressure in Africa may soon wipe out the species for which we should have the most empathy.

2. By causing the destruction of species like the chimps, we are, according to the Ehrlichs, bringing about our own destruction.

3. Some people argue that extinction is part of the natural evolutionary process. But, according to the Ehrlichs, the current rate of extinction is now between forty and four hundred times "normal."

4. Some people argue that we will miss extinct species no more than we now miss the dinosaurs. The Ehrlichs reply that the dinosaurs became extinct when evolution had a chance to replace them with mammals. Today the rate of extinction is beginning to overwhelm this process of replacement.

5. Some people argue that the value of some species such as the snail darter is very small compared to the benefits of technological developments that threaten them. According to the Ehrlichs, however, the issue is where to draw the line. There will always be someone willing to sacrifice one more species for short-term economic goals.

6. Some people believe that certain species are harmful to man and deserve to become extinct. This attitude, according to the Ehrlichs, ignores the complexity of the earth's ecosystems. It is impossible to remove one species without affecting the entire balance.

7. According to Paul and Anne Ehrlich, closer contact with ecosystems would increase people's understanding of their intrinsic beauty and importance.

Swain

1. According to Swain, agreeing with Ehrenfeld, current arguments for preserving wilderness are inadequate and may cause a public backlash against preservation efforts.

2. Ehrenfeld argues that we must replace our anthropocentric focus on the usefulness of wildernesses and preserve them for their intrinsic value. Swain argues, however, that we do not need to abandon our humanistic tradition to find reasons to preserve wilderness. He claims that all we need to do is expand our values to recognize the human need for a quality environment.

3. According to Swain, people have a gut-level desire to preserve wilderness areas in order to maintain their personal freedom of choice.

4. According to the theory of psychological reactance first formulated by Jack Brehm, people will react to preserve

Swain *(continued)*

the potential to see irreplaceable entities, whether or not they ever actually go into wilderness.

5. Krieger argues that after a while human beings will get used to unnatural environments and cease to desire wilderness. While Swain admits that this may be the case, he feels that it would be tragic for human beings to become accustomed to living in a world entirely of their own making. Krieger also underestimates, in Swain's opinion, how people would react just to knowing that they no longer had the choice.

6. Swain believes that we will have to lower our standards of living and adopt a renewable economy sooner or later. If we act now, however, we will preserve our sense of freedom of choice. If we wait until all wilderness is gone and our resources are depleted, we will have to cope with an overwhelming sense of oppression and restricted personal freedom.

Abbey

1. According to Abbey, his personal experience with Glen Canyon entitles him to evaluate the effects of damming the canyon. He admits that he is part of a growing number of Americans who prefer natural environments to man-made, industrialized, and urbanized settings.

2. According to Abbey, Lake Powell, formed when Glen Canyon was dammed, is a reservoir whose fluctuating water levels are intended primarily to generate electricity. This fluctuation, though, has caused an unsightly "bathtub ring," an instability in shoreline plant life, and a decrease in animal life.

3. Prior to damming, according to Abbey, Glen Canyon was teeming with plant and animal life that was drowned, buried, or crowded out afterwards. For all intents and purposes, Lake Powell is now a graveyard.

4. According to Abbey, the river above and below the dam today indicates the difference between Glen Canyon before and after the dam. Below the dam, the shores are overgrown with brush, the rapids are worsening, and the beaches are being washed away. While Abbey admits that Lake Powell is photogenic, it is no longer wilderness.

5. Defenders of the dam argue that Lake Powell is now more accessible to Americans for motorized boating and fishing. Abbey admits that the flooding has opened up more side canyons to motorboats, but he says even more of these canyons have been made inaccessible because they are under water. Furthermore, according to Abbey, the damming of Glen Canyon has led to a decrease in the accessibility of the area because motorboat trips are more expensive than raft trips.

6. According to Abbey, Lake Powell is doomed by the accumulation of silt and human waste and can be replaced by alternative methods of power generation anyway. Therefore, he argues, we should shut down the dam now and return Glen Canyon "to God, the people and the wild things that call it home."

FORMULATE TENTATIVE COMMON POINTS

The next step in imagining the conversation in your issue is to formulate a set of tentative common points of discussion. A **common point of discussion** is a claim about some aspect of an issue to which your authors can be said to respond. The basic strategy for formulating a common point is to create a claim on which at least two of your authors can be shown to disagree with each other. Look again, for example, at our cluster on the "access" topic for wilderness (pages 135–36). We tried to create a claim with which Julber and Nash might disagree. Since we began this cluster with their cross-citation, we found it easy to formulate a tentative common point to highlight this disagreement:

A TENTATIVE COMMON POINT

Julber's point:	According to Julber, we should open up our wilderness areas as they have done in Switzerland.
Nash's point:	According to Nash, Julber has confused wilderness with scenic beauty. Wilderness, according to Nash, would disappear with the kind of access Julber imagines.
Tentative common point:	We should open up our wilderness areas.

DRAW A GRID OF COMMON POINTS

After you have established tentative common points for your issue, the next step is to construct a grid to contain them. A **grid of common points** is a two-dimensional array of all the major positions in an issue constructed as shown below. Along the side of the grid, arrange the names of the authors you have selected. Across the top, arrange the tentative common points you have developed. Then fill in the boxes of the grid with authors' positions, using techniques discussed in the next section.

A GRID OF COMMON POINTS

	Common Point A	Common Point B	Common Point C	Etc.
Author 1	Position	Position	Position	
Author 2	Position	Position	Position	
Author 3	Position	Position	Position	

Etc.

A completed grid of common points is a ready index to the claims made in an issue. In constructing one, you break away from the one-dimensional, point-by-point organization of authors' lines of argument and put a single, more complex, structure in their place. By reading down a column, you will be able to review the diverse responses authors make on a given point. By reading across a row, you will be able to review the many beliefs held by a given author on a given issue. Thus, in a single format, you will have captured the current conversation in your issue.

Creating grids of common points can be a messy project. It is best to start out by putting each column on separate pages and only later try to put the columns together. Create a "form" for a single column by taking a piece of paper and evenly spacing the names of your authors down the side. Draw horizontal lines to separate them. Then add one vertical line to create your single column. Make several copies of this form, one for each of your clusters of points.

A FORM FOR A GRID OF COMMON POINTS

	Common Point
Author 1	
Author 2	
Author 3	

Then, in pencil at the top of the columns, write in the tentative common points you have developed for each cluster. Leave the boxes in the column blank for now.

FILL IN AUTHORS' RESPONSES

To fill in the boxes in your grid of common points, you must state each of your authors' positions with respect to the common point at the top of the column. An *author's position* is a single sentence that describes the author's basic response to the common point and elaborates on what makes the position distinctive.

State Basic Positions

Authors may take a position on a common point with one of four basic responses:

POSSIBLE BASIC POSITIONS

- They may *agree* with it.
- They may *disagree* with it.
- They may *qualify* it.
- They may *make no comment* on it.

If an author agrees with a common point of discussion, you can state the basic position by simply repeating the common point. On the topic of "access," for instance, we simply repeat the common point to capture Julber's position of agreement:

AN AUTHOR WHO AGREES

	We should open up our wilderness areas as much as possible.
Julber	We should open up our wilderness areas as much as possible.

If authors disagree with a point of discussion, you can describe their basic position by adding a negative like "not" or changing a word in the sentence to its opposite. This is how we initially handled Nash's basic position:

AN AUTHOR WHO DISAGREES

Nash	We should <u>not</u> open up our wilderness areas.

If authors' positions are more limited or more far-reaching than a common point of discussion, you can state their basic position with a qualification of the common point. That is, you can add the qualifying conditions that would make the common point acceptable. We tried, for example, to handle Tucker's position in this way:

AN AUTHOR WHO QUALIFIES

Tucker	We should open up our wilderness areas in accordance with the variety of American recreational tastes.

Finally, you may occasionally encounter an author who does not speak to a common point. If, in your best reading of a text, you find no clear statement about how an author stands with respect to a common point, you should enter the words "no comment" on your grid:

AN AUTHOR WHO MAKES NO COMMENT

Author	No comment

Use this entry sparingly. Columns filled with "no comment" will not help much to establish what the discussion in a community is all about; they only tell you what it's *not* about. If you find that you have overused this entry, you should rethink your common point of discussion.

Rephrase Common Points

Because you have created your common points tentatively—on the intuition that they would capture what's in dispute—their fit with authors' positions will often be less than perfect. Never be satisfied with this kind of situation. Whenever you aren't being fair to an author in stating the basic position, you should consider ways to rephrase the common point at the top of the column. The give-and-take between stating basic positions and rephrasing common points is what will give your grid of common points its power to capture the heart of your issue.

Our work on the topic of "access" provided two good examples of rephrasing common points. In the first case, our initial statement of Nash's position had made us uneasy:

AN UNFAIR CHARACTERIZATION

Nash	We should <u>not</u> open up our wilderness areas.

We felt it simply wasn't fair to characterize Nash's position that way. Nash, after all, was a wilderness advocate and saw many strong reasons for providing access. His real dispute with Julber seemed more a matter of degree—whether we should increase or decrease the current level of access. With this insight, we rephrased our common point of discussion and made changes in the basic positions going down the column:

A REPHRASED COMMON POINT OF DISCUSSION

	We should increase access to our wilderness areas.
Julber	We should increase access to our wilderness areas.
Nash	We should limit access to our wilderness areas.

Our second need to rephrase came when we tried to state Tucker's basic position in response to this newly phrased common point. Again, we felt the resulting characterization was less than fair:

A SECOND UNFAIR CHARACTERIZATION

Tucker	We should open up our wilderness areas in accordance with the variety of American recreational tastes.

Despite our statement, we knew that Tucker had said little about increasing access. In fact, he even wanted to see a decrease in the overall amount of wilderness set aside. Our problem was again in the verb, "increase." Tucker, we realized, said little about the level of access and probably wouldn't agree with "increasing" it. He did, however, speak to the *type* of access—canoeing versus motorboating, for example. To us, this concern seemed close to Julber's desire to provide mechanical transport to open up wilderness areas. With this final insight, we were able to rephrase the common point and complete the rest of our column:

A COMPLETED SET OF BASIC POSITIONS

	We should provide access to our wilderness areas.
Julber	We should provide access to our wilderness areas for all Americans.
Nash	We should limit access to our wilderness areas.
Tucker	We should provide access to our wilderness areas in accordance with the variety of American tastes in recreation.
Ehrlichs	We should provide access to our wilderness areas.
Swain	We should provide access to our wilderness areas.
Abbey	We should provide access to our wilderness areas.

For Class 6.2

In groups, create a column under *one of* the following common points by stating the positions of Julber, Nash, Tucker, the Ehrlichs, Swain, and Abbey in response to the given point. Use the points in "For Class 6.1" as the basis for your statements. Revise the common point if fairness dictates.

Common Point A: We are destroying our wilderness areas.
Common Point B: Wilderness is endangered by economic exploitation.
Common Point C: Wilderness is a source of peace and freedom.
Common Point D: Wilderness preservation has reduced our economic well-being.
Common Point E: Nature is a resource for human creativity.
Common Point F: We need to develop a new religious ethic.

Elaborate Each Author's Position

The basic positions of agreeing, disagreeing, qualifying, and no comment will go a long way in illuminating the major similarities and differences among your authors. In addition, however, your grid should capture what makes each author distinctive. You do this by adding a phrase to the basic position to elaborate on the rationale behind each author's stand.

On our topic of "access," for example, the basic positions made clear the differences among three authors (Julber, Nash, Tucker), but left unclear what made the others (Ehrlichs, Swain, Abbey) unique. By elaborating on the rationale of each author, however, we got a more complete set of distinctions:

A SET OF ELABORATED BASIC POSITIONS

	We should provide access to our wilderness areas.
Julber	We should provide access to our wilderness areas to allow all Americans to appreciate them.
Nash	We should limit access to our wilderness areas to preserve them from destruction.
Tucker	We should provide access to our wilderness areas to be fair to the variety of American tastes in recreation.
Ehrlichs	We should provide access to our wilderness areas to increase people's understanding of nature.
Swain	We should provide access to our wilderness areas to maintain our sense of freedom.
Abbey	We should provide access to our wilderness areas to provide a respite from civilized life.

For Class 6.3

For the following column from our wilderness grid:

a. Elaborate on the authors' positions to clarify their similarities and differences.
b. Revise the common point of discussion to avoid attributing "no comment" to Julber and Abbey.

	Wilderness is endangered by economic exploitation.
Julber	No comment
Nash	Wilderness is endangered not just by economic exploitation.
Tucker	Wilderness is hardly endangered by economic exploitation.
Ehrlichs	Wilderness is endangered by economic exploitation.
Swain	Wilderness is endangered by economic necessity.
Abbey	No comment

REVISE FOR ADEQUATE COVERAGE

We have already mentioned the kinds of revision you should consider if your statement of an author's position is not fair to the author. Now, however, you should turn your attention to several larger concerns.

First, read across the rows, author by author, to make sure that you have represented each one's position completely. Have your notes in hand as you conduct this check. Does your grid omit any important aspects of an author's position? If you uncover any incompleteness, it may arise because a particular author is idiosyncratic, spending considerable time discussing what you think is peripheral to the issue. But occasionally your review will turn up aspects of an issue that you do consider important or that do relate to more than one author. In this case, you should make appropriate additions to your set of common points and add a new column to your grid.

Second, make sure that, taken together, your columns cover the entire issue. In particular, make sure you have included points related both to the problem and to what the authors argue is a solution. If any points in either of these categories are missing, make additions to include them.

For Your Notebook #11

Create a grid of common points for your issue.

- Sort your notecards by topic using either a systematic or anchored review.
- Create a tentative common point for each cluster.
- Fill in each column of grid, working back and forth between stating authors' positions and rephrasing common points.
- Review your columns for adequate coverage. Make sure that you have a comprehensive view of each author's position and that you have included points relevant to both problems and solutions.

▢▢ 7 DISCOVER A PATTERN TO THE CONVERSATION

Once you have constructed a grid of common points, you have made extensive preparation for your own exploration. You have not only followed all the lines of argument suggested by others, but you have also compared their positions on points you will probably want to explore. What you have not yet done is construct a comprehensive and reliable map of the issue, one that lays out the decisions you will face in making your own journey.

To see why you need a comprehensive map, imagine for a moment that you are a nineteenth-century pioneer intending to move west. The success of your journey depends on starting with the best available knowledge. Many maps exist, but unfortunately they give conflicting advice. At points where one map says "head northwest," for example, another says "head southwest." Because the consequences of taking the wrong path can be serious, you need a way to avoid bad decisions—you need a map you can trust.

As a writer trying to synthesize an issue, you also need a comprehensive map. What are the consequences of accepting or rejecting an author's point? What are the choices that have led authors to take such different positions? What would happen if you disagreed with every author on some fundamental point? To answer these and other questions, you must construct a "synthesis tree" to serve as your comprehensive map of the issue.

BUILD A SYNTHESIS TREE

A **synthesis tree** is a structure that lays out your authors' arguments as alternative paths branching from crucial decision points in exploring the issue. In it, as shown below, you will locate three kinds of decision points: preliminary splits, the major split, and minor splits:

A SYNTHESIS TREE

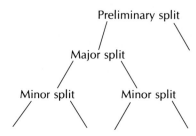

The **major split** in an issue is the dispute on which you find the most disagreement among your authors. The way the argument goes here will determine the entire issue in most people's eyes. It is where the action is. Most often a major split polarizes your authors into two, sometimes three, opposing camps. On the wilderness issue, for example, the major split appears to be between propreservationists and antipreservationists.

Preliminary splits, located prior to the major split, are disputes over decisions that most authors take as settled. In almost every issue, you will find a few authors disputing these settled decisions, arguing that everybody else is barking up the wrong tree. These preliminary disagreements are often serious and the authors taking these positions are often considered extreme. Among the preservationists, for example, Swain's argument that we will have to lower our standard of living whether or not we preserve wilderness puts him at a preliminary disagreement.

Minor splits are disputes within major splits. They usually have the flavor of differences among friends rather than disputes between camps. That is, most authors would agree that these controversies can be ironed out somewhere down the road. In the wilderness issue, for example, the disagreement between Abbey and the Ehrlichs on the best way to stop the economic exploitation of wilderness is a minor split between authors with the same fundamental goals.

Until this point, you have been able to think of authors as making many different points and taking many different positions. To create a synthesis tree, however, you must see each of them as representing a single final destination at the end of a series of preliminary, major, and minor splits:

AN AUTHOR'S POSITION IN A SYNTHESIS TREE

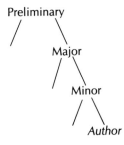

The rewards of such a perspective shift are large. With a synthesis tree, you will be able to identify the common concerns with which your authors begin and the series of disagreements by which they gradually diverge. With this understanding, you will have in hand the comprehensive map you need for your explorations. In the sections below, then, we will describe the steps you take in constructing this map.

Locate the Major Split

After you have constructed a grid of common points, one fact should be fairly obvious to you: authors disagree with one another. When you were just starting to read and summarize, the nature of these disagreements might have been hazy or unclear. But having stated each author's position on a number of common points of discussion, you should now have a firmer grasp of what they are. In constructing a synthesis tree, you take advantage of this understanding.

You begin constructing a synthesis tree by locating what you think is the major split in your issue. You can often do this by going back to what originally attracted you to the issue. If you read about the controversy in a weekly news magazine or on the opinion page of your daily paper, for example, you probably found it cast in terms of opposing camps: those who favor something and those opposed. Perhaps the dispute was so well recognized that the opposing camps had been given names. If so, this division is a strong candidate for the major split.

You can also locate the major split in a community by returning to your grid of common points. Looking over the common points that you listed across the top of your grid, try to decide on the one that represents the most serious controversy. Which of the points, in your opinion, lies at the heart of the issue, dividing the community into major opposing camps? Try using it as the major split in your community.

Once you have chosen a likely candidate for the major split in your synthesis tree, create two phrases, one to represent each side of the issue and divide the names of your authors between them. We have made this division below for our major split in wilderness:

THE MAJOR SPLIT IN WILDERNESS

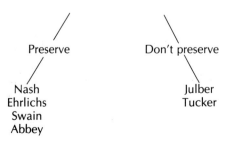

Add Preliminary Splits

Next, consider whether or not you need to add any preliminary splits to your tree. Preliminary splits occur prior to the major split. They indicate that one or more authors are taking issue with an assumption that the rest of your authors take for granted. To determine whether you should add preliminary splits to your map, check whether your common points of discussion neatly divide among the alternatives formed by your major split.

CHECKING THE DISTRIBUTION OF COMMON POINTS

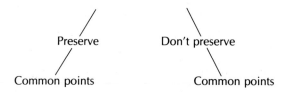

Preserve

Don't preserve

Common points

Common points

A. We should provide access to our wilderness areas (Ehrlichs, Swain, Abbey).

B. Our economic well-being will be affected by wilderness preservation (Swain).

C. Wildernesses must be protected because they are special (Nash, Ehrlichs, Swain, Abbey).

D. We are destroying our wilderness areas (Nash, Ehrlichs, Swain, Abbey).

A. We should provide access to our wilderness areas (Julber, Tucker).

B. Our economic well-being will be affected by wilderness preservation (Tucker).

When we checked the distribution of common points on wilderness, for example, we found that opinions did not neatly divide between the branches of our major split. In particular, Common Points A and B seemed to have advocates in both the propreservationist and antipreservationist camps. Thus, we knew we had to add preliminary splits to deal with this overlap.

If you find an overlap of opinions when you distribute your common points between your major split, you need to find the author or authors responsible and place them at preliminary splits. Our work on wilderness shows two different ways this can be done. In the first case, Common Point A, everybody on both sides of our major split agreed with the common point of providing access. The one exception was Nash, who wanted to limit access. To deal with this situation, we tried putting Nash at a preliminary split:

CREATING A PRELIMINARY SPLIT

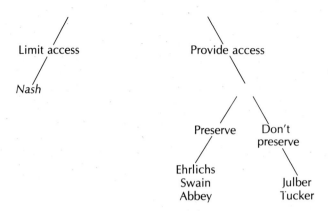

Once you have created a preliminary split, you should check whether the resulting arrangement matches your intuition. In particular, does the distance between the various authors reflect the actual differences between them? If not, you should play with the arrangement of splits. When we checked the preceding preliminary split for Nash, for example, we were dissatisfied. Tucker, an anti-preservationist, had ended up closer to the preservationists (Swain, Abbey, and the Ehrlichs) than Nash had. With a little shifting around, however, we succeeded in putting Tucker farther away:

REVISING A PRELIMINARY DISAGREEMENT TO REFLECT INTUITION

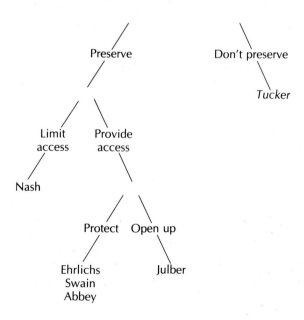

For Class 7.1

Add another preliminary split to the synthesis tree above to accommodate the overlap caused by Common Point B, "Our economic well-being will be affected by wilderness preservation." (See the diagram on page 152.) Notice that this overlap is caused by the agreement of two authors, Swain and Tucker, originally placed on opposite sides of the major split. How can you create a preliminary split to put them closer together?

Add Minor Splits

To complete your synthesis tree, you must add as many minor splits as necessary to put each author at a unique place on the tree. Search your grid of common points for disagreements between authors you still have clustered. On what issues do they seem to disagree despite their many agreements so far?

After adding preliminary splits to our synthesis tree on wilderness, for example, we still found ourselves with two sets of authors undistinguished: the Ehrlichs and Abbey, and Tucker and Swain:

REMAINING POSITIONS UNDISTINGUISHED

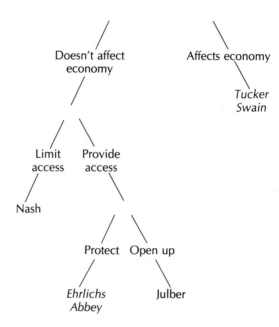

In our first cluster, we had the Ehrlichs and Abbey agreeing that we must protect wilderness. On what, we asked ourselves, do they still disagree? According to our grid of common points, the Ehrlichs focused on educational efforts as a means of preservation; Abbey focused on returning lands to their wilderness state. This seemed to be a relatively minor split over how to protect wilderness:

ADDING THE FIRST MINOR SPLIT

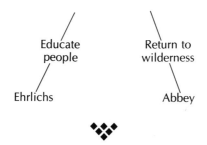

For Class 7.2

Create another minor split in the preceding synthesis tree to distinguish the positions on Tucker and Swain. Use this information from our grid of common points as a guide.

Common Point	A. We should provide access to our wilderness areas.	B. Our economic well-being will be affected by wilderness preservation.
Tucker	We should provide access to our wilderness areas to be fair to the variety of American tastes in recreation.	Our economic well-being will be affected by wilderness preservation which locks up needed natural resources.
Swain	We should provide access to our wilderness areas to maintain our sense of freedom.	Our economic well-being will inevitably be reduced regardless of our efforts at wilderness preservation.

Common Point	C. Wildernesses must be protected because they are special.	D. We are destroying our wilderness areas.
Tucker	Most wildernesses are protected not because they are of special value but because they serve as parks for the upper middle class.	We are hardly destroying our wilderness areas since we have as much open space now as we always have had.
Swain	Wilderness must be protected to preserve our sense of personal freedom.	We are destroying our wilderness areas in an effort to preserve our standard of living.

LABEL THE SPLITS

So far you have constructed a synthesis tree that traces your authors' positions as a set of alternative branches splitting off from common starting points. In the next step, you formulate central questions for each of these splits and phrase alternative responses to characterize each branch. Through these questions and responses, you will capture in language the common concerns and basic differences lying behind your authors' diverse positions.

As a rule of thumb, you can expect preliminary splits to occur close to the top of the tree, major splits to occur around the middle of the tree, and minor disagreements to occur near the bottom. That is, you should expect your central questions to refer to the three milestones of argument you first encountered in following a single author's line of argument: "seeing the issue," "defining the problem," and "choosing a solution." This is no coincidence. Just as a single author will try to move you past these three milestones in persuading you to accept and act on a position, a group of authors will usually offer you a number of alternatives in making this same journey.

The most fundamental questions dividing a community are usually *questions of issue*. Within the same issue, authors may disagree about which problem cases need to be dealt with. Such disagreements, when they occur, are serious because they indicate that authors are heading in quite different directions in their search for resolution. Not all issues contain questions of issue, but if yours does, you will find these disputes right at the top of your synthesis tree.

The wilderness issue offered us a classic question of issue. On the one side of our synthesis tree, we had placed a group of authors concerned with the problem case of decreasing wilderness experience. On the other, we had placed a group concerned with negative economic effects:

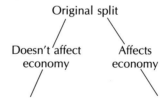

Original split

Doesn't affect economy   Affects economy

The efforts to eliminate these two quite different situations inevitably led the two groups of authors down divergent paths. To capture this disagreement, we inserted a question of issue in our synthesis tree and rephrased the labels on the branches to reflect the divergent responses:

A QUESTION OF ISSUE

What is at issue in wilderness?

Reduced wilderness experience   Reduced standard of living

A large number of questions dividing an issue-centered community concern *questions of definition*. These kinds of questions often appear at or near the major split in an issue and concern disagreements over the analysis of the problem to be solved. What is the nature of the problem? the source of the problem? the best way to describe the problem? You can capture disagreements over these questions with questions of definition.

In our synthesis tree for wilderness, we inserted one question of definition to distinguish the position taken by Nash from the position taken by Julber, the Ehrlichs, Abbey, and Swain. Originally, as you may remember, we had labeled the branches of the split "Limit access" (Nash) and "Provide access" (Julber, the Ehrlichs, Abbey, and Swain):

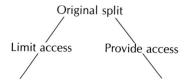

Original split

Limit access   Provide access

This split seemed to indicate a disagreement over what should be done to solve the problem. But, we realized, their disagreement started earlier and involved the way the authors saw the problem. Nash was concerned with increased recreational use; the others were concerned with economic exploitation. We used this insight to insert a question of definition and rephrased responses:

A QUESTION OF DEFINITION

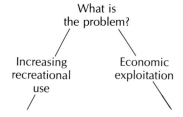

What is
the problem?

Increasing   Economic
recreational   exploitation
use

If a group of authors are in fundamental agreement concerning the definition of the problem, they may still have differences concerning the appropriate solution. As a result, you will often find it useful to create *questions of solution* to describe later, minor splits. Our wilderness tree, for example, required a question of solution to describe the minor disagreement between the Ehrlichs and Abbey:

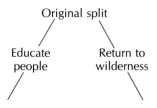

Original split

Educate   Return to
people   wilderness

A QUESTION OF SOLUTION

As you're formulating central questions and appropriate responses, aim to distinguish authors' positions in a way that is as informative as possible. To do this, avoid phrasing central questions that require simple yes/no, does/doesn't or should/shouldn't responses. Such answers say something about one of the alternative branches, but not about the other. For instance, in our original labels for the preliminary split between Tucker/Swain and the rest of the wilderness authors, we had used "Affects economy" and "Doesn't affect economy." These labels told us what Tucker and Swain believed (that preservation efforts affect the economy), but it didn't tell what the other authors thought. Thus, when we inserted a central question and rephrased alternative responses for this split, we moved away from this "does/doesn't" dichotomy and put more descriptive phrases in their place:

REVISING FOR MORE DESCRIPTIVE LABELS

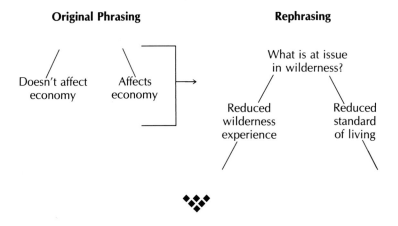

❖❖❖

For Class 7.3

In the tree on page 159, create a central question for the minor split between Tucker and Swain. Consider whether the question ought to be a question of issue, a question of definition, or a question of solution. (Refer to the grid of common points given in "For Class 7.2," if necessary.) Make sure to revise the labels of the alternative responses.

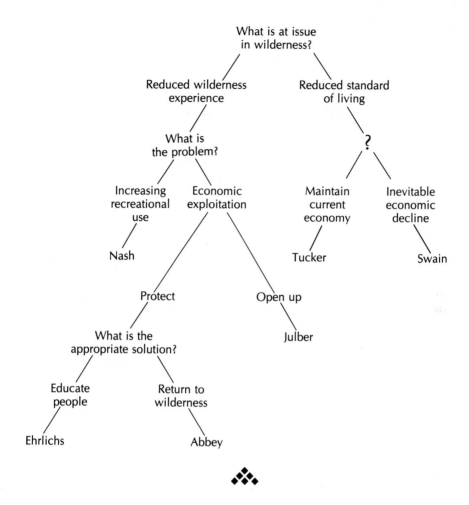

INSERT AUTHORS' POSITIONS

To complete your synthesis tree as a representation of your issue, place a characterization of each author's position at the end of its branch. This characterization should be a single shorthand statement that sums up your overall understanding of what the author is trying to persuade you to accept and act on. Often it will contain a reference to the action the author wants readers to take:

INSERTING AN AUTHOR'S POSITION

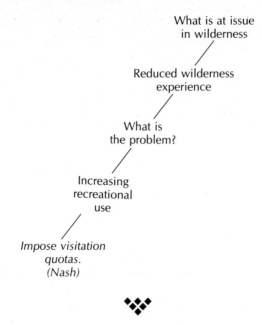

What is at issue
in wilderness

Reduced wilderness
experience

What is
the problem?

Increasing
recreational
use

*Impose visitation
quotas.
(Nash)*

For Class 7.4

Insert a characterization of the positions taken by Tucker and Swain in the synthesis tree given in "For Class 7.3."

REVIEW FOR OVERALL COHERENCE

Once you have finished delineating the branches of your tree with central questions and alternative responses, take the time to examine it carefully. Generally speaking, you should get a sense of coherent development when you follow the set of questions and responses leading from the top of the tree to each individual author's position:

CRITERIA FOR OVERALL COHERENCE

- General questions should precede specific questions.
- The answer to one question should lead naturally to the question following it.
- An author's position should be the logical result of the questions and responses preceding it.

If, as you trace the questions and responses, you have a sense of disorder or discontinuity, you will probably need to revise your tree.

Two examples of coherent sets of questions and responses were provided by our wilderness tree:

COHERENT SETS OF QUESTIONS AND RESPONSES

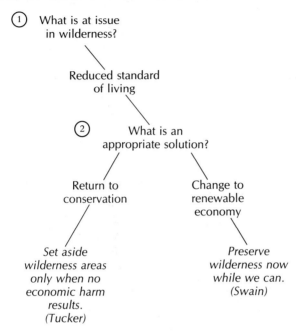

We checked these paths leading to Tucker and Swain as follows:

CHECKING OVERALL COHERENCE

- First, we asked ourselves, do general questions precede specific questions? Our answer was yes. The most general question, "What is at issue in wilderness?" comes before the more specific question, "What is an appropriate solution?"
- Second, does the answer to one question lead naturally to the question following it? Again, our answer was yes. The answer to Question 1, "reduced standard of living," gives rise naturally to Question 2, "What is an appropriate solution?"
- Finally, does each author's position seem the logical result of the questions and responses preceding it? For Tucker, our answer was yes. His position, "Set aside wilderness areas only when no economic harm results" follows from his concern with the economic consequences of preservation (Question 1) and his belief that we should follow a conservationist policy (Question 2).

For Swain our answer was also yes. His position for setting aside wilderness while we can follows from his concern with economic consequences (Question 1) and his belief that we must adopt a renewable economy (Question 2).

When we turned to the other half of our tree, however, we encountered more difficulty. Tracing the set of questions and responses leading to Julber's position, "Open up wilderness areas," we found our tree suggesting that his position followed from a belief that the issue is reduced wilderness experience (Question 1) and a belief that economic rather than recreational exploitation was the problem (Question 2):

AN INCOHERENT SET OF QUESTIONS AND RESPONSES

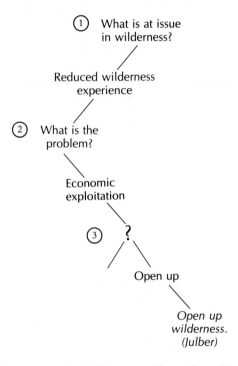

Our difficulty here was that Julber actually said nothing about economic exploitation. His position seemed to be prior to this question, not subsequent to it. Furthermore, we had no real question at 3. We knew we had to revise. Our solution was to move Julber farther up the tree to answer Question 2 rather than Question 3:

A REVISED SYNTHESIS TREE

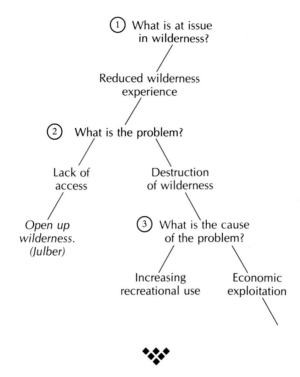

For Your Notebook #12

Build and label a synthesis tree for your issue.

- Include major, preliminary, and minor splits among the authors.
- Label these splits with central questions to reflect the movement from problem to solution.
- Revise the labels on the alternative branches so that they are informative.
- Insert a characterization of each author's position at the end of the branches.
- Review for overall coherence.

$\square$ 8 DRAFT THE SYNTHESIS

So far, you have been engaged in *synthesis*—the process of developing a comprehensive map for your exploration of an issue. First, your grid of common points helped you to establish the agreements and disagreements among your authors. Then, your synthesis tree helped you to see the significance of these differences. Now, in drafting a written synthesis, you transform these visual representations into a text designed to tell readers about what you know.

In a *written synthesis,* your aim is to help other readers survey the territory of an issue. Unlike your earlier annotated bibliography or set of summaries, a written synthesis should go beyond simply reporting on the major positions in an issue. It should also tell readers how you see the relationships among them. The framework of these relationships—which you now have in the visual form of a synthesis tree—is what you now have to contribute to your community in the cycle of reading and writing.

OUTLINE THE BODY

Think of your written synthesis as a tour, with yourself as the tour guide and your readers as the tourists. As in every tour, your readers are relying on you not just to describe things they stumble across, but to actually direct their attention in an orderly fashion. Order, then, is a very important concept in writing a synthesis. The order in which you present your authors' positions should never be arbitrary or unthoughtful. Readers will rely upon it; they expect you to have reasons for the choices you make.

Creating an outline can help you to discover these reasons. Generally, you begin an outline at the top of the synthesis tree and work your way down each of its branches in turn. In our work on wilderness, for example, we began with Central Question 1, "What is at issue in wilderness?," and then gradually worked our way down each of the branches:

A TOUR OF OUR SYNTHESIS TREE

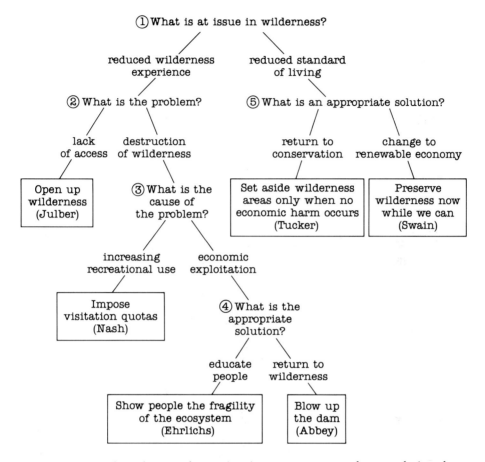

As you reach each central question in your tour, you have a choice about which of the paths to pursue. For Central Question 1 above, for example, we had to decide whether to tell our readers first about the positions arguing that the issue was reduced wilderness experience (the left-hand branch) or reduced standard of living (the right-hand branch). How you make these choices depends on the relationships you want your readers to see.

One of the most common relationships among positions is that of *chronology*. In most issues, some disagreements occur before others. If this is the case in your issue, your best strategy will probably be to give your readers a chronological perspective and discuss the earlier disagreements first, more recent disagreements later. Chronology helped us to decide, for example, which way to take our tour at Central Question 1, "What is at issue in wilderness?" We knew that, historically, the answer "reduced wilderness experience" had preceded the alternative response "reduced standard of living." Only later, after preservation policies had been implemented, did authors such as Tucker and Swain call attention to the reduced standard of living that might result. In constructing our outline, then, we pointed out this relationship:

OUTLINE USING CHRONOLOGY

What is at issue in wilderness?

   Early issue: reduced wilderness experience

   Later issue: reduced standard of living

   To determine whether you have a chronological relationship among the alternative paths in your synthesis tree, start with the dates of publication. Many issues go in and out of fashion. They stir up controversy in one time period and then lie dormant until a new set of circumstances arises. The issue of family planning, for example, was heavily discussed in the sixties and early seventies as concerns about the world population surfaced. Once policies were formulated, however, the issue dropped out of national attention until, in the eighties, these policies seemed to be failing. In this kind of situation, you will find more than one cluster of publication dates—in this example, many articles from the sixties followed by another cluster in the eighties.

   You may also find a chronology provided by the histories your authors give in "seeing the issue." We relied, for instance, on Tucker's history to order our discussion at Central Question 1. Tucker claimed that he had become concerned with the wilderness issue when he observed the negative economic consequences of preservation. Accepting his chronology, we planned our discussion of the preservationists' concern with declining wilderness experience (the left-hand branch) before Tucker's concern with economic consequences (the right-hand branch).

   Another common relationship is *idiosyncrasy*, which also provides a useful way to structure your outline for a synthesis. Using this criterion, your tour goes down shorter, more idiosyncratic paths before it continues down longer, more central paths. Idiosyncrasy, for example, helped us to decide which path to tour at Central Question 2, "What is the problem?":

AN IDIOSYNCRATIC POSITION

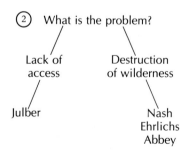

For this question, our tree indicated two alternative responses. On the left-hand branch, Julber stood alone in arguing that the problem was "lack of access." On the right-hand branch, Nash, the Ehrlichs, and Abbey all agreed that the problem was "destruction of wilderness." From this perspective, Julber seemed idiosyncratic. Thus, in our tour we decided to deal with him early before showing our readers the more central controversies. Our growing outline then looked as follows:

OUTLINE USING IDIOSYNCRASY

What is at issue in wilderness?
    Early issue: reduced wilderness experience
        What is the problem with reduced wilderness experience?
            Idiosyncratic problem: lack of access
            Julber: Open up wilderness.
            More common problem: destruction of wilderness
    Later issue: reduced standard of living

A final criterion to consider in completing your outline is the relationship of *merit*. Usually, you will want to discuss positions that have more merit *after* discussing those that have less, on the general principle of climactic order—saving the best for last. We haven't, of course, talked about formally evaluating authors' positions—this comes later in your work, in analysis (Part IV). Nevertheless, you probably already have some opinions about which positions seem more attractive than others. You can often go with this intuition in deciding which paths to leave until later in your tour.

Merit is a particularly useful way to decide which path to describe when the criteria of chronology and idiosyncrasy don't apply. We used it, for example, to determine our order at Central Question 4, "What is an appropriate solution?"

A MERITORIOUS POSITION

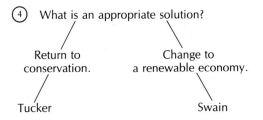

The two alternative responses, Tucker's "return to conservation" and Swain's "change to a renewable economy," seemed about equal in terms of chronology and lack of idiosyncrasy: Both had been offered at around the same time (1982 for Tucker; 1983 for Swain), and both seemed equally mainstream. But we had always found Swain's argument more plausible—thus more compelling—than Tucker's. For this reason, we wanted to make sure it was the final stopping point on the tour. With this decision, then, our outline looked as follows:

OUTLINE USING MERIT

What is at issue in wilderness?

    Early issue: reduced wilderness experience

        What is the problem with reduced wilderness experience?

            Idiosyncratic problem: lack of access

                Julber: Open up wilderness.

            More common problem: destruction of wilderness

    Later issue: reduced standard of living

        Less plausible solution: Return to conservation.

            Tucker: Set aside wilderness areas only when no economic harm results.

        More plausible solution: Change to a renewable economy.

            Swain: Preserve wilderness now while we can.

For Class 8.1

Review the tour of wilderness at the beginning of this section (page 165) and complete these exercises using the preceding outline.

1. In our tour, on what grounds might we have decided to take the path leading to Nash's position before the path leading to the Ehrlichs' and Abbey's positions? Based on your answer, insert this part of the tour into the outline above.
2. On what grounds might we have decided to discuss the Ehrlichs' position before Abbey's? Based on your answer, insert this part of the tour into the outline.
3. Revise the preceding outline to point out the chronological relationship between the Julber and Nash positions. Recall that Nash cited Julber's position as an argument on a faulty path. What kind of chronology does this imply? How can you indicate this relationship in the outline?

For Your Notebook #13

Create an outline for your synthesis following the structure given by your synthesis tree.

▪ Begin with the central question at the top of the tree.

- At each decision point, use chronology, idiosyncrasy, or merit to decide which path to tour first.
- Make the relationships among the paths clear.

DRAFT THE INTRODUCTION

In the introduction to a synthesis, you must get your readers to "see the issue"—that is, to care enough about the issue to be willing to take your tour. Your resources for generating this interest are the same as those you have seen other authors using:

STRATEGIES FOR GETTING READERS TO "SEE THE ISSUE"

- Provide a history of the controversy surrounding the issue.
- Describe one or more problem cases associated with the issue.

Here, for instance, is our introduction to wilderness taking the first approach:

AN INTRODUCTION USING A HISTORY OF THE CONTROVERSY

Wilderness was never an issue for our pioneer forebears. For them, wilderness was a thing to tame and develop, not something to be preserved. But now, in a time when we threaten wilderness more than it threatens us, wilderness has become the topic of heated discussion.

With issues that are less familiar, you will often find it appropriate to describe a problem case:

AN INTRODUCTION USING A PROBLEM CASE

The image of the Grand Canyon is one that is etched into our national consciousness: the deep gorge, the treacherous rapids, the inaccessibility, the beauty and the mystery. Now imagine, however, that this national landmark is gone, submerged under the water backed up to generate hydroelectric power for the ever-hungry cities on our western seaboard. True, we can now rent a houseboat for a week of leisurely fishing on this great expanse of water. But can we ever recover what we've lost?

This scenario, however implausible, is, according to author Edward Abbey, just what happened to another canyon on the Colorado, Glen Canyon. And it may, according to many authors, be the fate of our entire wilderness heritage if we are not vigilant.

For Class 8.2

1. Write an introduction to a synthesis of wilderness using one of the following problem cases:
   a. the problem case of the "purists" discussed by Eric Julber (page 11).
   b. the problem case of the Sierra Mountains discussed by Roderick Nash (pages 67–69).
   c. the problem case of the roadless areas discussed by William Tucker (pages 53–55).

2. Write an introduction to a synthesis of wilderness using one of the following histories of the controversy:
   a. the history of the controversy recounted by William Tucker (pages 52–53).
   b. the history of the controversy recounted by Eric Julber (page 11).
   c. the history of the controversy recounted by Roderick Nash (see pages 63–64).

DRAFT THE BODY

Once you have readers interested in taking a tour, you should set out to characterize each of the major positions in your issue in the order determined by your outline. For each position, you should do three things:

CHARACTERIZING AN AUTHOR'S POSITION

- Locate the author with respect to the immediately preceding central question and alternative responses.
- Explain the reasoning behind the author's overall position.
- Explain any conclusions the author draws as a result of this reasoning.

Here, for example, is how we translated the first section of our outline leading to Julber's position:

Outline	**Body**
What is at issue in wilderness? Early issue: reduced wilderness experience	Wilderness first became an issue when people recognized that the wilderness experience was no longer readily available to the majority of Americans.

Outline	**Body**

What is the problem with reduced wilderness experience?
    Idiosyncratic problem: lack of access
        Julber: Open up wilderness.
	Eric Julber, in a 1973 *Reader's Digest* article, for example, argues that wilderness should be opened up to more Americans by increasing the available transportation and accommodations in wild areas. The tendency of "purists" to restrict access to backpackers and canoers, he argues, is both undemocratic and unnecessary to preserve the scenic beauty of these areas.

More common problem: destruction of wilderness	While many authors would agree with Julber that the declining availability of wilderness experience is the major issue, most attribute the cause to something other than the purists' desire to keep scenic areas to themselves. Instead, these authors argue that the problem is an overall decline in the amount of wilderness available, caused by the increasing destruction of wilderness areas.

Notice that the first block of our text *locates* Julber's position with respect to the first central question (he agrees with the initial perception that wilderness experience is no longer readily available). The second block *explains the reasoning* behind Julber's response (restricting access to backpackers and canoers is undemocratic and unnecessary). It also explains the conclusions he draws based on this reasoning (we should increase the amount of transportation and accommodations available). The third section *identifies* Julber's location as idiosyncratic and prepares the way for discussing the next author on our tour, Roderick Nash.

For Class 8.3

Complete the next section of the body of our synthesis of wilderness using the following outline of points:

More common problem: destruction of wilderness
    What is the cause of this destruction?
        Recent explanation: increasing recreational use
            Nash: Impose visitation quotas.
        Traditional explanation: economic exploitation

You may begin with the transition we started above:

While many authors would agree with Julber that the declining availability of wilderness experience is the major issue, most attribute the cause to something other than the purists' desire to keep scenic areas to themselves. Instead, these authors argue that the problem is an overall decline in the amount of wilderness available, caused by the increasing destruction of wilderness areas.

DRAFT THE CONCLUSION

Once you have characterized each major position in the body of your text, conclude your synthesis with a general reflection on the state of the controversy. How do you see the issue now? Is there any general agreement in the community? Is the issue still stuck at the same place it was ten years ago? What seem to be major unresolved points? End your tour, in other words, by telling your readers where the community is and what remains to be done.

To conclude our synthesis of wilderness, for example, we noted the unresolved split between those concerned with reduced wilderness experience and those concerned with economic matters:

A CONCLUSION REVIEWING THE STATE OF THE ISSUE

> While many readers will deplore Swain's predictions that Americans must inevitably face a decline in their standard of living, he is one of a small number of authors trying to come to grips with the economic implications of preservation. As Nash documents, American appreciation for wilderness has increased dramatically in the last few decades. But it is only recently that we have had to face the economic consequences of this fact. How we resolve this tension, all authors acknowledge, will have enormous consequences on the quality of life for future generations.

For Your Notebook #14

Draft a synthesis of your issue.

- Begin with an introduction to convince your readers to "take the tour."
- Draft the body following the order of points in your outline.
- Conclude with your general reflections on the current state of the issue.

REVISE FOR YOUR READERS

Once you have produced a written synthesis, the next step is to turn your attention to ensuring your readers' understanding. You must make sure that they can follow the alternative paths you describe without getting lost. Often this will require you to add transitions and define or explain any technical terms in your first draft.

As in summary writing, transitions tell readers how to interpret upcoming information. You may wish to review some of the techniques for adding transitions that we discussed in Chapter 5. In addition, we list below a few examples of transitional phrases that are particularly useful for synthesizing. By no means a complete list, they do indicate the kinds of transitions that can keep your readers from getting lost:

TRANSITIONS FOR SYNTHESIZING

To Distinguish Majority from Minority Positions:

> Almost all authors believe that . . .
> Yet X thinks . . .
>
> Most authors agree that . . .
> One notable exception is Y, who argues that . . .

To Distinguish Major Camps:

> Even those who agree that . . .
> disagree on . . .
>
> Basically, most X think . . .
> while most Y think . . .

To Add Minor Disagreements:

> On X, two positions seem possible.
> First . . .
> Second . . .

Another problem you often face with a first draft is an abundance of specialized or technical terms. After working in an issue for a while, you will find you have developed certain "code words" that help you sum up a particular aspect of the issue, a particular approach to a solution, or a particular definition of the problem. Such code words are a positive outcome of your synthesizing effort because they enable you to manipulate complex information easily. The word "quota" for example, instantly conjured up a whole world of meaning for us in the wilderness issue. In a very real sense, this single word came to stand for Nash's whole line of argument.

The drawback to developing such code words, however, is that it makes communication with outsiders more difficult. You may be startled to think of yourself as an *insider* now; but indeed, in a fundamental way, you are: By synthesizing, you have a grasp of the issue and its language that is a hallmark of an insider. You have come to understand a community through your own eyes, and you have thus prepared yourself to make your own explorations.

But when you create a written synthesis, you have to share your understanding with outsiders who have not read all the essays you have. To do this, you need to turn back the clock—that is, you need to remember the confusion and distress that you felt as an outsider looking in; you need to try to recall the particular explanation or example that finally helped you to make sense of the community's language; and you need to try to provide that explanation or example for your own readers.

Defining code words for readers requires that you elaborate with either an explanation or an example. Here is how we defined the term "quota" when we revised our first draft:

DEFINING CODE WORDS

First Draft	**Revised**
According to Nash, for example, wilderness is being destroyed by the increasing recreational use of a generation of Americans newly fond of wilderness. Advocates of increased access, he argues, fundamentally misunderstand the nature of wilderness. True wildernesses require special handling in order to prevent their "carrying capacities" from being exceeded. Further, he argues, we should be willing to accept <u>visitation quotas</u> as the price we have to pay for our continued enjoyment.	According to Nash, for example, wilderness is being destroyed by the increasing recreational use of a generation of Americans newly fond of wilderness. Advocates of increased access, he argues, fundamentally misunderstand the nature of wilderness. True wildernesses require special handling in order to prevent their "carrying capacities" from being exceeded. Further, he argues, we should be willing to accept <u>visitation quotas, restrictions of the number of visitors who may enter an area at any given time</u>, as the price we have to pay for our continued enjoyment.

For Class 8.4

What follows is a first draft of our characterization of Julber's position on wilderness.

a. Circle the code words that readers unfamiliar with the issue might not understand.
b. Revise the text to define these code words.

Eric Julber, in a 1973 *Reader's Digest* article, for example, argues that wilderness should be opened up to more Americans by increasing the available transportation and accommodations in wild areas. The tendency of "purists" to restrict access to backpackers and canoers, he argues, is both undemocratic and unnecessary to preserve the scenic beauty of these areas.

One of the best ways to prepare yourself to revise is to ask a friend or classmate to read through your draft, answering the questions in the following checklist. Use the answers to plan your revisions.

REVISION CHECKLIST FOR SYNTHESIS

- What is the issue being addressed by this synthesis?
- Why, according to the synthesis, should you be concerned with this issue? Are you convinced by these reasons?
- Who are the major authors taking positions on the issue? List and number them.
- What is the relationship between the positions taken by the first and second authors?
- Between the second and the third?
- Between the third and the fourth?
- Between the fourth and the fifth?
- Between any others included?
- What is the overall state of the issue?
- Are there any authors whose positions you don't understand? List them.
- Circle all the words you don't understand.

For Your Notebook #15

Ask a friend or classmate to use the revision checklist to assess the draft of your synthesis. Review your reader's answers to see if you have any questions. Then use the results to revise.

⬚⬚⬚ 9 EXPLORE PROBLEM CASES

In this chapter and the three that follow, you will be engaged in a series of activities called *analysis*. The purpose of analysis is to explore your issue in enough depth to allow you to arrive at a position of your own or, at the very least, conclusions that you can develop into a position. The key word here is "explore" because, above all else, analyzing is a process of exploring until you have found something that is both worth saying and worth calling your own.

Bear in mind that no two people are exactly alike in the way they explore an issue, so you need to find a style of exploring that suits you best. As the following observations indicate, analyzing is much more open-ended than summarizing and synthesizing.

OBSERVATIONS ABOUT ANALYSIS

- *The exploration process is unpredictable.* By definition, you explore when you are looking for something *and* you don't know quite what that something is. Don't confuse exploration with search. When you search for a missing sock, you know what you are looking for—and you know when you have found it. The exploration process is not as well defined. You are looking for a position, but the position you are looking for does not exist, premade, before you explore for it. In large part you *shape* the position you discover by the process in which you explore.

- *The exploration process goes on in your head and on paper.* What goes on in your head will be richer and more interesting than anything you can put on paper. Still, if you are like many writers, you will find that the discipline of organizing on paper can help structure what's going on in your head and make it more accessible to you.

- *Exploring works best when you aren't in a hurry to find anything.* When writers explore for a position, they are tempted to want to find what they are looking for immediately. Who wouldn't be? It is human nature to want to accomplish our goals as quickly as possible—especially when we find ourselves under the pressure of deadlines. But, in spite of our human nature, exploring seems to work best when we don't expect results too soon. Should you be impatient and commit yourself to a position before you've had a chance to explore it fully, you may find, too late, that you've wasted your time on a badly flawed position. Writing is not a car race or a course in speed reading. You can't do it fast. And when it comes to exploring for your position, you have a vital stake in taking it slow.

- *Exploring depends on background knowledge.* Many writers start to explore an issue only to discover that they don't yet have the background to make their exploration as fruitful as they had hoped. What do they do? They seek out more texts to summarize, to add to their synthesis or to their general background knowledge. You would do well to follow their example.

- *Exploring is a flexible process.* Despite the fact that every book has no choice but to present information in a linear format, exploring is not a linear, step-by-step process. Writers have to find their own style and sequence for exploring. Don't be afraid to customize, to add to some of the techniques we provide here, or to look for your own short-cuts. But do try to understand the basic moves of analyzing before you make these adjustments.

- *You explore possible, not just previous, positions.* This is one of the most important differences in your advance from synthesizing to analyzing. While you summarize and synthesize the positions of previous authors, you use analyzing to explore the "space" of possible positions. You needn't feel confined to what others have said before you. Enlarge your exploration to what *could* be said. By doing so, you also increase the conceptual space within which to discover and design your own position.

To explore an issue, you must first *see* the issue. As we have said, authors see an issue through problem cases that cause tensions. Something about these cases leaves the author in a state of restlessness, dissatisfaction, or frustration. In part, the author writes in order to respond to these feelings of disquiet. In analyzing, it is your turn to settle yourself into the author's chair by focusing on the problem cases that evoke similar feelings of restlessness and disquiet in you.

SELECT YOUR PROBLEM CASES

Begin your exploration of problem cases by collecting them from your reading. Return to your notes from summarizing. What problem cases do your authors describe? What situations make them uneasy?

For Your Notebook #16

Review the problem cases you find in your summary notes. Start a new section of your notebook and label it "Cases." Make a separate entry for every problem case and leave blank pages after each one.

EXPLORE EACH CASE

With your problem cases in hand, you're now ready to explore them more fully. Right now, your notebook expresses these problem cases *in words*. Words are abstract and symbolic—at a distance from the experiences they refer to. To see the issue with your own eyes, you have to remove this distance. You have to take your focus off the words and place it on the human situations that existed before the words came along to abstract them. You have to change your perspective from that of a reader to that of an eyewitness. In doing so, you'll need to bring your senses and your imagination into play as you explore problem cases.

Narrate the Frustration

Think of the problem cases in your list as the source of someone's frustration. Someone had high hopes and those hopes were dashed. Someone was expecting a lot, only to feel let down. Now imagine that someone is you. For each entry in your list, tell or write a story that makes *you* the victim of the frustration. Tell the story from a first-person perspective. Tell it so that it appeals to your senses as well as to the senses of your listener or reader. Tell it in enough detail that it begins to explain, not just describe, the source of your frustration.

Let's start with a problem case from Julber (par. 2, 3, 4):

THE PROBLEM CASE OF THE PURIST

The purist standards were embodied in the Wilderness Act of 1964, which provides that in such areas there shall be "no permanent road . . . no temporary road . . . no mechanical transport and no structure or installation." The practical effect of this philosophy, thus frozen into federal law, has been to make many of the most beautiful areas of the United States "off limits" to anyone who is not willing and able to backpack into them. Statistics show that this means 99 percent of Americans.

In 1965, there were 1,475,000 visitors to the Wilderness Areas. In 1970, the number of visitors had increased only to 1,543,000. This represents use by less than one percent of our population. Moreover, a survey on behalf of the President's Outdoor Recreation Resources Review Commission (ORRRC) showed, by statistical analysis, that the users are the intellectual and financial elite of our nation.

Reports the ORRRC: "In the sample of Wilderness users interviewed, more than 75 percent had at least a college degree, and a high proportion have done postgraduate work or hold advanced degrees. . . . Wilderness users are disproportionately drawn from the higher income levels. Professional and semiprofessional people, and those in white-collar occupations, account for approximately three quarters of those interviewed.''

From this passage, you can gather the details that must go into your story. You need to be part of the 99 percent of Americans who feel shut out of wilderness. You need to have a bad back, asthma, small children, no wilderness training, or something else that keeps you from using a backpack. You need to be an average worker, with neither the time nor money to romp in the wilderness for extended periods of time. Perhaps you have only a few days vacation a year and touring by car would have been your only hope to enjoy nature. Perhaps you are yourself a child of ten and wonder why a grown-up back is required for seeing the most beautiful parts of America.

Whatever the details you invent, you need to plan a story that starts with great expectations and then leaves them unfulfilled. Your story would probably start with planning a visit to wilderness. The planning should seem responsible and well-motivated. You should leave yourself and your listener/reader with the impression that nothing could go wrong. Then somewhere in your story, you and your traveling companions run into Julber's "off limits" sign. You find out you are not welcome—and never were. You feel embarrassed, perhaps humiliated. How could my government do this to me? How could it leave me out? As an example, here is one possible narration of Julber's problem case:

A NARRATION OF A PROBLEM CASE

Two summers ago, my friend and I had planned a trip to a national park in a neighboring state. We both enjoyed fresh air and stunning landscapes and we had paged through some general brochures depicting the beautiful terrain of this particular park. Because neither of us was a hulking physical specimen or had ever been a Girl Scout, we assumed we would make our way by car. We planned to get out and stretch our legs at the sites that seemed most worth stopping for. Were we ever naive! When we reached the park we found to our dismay that only backpacking was permitted—by decree of a new and underpublicized government regulation. The park had good roads, but the state legislature had recently ruled that the public could not use them. To us, this restriction seemed unsafe as well as unappealing. One of the most beautiful areas of the country and only a few are permitted to look in!

You should practice telling/writing your story until you think you can make yourself hurt, bitter, angry, indignant. After telling/reading your story, you should see whether you've been able to communicate these feelings to your listeners/readers. Discuss with them how the story succeeded or failed to have impact. Discuss what details seemed to add to or take away from its impact. Use this feedback to compose a better story.

Now stand back and assess how well the story works. Perhaps no matter how well you compose the story, you won't be able to evoke much empathy for your situation. Perhaps you find you are unable to convince even *yourself* that things are all that bad (for you). You'll find this information helpful in deciding what problem cases provide you with a plausible lens on the issue.

Identify Important Aspects

Next break your narration apart to identify its important aspects. The **aspects** of a problem case are the components or factors that contribute to the frustrations and troubles—the tension—within it. You have already seen how problem cases can be broken down into the four aspects of agent, action, goal, and result. By breaking a problem case into these aspects, you can get a better understanding of what is generating the tension in your story. Here's our breakdown for Julber's case:

ASPECTS OF JULBER'S PROBLEM CASE

Agent: purists on the wilderness issue
Action: Wilderness Act of 1964
Goal: Protect wilderness from those who would plunder it.
Result: Most Americans are prevented from enjoying wilderness.

Vary the Aspects

Any breakdown is, at best, a first attempt to teach yourself the aspects that contribute to the tension in your story. You can be reasonably sure that the aspects in your first breakdown, taken together, produce the tension. It is unlikely, however, that you'll know which single aspect or which combination of aspects interacting or conflicting with one another is the most responsible. Thus, it's a good idea to explore further by varying aspects.

To vary aspects is to play a series of "what if" games with a problem case. What if the agent were different? What would happen to the tension? Would it increase? go away? stay the same? What if the action had been different? What would then happen to the tension? Sometimes, by varying an aspect, you change the overall tension. If so, you can be sure that the original aspect you varied makes an important contribution to the tension.

VARYING ASPECTS TO CHANGE THE TENSION

Agent: purists on the wilderness issue
Action: Wilderness Act of 1964

Goal: Protect wilderness from those who would plunder it.
Result: Most Americans can still enjoy wilderness.

Here, we have varied the result of Julber's problem case so that most Americans can still enjoy wilderness. The tension that Julber's case produced now seems to disappear. This observation indicates that the original information in the result aspect contributed largely to the original tension.

Conversely, if you find that varying an aspect, or combination of aspects, does not cause the overall tension to change, then you know that those aspects are not relevant to the tension.

VARYING ASPECTS TO LEAVE THE TENSION UNCHANGED

Agent: purists on the wilderness issue
Action: Wilderness Act of 1964
Goal: Protect wilderness without limiting visitation.
Result: Many Americans are prevented from enjoying wilderness.

Here, we have varied the goal so that the purists will not limit visitation. While this information seems important, the tension doesn't disappear as long as the information in the result role remains the same. That is, even had Julber described the purists as not intending to limit visitation, he still would have seen a problem, it seems, if their action (the Wilderness Act of 1964) ended with the same result. This might lead you to conclude that, for Julber, the intentions behind the Wilderness Act are not as relevant to the tension as the result to which it led. If you look further, you can isolate information even less relevant to the tension. For example, nothing about the tension would appear to change had the Wilderness Act been passed in 1965 rather than 1964.

By varying aspects, you can rank aspects of the problem case according to their importance to the underlying tension. In the example above, the result aspect would seem to be most important, followed by the goal aspect, followed by the agent aspect. Moreover, by breaking aspects apart, you can teach yourself more precisely how they combine to form the tension. For example, you can see that the agent, goal, and result aspects seem to work together to cause the tension. If the purists didn't have the attitudes they have as agents, they might not have the goals they have, and so might not adopt the actions that lead to the problematic results.

For Class 9.1

Consider the following problem case:

> Mineral companies, interested only in profit, will have mined over 60 percent of our best wilderness areas by the year 2010. This will leave our wilderness badly depleted.

Now consider the following variations of this case:

Variation 1. Corporations interested only in profit will have put roads and parking lots in over 60 percent of our best wilderness areas by the year 2010. This will harm our wilderness areas.

Variation 2. Mineral companies claiming to be interested in protecting the wilderness will still have mined over 60 percent of our best wilderness areas by the year 2010. This will harm our wilderness areas.

Variation 3. Mineral companies interested only in profit will have mined over 60 percent of our best wilderness areas by the year 2150. This will harm our wilderness areas.

Variation 4. Mineral companies interested only in profit will have mined over 5 percent of our best wilderness areas by the year 2010. This will harm our wilderness areas.

Variation 5. Mineral companies interested only in profit will have mined over 60 percent of our least interesting wilderness areas by the year 2010. This will harm our wilderness areas.

Variation 6. Mineral companies interested only in profit will have mined over 60 percent of our best wilderness areas by the year 2010. However, this will do no damage to our wilderness areas.

For each variation, ask yourself whether it reduces the tension in the original case, increases it, or leaves it unchanged. Write a short (two or three paragraph) analysis of the original case, indicating which aspects seem most responsible for the tension.

Write Your Own Description

After you have broken down a problem case into its aspects and varied those aspects to determine which are most responsible for the tensions, you're ready to write a short description of the case in your notebook—just a sentence or two to remind yourself of the aspects of the case and which of them are most responsible for the tension. Here's our description of the essence of Julber's problem case:

OUR DESCRIPTION OF JULBER'S CASE

In the name of trying to protect wilderness from the masses, a small and stubborn minority has in effect banned millions of Americans from our country's most beautiful wilderness.

Notice that our description added the idea of "stubbornness," which was not part of our original language for the agent. To fashion a graceful sentence, we found ourselves also making a contrast between the goal and the results—between what the purists claimed they wanted and the actual results. This new contrast offered further insight into the source of the trouble that we imagined Julber saw.

You'll learn even more from your written descriptions if you experiment with alternative wordings for each description. You'll find that these wordings not only describe tensions from your reading, but also help you tease out additional tensions from problem cases that come out of your own knowledge and experience.

Consider Similar Cases

As you experiment with wordings, always be aware of when you are describing the public commitments of an author and when you are describing something beyond those commitments. Such awareness serves a twofold function. First, it helps you understand the full range and limits of an author's publicly held commitments. Second, it gives you entry into a much larger territory of problem cases than the territory covered by previous authors.

See if any of your wordings spark your memory of problem cases from your general experience. If they do, explore these cases just as if they had appeared in your reading; narrate the frustration; identify and vary aspects; write a more precise description, and tuck it away in your notebook with *you* as the source.

For example, the strong language of "banned" proved helpful in drawing out a problem case from the experiences of one of our students. During her childhood, she had spent a number of family summers camping out at a particular wilderness site. In the intervening years, the wilderness site had closed down as part of a development project. She somehow felt that the closing of that site had "banned" her from reliving parts of her past. These revelations led her to compose the following description:

A PROBLEM CASE FROM PERSONAL EXPERIENCE

> By developing wilderness, many of us may be losing direct access to our childhood experiences.

To make your exploration of problem cases as rich as possible, you need to think of situations as objects that you can easily stretch, twist, and vary as you explore. You need to view cases from many different perspectives in order to decide which to keep with you as you move closer to formulating your own position.

For Class 9.2

From the list of problem cases on page 186, choose three and do the following:

A. Write a one-to-three-paragraph first-person narrative that illustrates the tension in the problem case.

B. Identify agent, action, goal, and result aspects for the problem case.

C. Vary aspects in order to determine which aspects seem most responsible for the tension and in what combination.

D. Write short (one-or-two-sentence) prose descriptions of the problem case.

E. Consider similar cases you know from experience.

Be prepared to compare your work with that of other students in the class.

1. the passing of the Wilderness Act of 1964 (Julber)
2. the boon in Wilderness Recreation (Nash)
3. the case of Old Sierra (Nash)
4. the case of the Boundary Waters Canoe Area (Nash)
5. the case of the Grand Canyon (Nash)
6. the case of overpopulation in Tanzania (Ehrlichs)
7. the case of the snail darter (Ehrlichs)
8. the case of the coral reef (Ehrlichs)
9. the campaign against wilderness development (Tucker)
10. the case of the vanishing wilderness(Swain)
11. the case of nonrenewable economies (Swain)
12. the case of Lake Powell (Abbey)

SELECT YOUR PARADIGM CASES

A **paradigm** is an important example—a model. The problem cases you consider most important are your paradigm cases. They are the problem cases that first come to mind when you think about the issue, the cases that you would never consider marginal to the issue. After you have explored problem cases from your reading and from your experience, decide on and make a list of your paradigms.

For example, you might decide that one or more of Tucker's problem cases are more important to the issue. Or you may decide that a certain case from your own experience, not raised by other authors, is most important. Whatever you choose as your paradigms, they have an important role to play. They will be the problem cases for which you will most want to account. As we will see later, you will be able to judge possible positions as "strong," in part, insofar as these positions can account for (can define and resolve) your paradigms. You will be able to judge them as "faulty," in part, insofar as they cannot account for (cannot define or resolve) your paradigms.

For Your Notebook #17

Analyze each problem case in your notebook.

- Write a one-to-three-paragraph first-person narrative that illustrates the frustration in the problem case and that makes you the victim of the frustration.
- Identify the aspects of the case.
- Vary the aspects in order to make your language as precise as possible.
- From your revised breakdown, write a short description of the problem case.
- Add similar problem cases from your experience.
- Decide which of your problem cases you regard as your paradigms.

⣿ 10 EXPLORE FOR POSSIBLE SOLUTIONS

When we think about issues, the first thing that usually comes to mind is solutions. In fact, the names we typically give to issues are also the names of specific *solutions* to them. For example, the label "gun control" names more than our discussion over the right to bear arms. It names a particular course of action recommended by some as a way of resolving that issue. The same is true of the labels "abortion" and "capital punishment," to name only two.

Why do solutions dominate the way we think about issues? One possible answer is that people are uncomfortable leaving issues unresolved. Life is not tidy, but we often wish it were. Rather than get involved in the complex detail of nursing an issue step by step from seeing to resolving, we have the tendency to dispose of the issue by a quick and tidy resolution.

We don't attempt a genuine contribution to the issue. That is, we don't try to push the discussion—from seeing to resolving—a bit farther ahead for a community. We simply report on how the issue would naturally be resolved *had we taken the time to compose a contribution*. We assume, that is, that our ultimate destination is correct, and we leave it to faith that somewhere in the back of our mind are the precise directions that lead convincingly to our destination.

Occasionally, we have more than faith to back us up. For our favorite issues, we sometimes have our favorite authors. Imagine that you hold a firm position on lotteries that you can elaborate into an explicit set of directions for others. Imagine further that you didn't compose these directions. You let George Will or William F. Buckley, Jr., or Ellen Goodman or Anthony Lewis or some other influential author compose them for you.

You had a commitment and a general destination point, but no clear path to get there. So you looked for an author who could provide directions for you, directions that could at least bring you within the vicinity of where you wanted to end up. You might think of this approach to authorship as "hitching a ride" authorship or —to change the metaphor to shopping—"off the rack" authorship.

There is nothing wrong with off-the-rack authorship if your goal is to sample a range of arguments and choose among them for your own persuasive

188

purposes. Standard debate training, relying heavily on off-the-rack authorship, is a case in point. So is the conventional term paper, insofar as the emphasis is on your ability to comprehend and apply a range of arguments rather than to compose your own line of argument from seeing the issue to resolving it.

In this book, however, off-the-rack authorship would be most inappropriate. Indeed, our working definition of "author" excludes such authorship as a legitimate form. At the same time, we don't want to leave you with the impression that authors of original argument ignore the solutions of others. They most certainly do not. They simply have a different orientation toward solutions than authors who shop off the rack. They rely on solutions as yet another tool with which to explore the issue for themselves.

In this chapter, you'll practice using the solutions of others on your issue as a further tool for exploring. How can solutions help you explore? Even though a solution is only part of a position or line of argument, it can help you explore the many possible positions and lines of argument that might contain it. Using solutions to explore many different positions and lines of argument will help you gain the perspective you'll need to develop your own.

GENERATE POSSIBLE SOLUTIONS

Begin by generating a starting set of solutions that you want to explore. To do this, use both your synthesis tree and your set of problem cases.

Use Your Synthesis Tree

Look at the endpoints of your synthesis tree, where you inserted a sentence that characterized your understanding of the position of each author you synthesized. Examine each of these sentences and ask yourself whether it recommends a plan of action. If it does, you can treat it as an author's solution.

For example, our synthesis tree of the wilderness issue included the following characterizations of Julber, Nash, Tucker, and Swain:

CHARACTERIZATIONS OF WILDERNESS AUTHORS

Julber: Open up wilderness areas.
Nash: Impose visitation quotas.
Tucker: Set aside wilderness areas only when no economic harm results.
Swain: Preserve wilderness now while we can.

These sentences clearly point to solutions. We thus found we could use them as a starting point for our exploration into solutions.

Use Your Problem Cases

Now look over the written descriptions of problem cases you included in the "Cases" section of your notebook. Working through each description, ask yourself, "What might be done to reduce or relieve the situation?" In response to this question, generate courses of action that you would recommend to remove or relieve the underlying tension.

For example, when we looked at our written description of the problem case offered by Julber, we generated the following possible solutions:

GENERATING POSSIBLE SOLUTIONS FROM CASES

Problem case

In the name of trying to protect wilderness from the public, a small and stubborn minority has in effect banned millions of Americans from our most beautiful wilderness.

Possible Solutions

1. Open up wilderness to the general public.
2. Build more tramways and roads.
3. Create routes for the handicapped.
4. Televise more programs on wilderness.
5. Defeat the wilderness lobby.
6. Sell more tourist packages.

We wrote down these solutions as they occurred to us, in no particular order of importance. Some of these solutions Julber would probably endorse, some probably not. It doesn't matter, because the object at this point is to get a list of possible solutions for exploration, not to quote Julber or any other author.

For Your Notebook #18

Generate a list of possible solutions on your issue.

- Begin by consulting the endpoints of your synthesis tree.
- Generate more solutions for your list by thinking of plans of action that would seem to remove or relieve the tension in your written descriptions of problem cases.

Call this entry your "List of Possible Solutions."

EXPLORE WITH SOLUTIONS

Once you have your list of solutions to work with, you are ready to use them to explore. For each solution in your list, the idea is to develop positions or lines of argument that might contain it. Suppose, for example, you are exploring the solution "Open up wilderness" (to the public). Visualizing this solution as part of a line of argument gives you the following picture:

Seeing the issue	Defining the problem	Choosing a solution
		"Open up wilderness."

$\longrightarrow$

Possible line of argument

Now try to develop lines of argument that can fit this solution. This effort requires exploring each solution for four kinds of information:

INFORMATION OBTAINED BY EXPLORING SOLUTIONS

- problem cases it helps resolve
- implications
- counterexamples
- strengths and faults

We discuss each type of information below.

Explore for Problem Cases Resolved

First search for problem cases that the solution seems to handle well. When the solution is applied to these problem cases, the underlying tension will seem to lessen, perhaps go away entirely. For example, in exploring the solution "Open up wilderness," we searched our written descriptions for the problem cases whose tensions would be resolved by opening up the wilderness. We found several such problem cases, which we listed in our notes as follows:

POSSIBLE PROBLEM CASES RESOLVED

Solution: Open up wilderness.
Cases resolved:
   1. difficulties of the handicapped in touring wilderness
   2. difficulties of children
   3. difficulties of the urban poor

Explore for Implications

Implications are the extreme endpoints of a line of argument moving from seeing an issue to resolving the issue. More specifically, the implications of a position or line of argument are the assumptions and principles associated with it. **Assumptions** are fundamental ways one must see the world in order to see the tension in an issue in a way that is consistent with the position. On the other hand, **principles** are patterns of reasoning or behavior that seem to follow logically when the solution endorsed by a position is carried out.

The following diagram illustrates the relationship between assumptions and principles in a line of argument:

ASSUMPTIONS AND PRINCIPLES WITHIN A LINE OF ARGUMENT

Assumptions →	Seeing	Defining	Choosing →	Principles
	the issue	the problem	a solution	

──────────────────────────────────→
Possible line of argument

Consider the different assumptions and principles implied by the following positions:

POSSIBLE POSITIONS ON WILDERNESS

(a) Wilderness needs to be protected for resource development.
(b) Wilderness needs to be protected from resource development.

These positions make different assumptions in their basic approach to the wilderness issue. Position (a) seems to assume that wilderness is a kind of factory, whose chief purpose is to serve the economy. Position (b) seems to assume that wilderness is a kind of sacred trust, removed from economic considerations. These positions also seem to imply different principles. From the solutions implied by position (a), it would seem to follow that economic development is more important than the protection of wilderness. From the solutions implied by position (b), however, it would seem to follow that wilderness protection is more important than economic development.

You can learn a great deal about a proposed solution (and the possible lines of argument that contain it) by trying to insert it between the assumptions that precede it and the principles that seem to follow from it. For each solution in your list ask yourself, "What assumptions precede it?" and "What principles follow from it?" Generate a number of assumptive statements that begin with the words, "We must assume that . . ." and a number of statements of principle that begin with the words, "We should always/never do/believe this or hold this above that."

When we asked ourselves the above questions in exploring the implied assumptions and principles of the solution "Open up wilderness," we came up with the following statements:

SOME STATEMENTS OF IMPLIED ASSUMPTION AND PRINCIPLE

Assumptions	**Principles**
"We must assume that the best thing about wilderness is to witness it."	"We should always give the public open access to things of beauty."

"We must assume that getting into nature is basically good for people."

"We should always give people free access to wilderness."

"We should never restrict people from environments where they can learn about nature."

Notice that assumptions and principles may or may not include information about the immediate issue—such as wilderness. Often, they will refer to ways of seeing the world or approaches to resolving problems that are much broader than the immediate issue. In your own work, you will want to explore for the assumptions and principles implied by a solution in order to give yourself this broader perspective both on your issue and on the particular lines of argument you are trying to trace through it.

Refine Implications with Counterexamples

We mentioned that you can learn much about a solution by trying to insert it between a set of assumptions and principles that seem consistent with it. However, if the assumptions and principles you formulate are too broad, they won't tell you as much about the solution as you would like. To make the assumptions and principles you formulate as specific and as plausible as possible, you need to refine them. We'll use a statement of principle to illustrate how such refinements are made. The same technique can be used to refine assumptive statements.

When we explored the solution "Open up wilderness," we generated the principle "We should always give the public open access to things of beauty," which seemed, at first, to follow from this solution. However, this principle is so broad that we suspected it is not always true. We decided to try to refine the principle so that it would be more specific and informative. In that way we felt we'd get a better idea of what principles actually followed from the solution "Open up wilderness." We did this by searching for a **counterexample,** which is any concrete thing or situation that does not fit an assumption or principle. When searching for a counterexample to the above principle, we thought of an adorable newborn baby. Should the public be allowed unlimited visiting rights to this beautiful baby? Of course not. The example of the baby is counterexample to the general principle that the public should be given open access to things of beauty.

In particular, the baby example shows that the original principle is *too strong.* This means that the principle covers more cases than it should. A counterexample can also be used to show that a principle is *too weak.* This means that the principle covers fewer cases than it should. For example, from the same solution, we also generated the principle that the public should be given free access to the wilderness. We then thought of situations that seemed compatible with the solution but not with the principle. Visitors pay a fee to get into Yellowstone National Park. This case violates the principle of free access. But it doesn't seem to violate the solution of open access. As a result, we felt we needed to reformulate the principle before we could say that it truly followed from the solution.

Once you find a counterexample in your own exploring, you need to determine whether it shows the original generalization to be too weak or too strong. If it shows the generalization to be too strong, you must qualify the generalization so that it no longer includes the counterexample (for example, the case of the baby). If it shows the generalization to be too weak, you must strengthen the generalization so that it can now include the counterexample (for example, the case of Yellowstone).

There is no limit to how many times you can thus qualify or strengthen assumptions and principles. You should continue doing so as long as you find it profitable, as long as you feel the exercise teaches you more about the solution (and ultimately the line of argument and the issue) you are exploring. For example, once we discovered the counterexample of the baby, we reformulated the principle of the public's right to access to things of beauty as follows:

REFORMULATED PRINCIPLE

"We should always grant the public open access to publicly owned sites."

This rewording weakened the original principle so that it no longer included the case of the baby (babies aren't publicly owned sites). But we now recognized that this revised principle could also be the object for further refinement, for further weakening or strengthening. We quickly thought of counterexamples that showed this revised principle to be too strong. Nuclear power plants are publicly owned sites. We certainly don't want to grant the public full access to them.

This led us in search of a new wording of our principle that would exclude the case of nuclear power plants. Our new wording of the principle went as follows:

SECOND REFORMULATION

"We should always grant the public open access to publicly owned sites known for their beauty."

This rewording eliminated the power plant example since power plants are not known for their beauty. We found it difficult to find easy counterexamples to this new principle, but we still found it worthwhile to search for them. We noticed that this principle seems to cover the public's access to museums of art. To our knowledge, there is no issue about the public's access to such museums. Why is there such an issue about wilderness? We found it worthwhile to raise questions like these, questions that compared assumptions and principles at stake on the wilderness issue with other cultural contexts. As we will see later on, you can often base an original essay on analogies between your immediate issue and these other contexts.

For Class 10.1

Imagine that you are exploring the solution "Open up wilderness." You have proposed the following principle as following from that solution: "We should never restrict people from environments where they can learn about nature."

You now want to refine that principle so that it more precisely follows from the solution. You discover counterexamples that convince you that the principle is both too strong and too weak. It is too strong because it allows for examples that we normally wouldn't allow for, as these two counterexamples show:

1. allowing people to enter cages of dangerous animals in the zoo
2. allowing people access to other people's gardens

But it is also too weak because it fails to allow for examples that we normally do allow for, as these two counterexamples show:

3. allowing people to visit wilderness to have fun (not to learn)
4. allowing people to visit wilderness to meditate (not to learn)

Refine the original principle through these counterexamples. Qualify the wording so that your revised principle no longer includes the first two counterexamples. Strengthen the wording so that your revised principle now includes the last two counterexamples.

For Your Notebook #19

Start a new section of your notebook labeled "Possible Solutions." This section should have a separate entry for each solution in your list of possible solutions. Leave space to keep notes on (1) the problem cases resolved, (2) implications, (3) counterexamples, and (4) strengths and faults of each solution (to be discussed in the following section).

For each possible solution you have listed in your notebook:

1. Explore problem cases it would seem to resolve.
2. Explore its implications.
3. Explore further by refining its implications through counterexamples.

EXPLORE FOR STRENGTHS AND FAULTS

Thus far, you've explored solutions more to identify than to test them. Now you should explore possible solutions for their strengths and faults. A solution is *strong* insofar as it can resolve the tensions in problem cases; it is *faulty* insofar as it can't. As a result, exploring a solution for its strengths and faults means deciding whether and how well it resolves the tensions in problem cases.

Whether a particular solution resolves a particular case or not is often an intuitive judgment—and consequently difficult to describe. Nonetheless, we can offer some guidelines that may help sharpen your intuition. First, recognize that every solution will both succeed and fail to resolve a particular problem case. This is a good assumption to begin with because it will remind you of the likelihood that every solution will have both strengths and faults.

Second, don't think of success or failure as an either/or judgment, but as a "to the extent that" judgment. A solution succeeds with respect to a problem case *to the extent that* it permanently removes or lessens the tensions that underlie it. A solution fails with respect to a problem case *to the extent that* it doesn't reduce the tensions at all, or reduces some but not others, or perhaps even creates new tensions (or problem cases) of its own. Of two strong solutions, one may be stronger. Of two faulty solutions, one may be faultier. In other words, your overall assessment of a solution as strong or faulty often involves weighing its comparative strengths and faults.

Third, to come up with an overall assessment of a solution as strong or faulty, you must balance two factors: *positive effects* of a solution and its *negative effects*. Positive effects refer to the degree to which a solution eliminates the original tension in a particular problem case. Negative effects refer to the degree to which a solution would create new tensions (or generate new problem cases) as a result of being implemented. The overall strength of a solution is a combination of its positive effects minus its negative effects.

Naturally, if a solution seems to cause more problems than it solves, you should judge it faulty. For example, if the tension in the wilderness issue involves too many people visiting a beautiful forest, the idea of quotas would seem to be a strong solution. However, if you judge that setting up quotas would create more problems than it solves, you would still want to judge the solution faulty.

Sometimes you find yourself with a solution that seems to relieve some part of the tension, but not other parts. Here, the solution will show some positive effects, but they will seem insufficient. For instance, one solution might prevent tourists from trampling some wilderness areas by building fences. While this solution wouldn't do away with the overcrowding problem as neatly as quotas, it might resolve part of the tension. Still, aspects of overcrowding might persist.

Whether you finally judge such partial solutions as strong or faulty overall depends on several factors. Can these solutions combine with other partial solutions to eliminate the tensions more completely? Can these partial solutions minimize the negative effects so that they are worth implementing? Can you be sure there are no alternative solutions that provide a more complete reduction of tension with no more negative effects? To the extent you can answer yes to these questions, you have reasons for judging partial solutions strong overall.

Last but not least, an important criterion for judging the overall strengths and faults of a solution is how well it handles the problem cases that function as your paradigm cases—the problem cases you judge to be most important. You will want to give greater weight to a solution's positive effects if those effects extend to your paradigm cases. Thus, if two solutions seem to have the same positive effect overall, but only one relieves the tension in one or more of your paradigm cases, you will want to judge as stronger the solution that resolves the tension in your paradigms.

For example, one of our paradigm cases in the wilderness issue was the fact that it is now hard to go camping without hearing radios blasting. We had explored two possible solutions. One would restrict visitation. The other would restrict pollution levels, including the level of noise pollution. We had judged both of these solutions as carrying pretty much the same positive effects overall. However, only one solution—the one dealing with pollution—directly addressed a paradigm case. So we judged it the stronger of the two.

For Class 10.2

Refer to the problem cases discussed by Nash, Tucker, and Swain. Decide which of these problem cases are the most important to you and call them your paradigm cases. Now consider the three solutions below:

1. Impose visitation quotas on wilderness.
2. Protect only the wilderness lands we can't develop for economic purposes.
3. Prohibit all visitation to wilderness. Hire a production company to videotape the sights and sounds of wilderness. Wilderness lovers can then buy the tapes, comforted by the knowledge that the wilderness will not be touched in any way.

For each solution do the following:

A. Decide which tensions in your paradigm cases the solution in question would seem to resolve.
B. Decide which tensions in your paradigm cases the solution would miss.
C. Decide whether the solution is strong or faulty overall by
   (1) balancing its positive effects against its negative effects.
   (2) judging whether its positive effects affect your paradigms.

For Your Notebook #20

Take notes on strengths and faults for each possible solution you've explored and make an overall assessment for each. For each solution in the "Possible Solutions" section of your notebook:

1. Take notes on its strengths.
2. Take notes on its faults.
3. Take notes on your overall assessment of it.

⬚⬚⬚ 11 EXPLORE
POSSIBLE PROBLEM
DEFINITIONS

Thus far, you've explored possible lines of arguments in your issue from the perspective of two milestones, seeing the issue and choosing a solution. You've broken down problem cases and studied how well particular solutions handle them. You've also studied the implications of particular solutions, and their overall strengths and faults. In this chapter, you'll complete the exploration of your issue by exploring the remaining milestone—"defining the problem."

FORMULATE ALTERNATIVE PROBLEM DEFINITIONS

You'll begin by formulating alternative **problem definitions.** A problem definition is a formal way of representing the tension at the heart of an issue. We'll elaborate this definition more fully below.

Locate Possible Alternatives

The work you have done so far provides you with two potentially rich sources for locating alternatives to formulate. First, return to your notes from summarizing. There you should find notecards labeled "defining the problem," which characterize the claims your authors have made.

Second, refer to your written descriptions of problem cases in the "Cases" section of your notebook. Working through each description, ask yourself, "Can this wording be used to express the tension at the heart of the issue? If not, can it be revised slightly to do so?" In response to your questions, list alternative ways of defining the problem as suggested by your descriptions.

Formulate the Tension

The list you compile should provide a good idea of the range and variety of words that you and others can use to describe the source of the underlying tension. In order to test these alternatives, you'll want to turn each wording of the problem into a problem definition. When you formulate a problem definition, you describe the tension in the issue as a conflict between two activities, X and Y, involving the same agent. The general form for every problem definition is the following:

A GENERAL FORM FOR PROBLEM DEFINITIONS

Some agent is involved in X
but
the same agent is involved in Y
[where X and Y are activities that conflict].

By giving a problem a formal definition, you are trying to pinpoint the exact nature of the tension giving rise to your problem cases, or at least to the problem cases you deem most important to the issue (your paradigms). In addition, a well-chosen problem definition can narrow your search for possible solutions to two courses of action: Either do something to change X or do something to change Y. Its capacity to focus the tension and to narrow your search for possible solutions is what gives a problem definition its power.

Beyond the basic form we have just presented, problem definitions generally fit into one of three other specific categories. The first category, *conflicting goals,* is a problem definition in which X and Y are two goals that a single agent pursues and that seem incompatible. That is, if the agent pursues goal X, the path to Y seems blocked, and vice versa. As a refinement on the basic form, the conflicting-goals definition takes the following form:

FORM FOR PROBLEM DEFINITIONS BASED ON CONFLICTING GOALS

Some agent wants to X
but
the same agent wants to Y
[where X and Y are goals that conflict].

For example, one way of stating Nash's problem definition is a problem of conflicting goals:

A PROBLEM OF CONFLICTING GOALS IN WILDERNESS

X: Americans want to enjoy free access to wilderness
but
Y: Americans want to prevent themselves from loving wilderness to death.

Defining a problem as one of conflicting goals is to suggest that the agent who has both goals must change one of them. By stating the problem as one of conflicting goals, Nash is suggesting that Americans must either give up the goal of having free access to wilderness (X) or the goal of not destroying wilderness (Y). Nash, of course, goes on to argue for changing our policy of free access.

The second category of problem definition is a variation on the first, a *belief/goal conflict*. In this case, the agent holds a belief that conflicts with a goal he or she wants to achieve. A belief/goal conflict takes the following form:

FORM FOR PROBLEM DEFINITIONS BASED ON BELIEF/GOAL CONFLICTS

Some agent wants X
but
the same agent believes Y
[where goal X is in conflict with belief Y].

We can, for example, attribute this kind of problem definition to Julber. According to Julber's analysis, the American public wants to preserve the beauty of wilderness but also believes that this preservation effort requires us to limit public access:

A BELIEF/GOAL CONFLICT IN WILDERNESS

X: Americans want to preserve wilderness
but
Y: Americans believe that preservation depends on limited access.

When you see a belief/goal conflict, you explore solutions by trying to change one or the other. Julber asks us to change our beliefs. Citing the example of the Swiss, he tries to show us that we can preserve the wilderness and still provide free access.

The final category of problem definition is a *goal/knowledge conflict*. In this situation, an agent has a goal, but lacks some important information needed to achieve it. The form for this kind of conflict is illustrated below:

FORM FOR PROBLEM DEFINITIONS BASED ON GOAL/KNOWLEDGE CONFLICTS

Some agent wants X
but
the same agent doesn't know Y
[where goal X requires knowledge Y to be achieved].

The Ehrlichs' problem definition can be formulated in these terms:

A GOAL/KNOWLEDGE CONFLICT IN WILDERNESS

X: Humans want to preserve the ecosystem
but
Y: humans do not yet understand the effect of resource development on the ecosystem.

Your goal is to formulate as many plausible alternative problem definitions as you can—and then explore the alternatives. Start by trying to formulate the problem definitions of the authors you have read. Then try to formulate any other conflicts that occur to you. In your work, keep in mind the following two rules of thumb:

RULES OF THUMB IN FORMULATING PROBLEM DEFINITIONS

- The agent must be the same on both the X and Y sides of the definition.
- Every time you formulate a problem definition, test whether the X and Y are really in conflict by considering whether plausible solutions will eliminate either the X or the Y. If you can't trace the effect of solutions on the X or the Y, you probably haven't formulated the X and the Y as precisely as you need to.

For Class 11.1

Consider the following descriptions of how to define the problem in the wilderness issue:

1. It's hard to tour a national park without ending up in a trail of pollution-causing cars.
2. Only a few Americans can see some of our most beautiful wilderness because wilderness freaks refuse to allow even small roads and trails to be run through it.

For each description,

1. Formulate the tension as a problem of conflicting goals, a goal/belief conflict, or a goal/knowledge conflict.
2. Discuss how your formulation of (1) agrees with Nash's understanding of the problem, and how it differs from it.
3. Discuss how your formulation of (2) agrees with Julber's understanding of the problem, and how it differs from it.
4. Revise your formulation of (1) so that Nash's solution (a quota system) would eliminate the "but."
5. Revise your formulation of (2) so that Julber's solution (an access philosophy) would eliminate the "but."

For Your Notebook #21

Formulate the problem definitions in your issue.

- From your summary notes and written descriptions of problem cases, generate a list of possible ways of defining the problem on your issue. Call this entry your "List of Possible Problem Definitions."
- Start a new section of your notebook called "Possible Problem Definitions". Give a separate entry to each written description in your list. Following each entry, allow space for recording information under two subentries: (1) Formalizations and (2) Evaluations. Here you'll be filling in the first of these subentries. (We'll defer Evaluations to the next notebook entry.)
- For each entry in your list, formulate the description as either a problem of conflicting goals, a goal/belief conflict, or a goal/knowledge conflict. Experiment by giving each entry different formulations and try to decide if some formulations are better than others. Record your alternative formulations and your reasons after each entry.
- Check the validity of a particular formulation by considering whether there are reasonable solutions to the issue that would eliminate the X or the Y.

TEST PROBLEM DEFINITIONS

You'll test your problem definitions by seeing how well each describes the problem cases you have so far discovered. A problem definition seldom provides an apt description for all the cases a community finds problematic. However, you will want your problem definition to cover those problem cases you consider most important to the issue—your paradigm cases.

Test a Single Definition Against a Single Case

Compare your alternative problem definitions with your paradigm cases. Ask yourself, "How many aspects of the problem definition match aspects of these cases?" The more aspects that match, the more relevant the definition is to the case. You can judge any problem definition as strong or faulty depending on the extent to which its aspects match the aspects of your paradigms.

For example, suppose you have formulated a problem definition for wilderness based on conflicting goals:

PROBLEM DEFINITION WITH CONFLICTING GOALS

X: Americans want to protect wilderness
but
Y: Americans want to consume its resources.

Now assume you want to test that problem definition against the written description of the following paradigm case:

DESCRIPTION OF PARADIGM CASE

"By developing wilderness for business, Americans are destroying it for everyone."

In judging the relevance of the problem definition to this paradigm case, ask yourself, "What aspects do they have in common? What aspects are different?" It is clear that both the problem definition and the paradigm imply that Americans have the goal of developing our wilderness for economic reasons. Insofar as they overlap in that implication, the problem definition is relevant to the case (and thus strong).

However, there are also differences. The paradigm case, but not the problem definition, conveys the idea that we are actually developing our wilderness and causing its destruction. The problem definition, but not the paradigm case, conveys the idea that we also have the goal of protecting wilderness. Insofar as they convey aspects that do not overlap, the problem definition is irrelevant to the case (and thus faulty).

Note that judging the relevance of a problem definition means judging the extent to which its individual aspects match the individual aspects of a single problem case. Judgments of relevance are made with respect to single problem cases. When you wish to judge the *overall* relevance of a problem definition, you must judge its relevance against a *set* of problem cases. We'll say more about this in the next section.

Often, you'll find very little overlap between a problem definition and one of your paradigms. That gives you grounds for judging the problem definition irrelevant. In other cases, you will sense that the problem definition seems not only irrelevant to a paradigm case, but actually *incompatible* with it. A problem definition is incompatible with a paradigm case when the definition carries assumptions about seeing the world that would prevent you from acknowledging the tension in the case at all. For example, take the following problem definition of the wilderness issue, based on a goal/belief conflict:

PROBLEM DEFINITION WITH GOAL/BELIEF CONFLICT

X: Americans want resources only wilderness can provide
but
Y: Americans have been slow to develop these resources.

Now imagine we want to test this definition against the previous description of a paradigm case: "By developing wilderness for business, Americans are destroying it for everyone."

You can see aspects of the problem definition and the paradigm that do *not* overlap. You thus have grounds for judging the problem definition irrelevant. And yet you may notice that the distance between the problem definition and the paradigm seems to go beyond mere irrelevance. The problem definition seems to be based on a set of assumptions for seeing the world that are markedly different from the assumptions that are required to appreciate the tension in the paradigm case. More specifically, the (pro-business) perspective of the problem definition would seem to block the (anti-business) lens you need to appreciate the tension in the paradigm.

If you accept the problem definition, it seems likely that you won't see the tension in the paradigm case—and so you won't even acknowledge the situation as a problem case. Conversely, if you acknowledge the tension in the paradigm, you can't accept the problem definition. These are the practical outcomes of judging a problem definition incompatible with one of your paradigms.

To test a problem definition against your paradigms, match each alternative definition against each paradigm. Search for overlapping aspects. If you find many, you can judge the definition relevant and thus strong relative to the paradigm. If you don't find many, judge the definition irrelevant and thus a faulty description of the paradigm. Explore further to see whether you also want to call the problem definition incompatible with the paradigm, as well as irrelevant to it.

Test a Single Definition Against a Set of Paradigms

Thus far, we have tested single problem definitions against single paradigm cases. However, it is more efficient (and usually more illuminating) to test a problem definition against a set of paradigms. In doing this you are, in effect, setting up a competition among your problem definitions. We call this activity a *competitive test* of problem definitions.

The purpose of this competition is to judge which *single* problem definition does the best job of describing the tension underlying *the set* of your paradigms. Take any three problem definitions from your list of alternative definitions and call them PD 1, PD 2, and PD 3. Take any three written descriptions of paradigms in your issue and call them PC 1, PC 2, and PC 3. Your aim is to explore the comparative strengths and faults of each problem definition with respect to the set of three paradigms.

To see how this notion of competition works with real examples, turn to the section in your notebook called "Possible Problem Definitions" (which you created earlier in this chapter). For each problem definition in your list, you should have a third subentry called "Evaluation." Fill in this subentry with the following headings:

EVALUATION ENTRY

(List problem definition here)
   Evaluation:
      Strong (relevant) with respect to
         (List paradigms here)
         (List aspects here)

Faulty (irrelevant) with respect to
>(List paradigms here)
>(List aspects here)

Incompatible (conflicting) with
>(List paradigms here)

Because of
>(List incompatible assumptions here)

For each problem definition, you'll want to keep a similar record of its strengths and faults. More specifically, you'll want to keep a record of the paradigms and the aspects of those paradigms that you find the definition relevantly describes. Second, you'll want to keep track of the paradigms and aspects that the definition misses (is irrelevant to).

Third, you may want to keep track of the paradigms that seem incompatible with the definition, as well as the conflicting assumptions behind the incompatibility. By keeping track of which problem definitions are incompatible with your own lens on the issue, you can learn a good deal about the assumptions with which you approach the issue.

Let's take a brief example. Consider the following alternative problem definitions in the wilderness issue:

COMPETITIVE PROBLEM DEFINITIONS IN WILDERNESS

PD 1

X: Americans want to protect wilderness

but

Y: Americans want to consume wilderness.

PD 2

X: Americans want to know how much damage to wilderness commercial development causes

but

Y: *Americans don't yet have the knowledge they need to achieve this goal.*

Now imagine we want to competitively test these alternatives against the written descriptions of our two paradigms in the issue:

PARADIGM CASES

PC 1

"In the name of trying to protect wilderness from the masses, a small and stubborn minority has in effect banned millions of Americans from our country's most beautiful wilderness."

PC 2

"Wilderness lands are disappearing faster than we can replenish them because of commercial development."

Here's how we competitively tested the two problem definitions against these two paradigms. First, we noticed that both problem definitions seem equally strong and faulty as a description of PC 1. Both definitions capture the goal aspect ("to protect wilderness") in PC 1. But neither captures the tension aspect ("a minority is banning millions from wilderness").

We further noticed that both definitions seemed equally faulty when it came to judging their relevance (matching aspects) to PC 2. PC 2 speaks of what is now happening to wilderness (being destroyed faster than it is being replenished). Neither problem definition speaks of what is happening now—only of what our goals are or what is missing from our knowledge.

On the other hand, we did notice a sizable difference in the strengths of these problem definitions when it came to making judgments of compatibility. While PD 1 seemed compatible with PC 2, PD 2 did not. The second definition seems to assume that it is not yet certain how much actual "destruction" wilderness development causes. Yet PC 2 seems (to us anyway) to convey the certainty that commercial development *does* wreak irreparable harm on wilderness.

In essence, PD 2 implies assumptions that seem to view the world in ways inconsistent with PC 2. Thus, an author committed to that problem definition would have a difficult—if not impossible—time committing to PC 2 as a problem case in the issue. Conversely, an author committed to PC 2 as a central problem case in the issue could never generalize the problem in the terms of PD 2. Notice that by examining the strengths of competing problem definitions, you can't help examining faults and even incompatibilities as well.

Based on our competitive testing, our notebook entries under "Evaluation" for PD 1 looked like this:

EVALUATION OF THE FIRST PROBLEM DEFINITION

PD 1: We have the incompatible goals of wanting to protect wilderness and wanting to consume its resources. (We can't do both.)

Evaluation:

Strong (relevant) with respect to PC 1 (banning in the name of protecting)
Aspects: goal (to protect wilderness)
Faulty (irrelevant) with respect to
  PC 1
  PC 2 (disappearing faster than replenished)
  Aspects: agent (millions are banning)
  Result (disappearing faster than replenished)
Incompatible with
  None

We filled in our entry for PD 2 as follows:

EVALUATION OF THE SECOND PROBLEM DEFINITION

PD 2: We want to know how much permanent damage the commercial development of wilderness causes. (We don't know enough to achieve this goal.)

Evaluation:

Strong (relevant) with respect to PC 1 (banning in the name of protecting)
Aspects: goal (to protect wilderness)
Faulty (irrelevant) with respect to

PC 1
PC 2 (disappearing faster than replenished)

Aspects: agent (millions are banning)
result (disappearing faster than replenished)
Incompatible with: PC 2
Because of

Conflicting assumptions behind incompatibility: PC2 assumes that commercial development causes destruction. And yet PD 2 assumes that this is exactly what we don't know and want to find out.

Recording evaluations across a wide range of problem definitions and problem cases can help you see at a glance the comparative strengths and faults of multiple definitions across multiple cases.

As you gain experience making these judgments, you'll find you will be able to make them lightning quick, in your head. You'll come increasingly to realize that the reason for keeping your judgments organized and up-to-date in your notebook is so they can remain that way in your head. The sections of your notebook will become, more and more, file folders of the mind. Eventually, you may find yourself relying on paper less and less, using it only when the going gets unusually detailed or rough.

For Class 11.2

Using the paradigm cases listed below, run competitive tests on the following problem definitions:

PD 1. We want to maximize the yield of resources we derive from wilderness, but we don't know if that's the goal we should be pursuing (we think our goals can't work together).

PD 2. We want to maximize the yield of resources we derive from wilderness, but we don't know how to attain that goal (we lack the knowledge to reach a goal).

PD 3. We'd like to keep wilderness as a version of the past and a vision of the future, but we can't decide which vision is most important to us.

Fill in strengths, faults, and incompatibilities for PD 1, PD 2, and PD 3 that you find as a result of your testing.

Paradigm Cases

1. In the name of trying to protect wilderness from the masses, a small and stubborn minority has in effect banned millions of Americans from our country's most beautiful wilderness.
2. Wilderness lands are disappearing faster than we can replenish them.
3. America must import many mineral and paper products at a high cost and starve her own mineral and paper industry. While we have these resources in abundance, they lie on land which is protected by the Wilderness Protection Act.

For Your Notebook #22

You'll use this notebook entry to fill in the "Evaluation" section for problem definitions.

• Judge the relevance of each problem definition to each of your paradigm cases. Note which aspects of the case match aspects of the description; note which do not. Use this information to fill in information about the strengths and faults of each definition.
• Judge the compatibility of each problem definition to each case. Focus on those problem definition/paradigm case pairings that seem not only irrelevant to each other, but incompatible. Record the conflicting assumptions behind the incompatibility.

DRAW YOUR OWN CONCLUSIONS

Thus far, we've seen how exploring problem definitions against cases can help you test them. Now we'll consider how testing problem definitions can help you draw some of your conclusions about the issue. Your own values and commitments have informed your exploration throughout. Your selection of certain problem cases in the issue as paradigm cases, for example, was your own signature on the issue. And since you test solutions and problem definitions against your paradigms, your exploration has borne your personal stamp throughout—although implicitly.

At this point, though, you'll want to try to make the implicit explicit. You'll want to draw from your exploration a set of conclusions that can become the germ of your own position and, eventually, your own original essay.

Recheck Your "Faulty" Problem Definitions

Before you work on drawing out your conclusions directly, you'll want to make sure that your competitive testing of problem definitions hasn't forced you to discard problem definitions that may still strike you as compelling. It's therefore a good idea to go back and explore why any such definition failed to "cover" your paradigms. By trying to understand why certain problem definitions failed, you can accomplish a couple of worthwhile things.

First, you can check whether your set of paradigms needs to be expanded or reduced. Perhaps you judged a problem definition faulty because it failed to describe one of your paradigms. In retrospect, however, you come to believe that this paradigm case is not so important after all. You will then want to reconsider a problem definition you might earlier have dismissed.

Second, you can check whether your evaluation of a problem definition as faulty can be reversed simply by rewording the X and Y components of the definition. Sometimes you'll find that a slight rephrasing can make a problem definition cover a paradigm case that the previous phrasing seemed to miss.

In sum, before drawing your conclusions, focus on the problem definitions you judged faulty and see if you can salvage them before dismissing them.

Come to Some Commitments

Having thoroughly explored the issue, you are now ready to see what your commitments look like against the context of your exploration. You're ready to draw some conclusions about the issue. By "conclusions," we don't mean anything as careful and elaborate as a line of argument. We don't even mean anything as definite as a position. Instead, we mean statements that are likely to lead you—after further exploration, testing, and revision—to ideas that you can eventually refine into an original position, line of argument, and finally an original essay or contribution.

Once you have what you think is a consistent orientation on the issue, you are ready to state what you believe. Simply write down, in a sentence or two, the conclusions you believe you can draw about your approach to the issue. Your words needn't be refined or elaborate. If all goes well, they may be the first germ of what will turn into your own position and, eventually, your own line of argument. When one of our students stated her conclusions about the wilderness issue, her statement of conclusion was simply this:

A STATEMENT OF CONCLUSION

I think our need for wilderness is really a need for security.

Certainly, you might want to write more than this. But you don't have to. More important than what gets written down is the feeling that your conclusions give you an "angle" on the issue—a vantage point from which you can see an opportunity to say something new about the issue to the community. Our observation of experienced writers suggests that they see, and get excited about, opportunities to say something new long before they work out the details of exactly what they will say.

For Class 11.3

The following are two lines of argument. Each line of argument includes a problem case, a problem definition, and a solution.

Line of Argument #1

PC 1: We are losing money by not developing wilderness.

PD 1: We place fantasies ahead of hard economic realities (we have the wrong priorities).

S 1:   We should develop more wilderness.

Line of Argument #2

PC 2: We are losing our sense of values by developing wilderness.

PD 2: We place money ahead of what's really valuable (we have the wrong priorities).

S 2:   We should develop less wilderness.

Select a partner and do the following:

1. With your partner, decide on PC 1 or PC 2 as your paradigm for the wilderness issue. If your partner chooses PC 1, you must choose PC 2, and vice versa.
2. Working separately, try to build a pathway up from your paradigm. Try to show why you think the problem case you have chosen for your paradigm is more important to the issue than the problem case your partner has chosen. Try to repair the faults you perceive in the problem definitions and solutions associated with your paradigm. (If your paradigm is PC 1, these will be PD 1 and S 1.) Try to diminish the strengths in the problem definitions and solutions that are *not* associated with your paradigm. (If your paradigm is PC 1, these will be PD 2 and S 2.)
3. Working together in class, report to your partner what you have found. Indicate whether you have gained or lost confidence in your original problem case as a lens on the issue.

For Your Notebook #23

Record your conclusions on your issue.

- Turning to the "Cases" section of your notebook, decide on your paradigms for the issue. Search your own experience for paradigms as well.
- Try to establish a unified orientation toward the issue by building a pathway up from your paradigms. Try to convince yourself why you have chosen the paradigms you have—why they provide a lens on the issue that is more central, more important, than other problem cases provide. Scan the "Possible Solutions" and "Possible Problem

Definitions" sections of your notebook. Determine which possible solutions and problem definitions fit (are compatible and relevant to) your paradigms and which do not. Try to repair the faults in problem definitions and solutions that fit your paradigms. Try to diminish the strengths in problem definitions and solutions that don't. If you find it hard to apply these strategies effectively, rework your paradigms and explore new pathways.

- State what you believe. Write a sentence or two stating your general conclusions about the issue.

⊞ 12 DRAFT THE ANALYSIS

You're now ready to draft a written analysis. In your analysis, you group positions that share important aspects at one milestone or at a sequence of milestones. Such positions are said to share the same **approach**. For example, positions on wilderness that are similar at "seeing the issue" may constitute an approach to the issue. As you explore for your own position, it is useful to work at the level of approaches rather than the level of individual authors and positions. Authors first decide on their general approach to an issue and then work within that approach to construct a position.

Though you may not have realized it, you have taken a number of steps in analyzing to help you reorganize your understanding of your issue away from individual authors and positions and toward approaches. You've kept records on problem cases, paradigms, possible solutions, and problem definitions in your issue. These items of information represent "spare parts" that can fit into and help you identify, characterize, and evaluate groups of positions—that is, approaches.

The records you've thus far kept in analyzing pay off if they allow you to identify different approaches to your issue. In a written analysis, you teach yourself and your readers about the possible approaches to your issue. You characterize these approaches and evaluate them as best you can. In the conclusion, you connect your own conclusions on the issue to existing approaches. In making these connections, you can express a preference for one of these approaches (or some or none).

LABEL APPROACHES TO THE ISSUE

The first step in drafting your analysis is to work across your notes to label approaches. The way you make these labels is easier to do than to explain. You simply create names. There's more to it than that, but not much.

Let's see how this naming strategy works. After collecting our notebook information on the problem cases, solutions, and problem definitions in wilderness, we began organizing approaches to the issue. We had to think of names describing groups of positions. To find names, we looked for contrasting information from common milestones. More simply put, we looked for two problem cases that we thought represented two different approaches to the issue; or two problem definitions; or two solutions.

We then assigned short names to each problem case, problem definition, or solution that distinguished it from its opposite pair. For example, we decided to focus on approaches based on contrasting information at "seeing the issue." We chose two problem cases that, for us, seemed representative of two quite different approaches to seeing the issue in wilderness.

PROBLEM CASES REPRESENTING DIFFERENT APPROACHES

PC1: The cost of paper is on the rise because we refuse to cut trees in protected areas.

PC2: Many children no longer know the difference between roughing it outside and driving in a convertible.

While we believed that each problem case represented a particular approach to the wilderness issue, we didn't have names for these approaches. We used the problem cases to help us find names. We asked ourselves, what can we call an approach that would see the issue through PC1? an approach that would see the issue through PC2?

We wanted words that would be good labels—short, memorable, and catchy. Names for approaches should be adjectives because the name has to modify the noun "approach." We need to be able to refer to the "(blank) approach to the issue of wilderness."

We decided on the adjective "economic" to describe the approach implied by PC1. That was pretty easy. Deciding on a good adjective describing PC2 was not. The first description that came to mind was "lack of wilderness." But that was not an adjective. We finally decided on the adjective "deprivational" (a bit clumsy, but adequate) since this approach to the issue seemed to assume that too many of us are deprived of wilderness too much of the time.

For Class 12.1

A. Below are pairs of problem definitions and solutions. Assume that each member of the pair is representative of an approach to the issue. That is, problem definitions 1 and 2 represent different approaches to the wilderness issue as do solutions 1 and 2. Find one-word descriptive adjectives to label each approach. You should end up with four labels. Discuss your labels in class.

PC1: We want to preserve wilderness but we also want to consume its resources.

PC2: We want to save the wilderness from pollutants but we don't know how to do that.

S1: Let's set aside more wilderness.
S2: Let's set aside less wilderness.

B. Imagine that you have isolated the "economic" and "deprivational" approaches to wilderness based on the discussion in this section. Read the following excerpt from a speech by the late Senator Henry M. Jackson on wilderness and decide whether you would classify Jackson's position as belonging to either of these approaches. If not, generate a third label for his approach. Give reasons for your answers.

SHOULD CONGRESS ENACT THE WILDERNESS PROTECTION ACT OF 1982?

Henry M. Jackson

I am introducing the Wilderness Protection Act of 1982. This legislation 1 is a very straightforward bill. It would immediately and permanently withdraw lands in the National Wilderness Preservation System—except for lands in Alaska—from oil, gas, oil shale, coal, phosphate, potassium, sulfur, gilsonite, and geothermal leasing. National Forest System lands recommended to Congress for designation as wilderness, wilderness study areas, and further planning lands identified in RARE II would be temporarily withdrawn from such leasing. The bill also provides for mineral inventories of withdrawn areas, revocation of withdrawals in the case of urgent national need, the protection of valid existing rights, and for leasing under wilderness if exploration and extraction is below the surface and is accomplished from outside the wilderness.

The Congress has been embroiled in a debate over mineral prospecting, 2 exploration, leasing, and development in wilderness and so-called wilderness candidate areas for the past 1½ years. This debate began early in 1981 when the Forest Service announced that it was considering issuing permits for seismic activities involving the use of explosives in the Bob Marshall Wilderness in Montana. At the same time, it was discovered that some 340 applications for oil and gas leases were pending within the so-called Bob Marshall Wilderness "complex"—the Bob Marshall, Scapegoat, and Great Bear Wilderness Areas. In response, the House Interior and Insular Affairs Committee voted on May 21, 1981, to invoke its emergency withdrawal authority pursuant to section 204(e) of the Federal Land Policy and Management Act and requested the Secretary of the Interior to make an emergency withdrawal of

Henry M. Jackson, "Should Congress Enact the Wilderness Protection Act of 1982?" *The Congressional Digest*, December, 1982.

the Bob Marshall complex from mineral leasing. The Secretary made the withdrawal and the matter is now being litigated in the Federal district court in Montana.

In the ensuing months the controversy over wilderness leasing height- 3 ened when leasing recommendations were developed for wilderness areas in California, Washington, Wyoming, and Arkansas, and when three leases were actually issued by the Department of the Interior in the Capitan Mountains Wilderness Area in New Mexico.

In November 1981, the Secretary of the Interior agreed to place a 6- 4 month moratorium on leasing in wilderness areas in order to give Congress time to consider changes in the law. In late January, the Secretary extended the moratorium until the end of the current session of the 97th Congress. In the meantime, the Congress continues to consider a variety of statewide wilderness proposals, some of which withdraw wilderness lands from further leasing and others that do not.

I am introducing this legislation because the debate over the past 1½ 5 years has convinced me of three things. First, the people of this country are, for the most part, overwhelmingly opposed to oil and gas development in wilderness areas. In every instance, where leasing has been an issue, public reaction has been swift and negative. The strong sentiment in my State and elsewhere in the country is that wilderness and potential wilderness areas should be the last places to be leased. I concur in this view, and the bill I am introducing today will help insure that other lands are explored and developed first.

Second, I am convinced that the amount of oil and gas involved is very 6 small. There are millions and millions of acres of Federal lands available for leasing that are not components of the Wilderness Preservation System. Secretary Watt, for example, has recently announced the implementation of a 5-year plan for leasing over 1 billion acres of the Outer Continental Shelf. By comparison, the amount of acreage withdrawn under his bill is quite small indeed. Further, experts at the Oak Ridge National Laboratory have indicated at hearings conducted by the House Interior and Insular Affairs Committee that wilderness and wilderness-candidate areas may only contain on the order of 3 percent of the Nation's undiscovered gas resources. Obviously, this figure is quite speculative, but even if it is 100 percent too low, it is clear that the potential energy loss is a relatively small price to pay for preserving our Nation's wilderness system.

Finally, I think it is very important that the Congress act before the end 7 of this year. Secretary Watt has urged us to address this issue legislatively, and I think we should respond. Once the current moratorium expires at the end of this Congress, we will again be forced to deal with the leasing question through administrative confrontation, FLPMA, and the courts. It is clear that Secretary Watt intends to issue oil and gas leases between the end of this Congress and December 31, 1983, when the leasing authority expires under the terms of the Wilderness Act. I think we should deal with that eventuality now rather than wait to legislate in the crisislike and emotionally charged atmosphere that pervaded the Congress and the administration last year.

For Your Notebook #24

In this notebook entry, you'll work through your notes on analyzing and identify approaches to your issue.

- Select contrasting problem cases, definitions, and solutions that you think represent different approaches to your issue.
- Give names to these contrasts using short descriptive adjectives. You can experiment with many approaches, but avoid ending up with too many approaches. The more approaches you allow, the more your "approaches" will collapse into positions, and you'll defeat the purpose of looking for approaches. A good rule of thumb is to keep the number of approaches in an issue to a number between two and five per milestone. That is, no more than two to five approaches for seeing, two to five for defining, and two to five for resolving.

DESIGN A TREE OF APPROACHES

The next step in drafting your analysis is to design a tree of approaches. This tree is like your synthesis tree in that it is made up of questions and responses that move downward in a coherent chain. However, the branches that split at the top of this tree represent the major approaches you've identified in your issue. For example, had you identified three major approaches (deprivational, psychological, and economic) to the wilderness issue, you would begin your tree of approaches in this fashion:

APPROACHES TO WILDERNESS

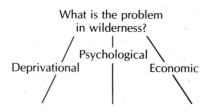

Limit your top split to two to five approaches. Suppose you've identified a cluster of approaches at "see the issue," a cluster at "define the problem," and a cluster at "choose a solution." Which of these do you pick for the top split of your tree? If you've identified important differences in approach at "seeing the issue," start with those at the top. If you think interesting differences of approach don't reveal themselves until the milestone of "defining the problem," start with those differences at the top; if not until the milestone of "choosing a solution," start with differences in solutions. In general, always start your tree at the earliest milestone where important differences of approaches begin to appear.

In our case, sorting out the differences among the three approaches to the wilderness issue was straightforward. As we saw it, the paradigms of each of these approaches differed markedly. The deprivational approach (exemplified by Julber, Nash, and Abbey) relied on paradigms where the goal was to define a person's right to enter a physical territory. Authors taking this approach differed in the degree to which they wanted to see this goal restricted. The economic approach (exemplified by Tucker and the Erhlichs) relied on paradigms where the goal was to define rights on exploiting a wilderness, not entering it. The psychological approach (exemplified by Swain) relied on paradigms that did not limit wilderness to a physical territory at all.

Once you've drawn your top split of approaches, build the tree downward by relating the various positions that fall within each approach. You can find some of these positions from your notes. But you can also discover many of these positions in the very process of building the tree downward from an approach. Thinking from the perspective of an approach makes it easier to explore, generate, differentiate, and refine positions that fall within it.

How can thinking at the level of approaches make you more productive in thinking about positions? Every time you think about a position, you can think about it as belonging to a certain approach. And that gets you to thinking about the other positions within the same approach. Which can make you curious about what distinguishes these positions from one another. Which leads to a greater differentiation of positions. And on and on.

It is this exploration, generation, differentiation, and refinement of positions within approaches that guides the downard design of your tree. Watch how we used this chain of exploration, variation, and differentiation to extend our own tree. We'll focus on our work beginning at the top-level structure:

TOP OF OUR TREE

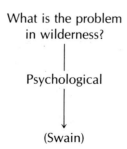

Exploring Swain's position, we were able to identify and name its approach—"psychological." Now we knew we could seek out and try to classify other psychological positions in the issue as long as they linked the wilderness issue to psychological needs, as did Swain's position. We also knew that by finding and refining these other psychological positions, we could build our tree downward.

We focused our search on other possible psychological positions that differed from Swain's in interesting ways. We discovered a large class of such positions, identifying wilderness with our psychological need for religion. In order to differentiate this class further, we found ourselves asking pointed questions, such as: "For those who associate the wilderness issue with our psychological need for religion, does the death of wilderness mean the death of religion and the psychological loss this brings? What could be done in the face of this loss?"

We could now imagine splits forming at this question. We could imagine some wilderness enthusiasts arguing that this psychological loss would be unbearable and that, to prevent it, we should encourage a religious attitude toward wilderness. On the other hand, we could imagine some defenders of traditional religion arguing that the personal loss many in our modern civilization now feel is caused when people turn to wilderness as a replacement for traditional religious values.

By thinking of the issue in terms of approaches, we were able to break an approach down into broad positions and those positions into finer-grained positions. Of positions representing a psychological approach to wilderness, we came to see that Swain's was only one of many possible positions associating wilderness with "the psychological loss of freedom." And Swain's position contrasted with other psychological positions that took a greater interest in our psychic need for religion than for freedom.

Whether you completely agree with our reasoning is not important. What is important is that you understand what our reasoning allowed us to do—to build our tree downward from within each general approach to the wilderness issue. By exploring, contrasting, and differentiating positions within the psychological approach, for example, we were able to revise our tree downward from the preceding to this one:

BUILDING DOWNWARD WITHIN THE PSYCHOLOGICAL APPROACH

Note that of all the positions we represented as falling under the psychological approach in this tree, only one is directly linked to an author (Swain) we had previously read. We discovered the remaining positions by searching, varying, and distinguishing increasingly fine-grained positions within that approach.

For Class 12.2

In this exercise, you'll practice exploring, varying, and differentiating positions within a general approach. Start with the following tree:

What is the
problem in wilderness?

Deprivational
(Too many are deprived of wilderness)

You can think of the deprivational approach to wilderness in different ways. It can mean "deprived of visitation" in which case it comes close to Julber's position. But it can also mean "deprived of quality visitation," in which case it resembles the position of Nash or Abbey. Using any *one* of these authors as your starting point (just as Swain was a starting point in the discussion above), explore, vary, and differentiate positions that fall within the deprivational approach. Design a tree that builds downward that shows how these deprivational positions relate to one another.

For Your Notebook #25

In this notebook entry, you'll design a tree of approaches for the issue you are addressing.

- List the most important approaches in your issue as branches splitting off at the top of your tree.
- Build down under each approach by exploring, varying, and differentiating positions that fall within it.

OUTLINE THE BODY

Schematically, you can think of the body of a written analysis as being composed of the following parts:

THE BODY OF A WRITTEN ANALYSIS

For each major approach you've identified:

  I. Characterize it.
 II. Break it into classes of positions.
    A. Discuss its strengths.
    B. Discuss its faults.
III. Break the classes into subclasses (until you reach the bottom of your tree).

Your tree of approaches gives you a coherent structure with which to organize the body of your analysis. It gives you a listing of the major approaches taken in your issue and a structured account of how positions subdivide within each approach. All that remains is to transform your revised tree into a linear outline. As with outlining the body of a synthesis from a synthesis tree, there is no rigid formula for translating your revised tree into a linear outline. Use the following criteria to guide your judgment.

CRITERIA FOR ORGANIZING THE BODY

- *Organize by approaches.* Since a written analysis reflects your understanding of how positions naturally group into approaches, you should organize your discussion by approach. Discuss all the positions that fall under one approach; then all the positions that fall under a second; then all falling under a third, and so on.
- *Use chronology, idiosyncrasy, and merit to sequence approaches.* Organizing by approaches does not tell you the order in which to discuss approaches. To

decide how to arrange your approaches, use the strategies you learned about in synthesizing. Generally speaking, you'll want to start with approaches that you see as historically prior, less often discussed, and less promising than approaches that arose later in time, that are more often discussed and more promising.

The criterion of organizing by approaches prompted us to discuss the economic approach to wilderness and all the positions associated with it; the deprivational approach and all its positions; and the psychological approach with all its positions.

The conclusions we had drawn on the wilderness issue seemed to us most consistent with the psychological approach, so the criterion of merit prompted us to discuss the psychological approach last. By saving the best approach for last, we knew we'd be able to maintain a smooth transition between the body and the conclusion, where we'd have a chance to discuss our own conclusions and our preferences for an approach.

The criterion of idiosyncrasy prompted us to discuss the economic approach before the deprivational. We judged the economic approach less often discussed than the deprivational; thus, we decided to bring it up early and be done with it early.

We could now refine the outline of the body of our analysis into a more detailed one.

A MORE SPECIFIC OUTLINE OF THE BODY

 I. Discuss the economic approach.
     A. Characterize positions associated with it.
     B. Evaluate them.
 II. Discuss the deprivational approach.
     A. Characterize positions associated with it.
     B. Evaluate them.
 III. Discuss the psychological approach.
     A. Characterize positions associated with it.
     B. Evaluate them.

DRAFT THE INTRODUCTION

The introduction of an analysis paper should familiarize readers with the issue you are discussing. It should discuss problem cases that are most widely recognized as problem cases in the issue, and it should discuss the history of the issue. Most importantly, the introduction should prepare readers to hear about the variety of approaches that can be taken toward the issue. By the time readers finish your introduction, they should have enough background and interest to want to hear about the various approaches you'll be discussing in the body.

It isn't easy to reconcile the frequently conflicting aims of (1) discussing problem cases and history, (2) preparing your reader to hear about the multiplicity of approaches, and (3) writing a short introduction. This conflict can occur because different approaches to the issue will often emphasize different problem cases and even different histories. To prepare your readers for each of the approaches you'll discuss in the body, you might find yourself having to include multiple sets of problem cases and histories. This, in turn, will make your introduction long—often, too long.

When you sense this conflict, as we did in the wilderness issue, you'll want your introduction to give your readers a glimpse of the different approaches without commiting them to the details they'll need to follow any one. That was our decision when we wrote the following brief introduction:

INTRODUCTION OF THE ANALYSIS

> For our ancestors in generations past, the wilderness was a hardship to tame and develop. Now, we often think of wilderness as the spot for an idyllic vacation, a place for peace and quiet. Above all, perhaps, we think of wilderness as a retreat from issues, not as a starting point for them. But in fact, wilderness has become an important issue. We can't seem to agree on whether maintaining it will ruin the cost of living; whether losing it will ruin our quality of life; whether it fills holes in our personal lives that we desperately need to fill; or whether it fills holes that it shouldn't be trying to fill.

DRAFT THE BODY

In a sense, drafting the body of an analysis is like drafting several papers in one. Your aim is to describe approaches to the issue and the positions associated with them. Yet each approach represents a way of "seeing, defining, and resolving" that is distinctive. For this reason, you'll need to think of each approach in your body as requiring its own stage-setting and elaboration of positions.

Set the Stage for the Approach

For each approach you draft in the body, decide what information you need to include in order to set the stage for your reader. As we have already mentioned, each approach you plan to discuss may have a set of problem cases and a written history that is unique to it. In that case, you'll need to introduce these cases and that history to give your readers a frame of reference. In addition, even if a particular approach shares problem cases and a history with others, it may still rely on certain unique assumptions for seeing the issue. In that case, you'll need to include these assumptions in order to set the stage adequately.

In brief, you need to include in your stage-setting any information about the particular approach you are discussing that distinguishes it from your other approaches. For example, when we thought about setting the stage for the psychological approach to the wilderness issue, we recognized a host of problem cases and historical accounts that applied to it but that didn't apply to our other two approaches, such as:

INFORMATION UNIQUE TO THE PSYCHOLOGICAL APPROACH

- the intensity and passion behind the arguments to preserve wilderness
- the psychological implications of a vanishing frontier
- cultists worshiping wilderness in the Pacific Northwest
- a historical account of the decline of traditional religion
- a historical account of the research on personal alienation
- a historical account of the psychological importance of religion

Because this information seemed to us both relevant to the psychological approach and unique to it, we knew any of it would be appropriate to use for introducing the psychological approach to wilderness. For example, relying on the first item in this list, the following paragraph sets the stage for the psychological approach:

A STAGE-SETTING PARAGRAPH

Another approach to the wilderness issue emphasizes our psychological relationship to it. In this approach, wilderness is not so much a physical fact but a state of mind, a human need. What is interesting about the issue from this approach is why there is an issue at all and why it is discussed with such intensity and passion.

Often, as in our case, you'll find more background research is necessary if you are to include some stage-setting material. For example, we recognized that the literature on the "vanishing frontier" would probably be relevant to introducing the psychological approach to wilderness. But we needed more library research to cite this literature with authority. If you are writing under a tight deadline, with no time for research, you will have to limit your stage-setting to information you already have. If you do have time for research, however, you'll be on your way to serious writing. Much earlier, we discussed using the library to find issues and sources. You'll find it far more productive to research your issue from a particular approach. With a specific approach in hand to guide your search through an issue, sorting the relevant from the irrelevant becomes a much simpler matter.

Elaborate the Positions Associated with the Approach

Once you've set the stage for an approach, you're ready to discuss the positions you've associated with it. As we saw in the outline, you'll want to characterize the positions associated with each approach and then evaluate them as best you can. What follows is our elaboration of the positions associated with the psychological approach to the wilderness issue:

ELABORATING THE POSITIONS TAKING THE PSYCHOLOGICAL APPROACH

Positions formulated from the psychological approach can try to explain the intensity of the debate on wilderness in two quite different ways. They can explain the wilderness issue as affecting our sense of personal freedom: The decline of wilderness is a decline in our sense of freedom. Or they can explain the issue as affecting our sense of religion: The decline of wilderness is a decline in our sense of the spiritual or of God.

Of positions associating the decline of wilderness with a decline in freedom, some might suggest that the loss of freedom comes when we know we no longer have the freedom to visit wilderness. The problem with this position is that many of us "city slickers" never visit wilderness and never seem to feel less free. A stronger position would be to associate our loss of freedom with our loss of choice. Whether you want to visit a wilderness or not, you would feel less free if you knew the option had been taken away from you.

Edward Swain takes this position, noting that we need the *knowledge* that wilderness exists in order to maintain our sense of personal freedom and choice. Swain likens our need for wilderness to our need to know that we still have options. What makes an insurance policy valuable to us is the knowledge that we have the option to keep it or cash it in. Similarly, what makes wilderness valuable is that we have the option to visit it, whether we exercise our option or not.

Swain suggests that our energy policy of using fossil fuels (nonreusable sources of energy) is leading us down a road where all our wilderness lands will eventually be destroyed. He observes that for our economy to survive in the long run, we must convert to an energy policy based on resources that are reusable (sun, wind). Why not speed up that conversion, he suggests, so that we can save our wilderness (and our sense of personal freedom) in the process?

The value of Swain's position is that it looks into the future and anticipates what most positions simply ignore—a future where we find ourselves yearning for stable energy sources and wilderness all at once. Swain's solution would prevent that future. At the same time, Swain never discusses the feasibility of changing our energy policy so abruptly. How hard would it be? How much would it cost?

As important as wilderness is, it is hard to imagine that we would be willing to give up our reliance on fossil fuels for the sake of having a wilderness experience in the year 2050. The only argument serious enough to justify changing our policy is a feasibility argument—which Swain does not provide. Equally important, Swain may have the wrong answer to the question of why we need wilderness.

Of positions associating the decline in wilderness with a decline in our religious sense, there seems to be a major split in the arguments about what we can do to restore it. One can argue that traditional religion is dead and that wilderness has replaced it. In this argument, destroying wilderness represents a sin against religion. But a traditionalist might argue that this reasoning is backward. If traditional religion is dead, it is because humankind has turned to false gods (such as wilderness) as a poor substitute. The traditionalist would then argue that the only way to replace traditional religious values is to restore traditional religious values. Both sets of positions assume we need wilderness in the way we need religion. But neither answers why we need religion.

Notice the language in this text. The prose is not about authors, but about positions. If you read the above passage carefully, you can identify a number of syntactic techniques you can use to help you write about positions. Here's a list of these techniques with examples:

TECHNIQUES FOR WRITING ABOUT POSITIONS

Technique	**Example**
1. Use the word "position" as an active agent (and subject of the sentence) that can explain, clarify, suggest, or resolve issues.	"These positions can explain . . ." "This position suggests that . . ."
2. Use the word "position" as the subject of the sentence with its potential explained by a preceding adjective.	"A good position would . . ." "A stronger position would be . . ."
3. Use the names of authors as agents who represent positions.	"Nash represents this view." "Edward Swain takes this position."
4. Use indefinite human agents who take, argue, or represent positions.	"One might argue that . . ." "One could take that position but . . ."
5. Name human agents by the position they represent.	"Traditionalists argue that . . ." "Wilderness fanatics might deny that . . ."

For Class 12.3

In this exercise, you'll practice the syntactic techniques you'll need to rely on in order to turn prose about authors into prose about positions. Each paragraph below discusses an author (or authors) in the wilderness issue. Using the five techniques provided above, rewrite each paragraph so that it focuses on positions, not authors.

A. Eric Julber sees the wilderness issue from the point of view of these situations. He notes that a small elite was responsible for passing the Wilderness Protection Act of 1964. This act made it illegal to establish permanent roads or other convenient means of access to our most scenic wilderness lands. According to Julber, the result of the act was to bar 99 percent of the American public from these lands. The fear of the "purists," as Julber describes this elite, was that the public would destroy the wilderness once it was given convenient access to it. Julber argues that this fear is unfounded. He describes the situation in Switzerland, where wilderness areas thrive despite open access to the public. He defends what he calls an "open access" philosophy.

B. Roderick Nash defines what he calls the "carrying capacity" of a wilderness. That is, a quality wilderness can be said to disappear when its carrying capacity is exceeded. Nash classifies carrying capacity into three types: physical, biological, and psychological. Physical carrying capacity, according to Nash, refers to the "effects of human visitation on the nonliving environment." Biological carrying capacity refers to the effects of human visitation on wilderness ecosystems. Psychological carrying capacity refers to the effects of "other people's presence" on the experience of one who visits a wilderness.

C. Like Nash, Edward Abbey insists on a quality wilderness experience. Unlike Nash, however, Abbey focuses on one example—Glen Canyon (along the Colorado River) and Glen Canyon Dam, forming Lake Powell. Abbey knew Glen Canyon both before and after it was dammed and he devotes most of his article to making before-and-after contrasts. Abbey describes how the damming of the canyon changed both its physical landscape and its wildlife for the worse. He describes in effect how human visitation, in the form of technology, exceeded (to use Nash's terms) the physical and biological carrying capacity of Glen Canyon.

DRAFT THE CONCLUSION

After you draft the body of your analysis, you are ready to draft the conclusion, where you present the general conclusions you've drawn from the issue and, on the strength of these conclusions, express a preference for an approach. This does not mean you must accept an existing approach. It means that you should explore connections between your conclusions and these approaches. It may be immediately clear to you what approach you prefer. It may be immediately clear that you prefer none and that you will need to define your own.

Drafting our analysis taught us about the psychological approach and also taught us that our general conclusions on the issue fitted within it. Here is our attempt at drafting a conclusion:

A CONCLUSION ON WILDERNESS

In the final analysis, wilderness seems important because it provides security. When we think about leaving society behind to visit the wilderness, we yearn for fewer surprises, not more. In a world where everything changes rapidly, wilderness changes at a slower rate, insulates us from "future shock," provides stable landmarks to mark the passing of time. If we understood this function of wilderness better, we would perhaps be in a better position to know what we were jeopardizing every time we decided to turn a wilderness area into a development project. Psychological approaches to the issue, though on the right track, have yet to push these ideas far enough.

For Your Notebook #26

In this notebook entry, you'll draft your written analysis. To write your draft, do the following:

- Label approaches to your issue.
- Design a tree of approaches.
- Use your tree to outline the body.
- Draft the analysis.

REVISE FOR YOUR READERS

After drafting your analysis, you should get comments for revision. The following are questions you'll want a reader to answer about your text.

CHECKLIST FOR REVISING THE ANALYSIS

- Does my introduction prepare you to hear about the various approaches taken in the issue?
- Does my body set the stage for each approach and the positions associated with them? Are my progression within an approach and my ordering of approaches clear and well motivated?

- Does my conclusion indicate how I align myself with existing approaches?
- Do I give clear and valid reasons for the strengths and faults I attribute to positions? What elaboration would I need to make my reasons clearer or more valid?
- Did I adjust my prose to talk about approaches and positions rather than authors?

For Your Notebook #27

Ask a friend or classmate to read the draft of your analysis using the revision checklist. Use the responses to guide your revision.

PART FIVE

CONTRIBUTE

⊡ 13 VISUALIZE THE LINE OF ARGUMENT

The ultimate goal of composing written argument is to use your writing to make a contribution. What does "contribute" mean in this context? Your community has formed around an issue. It would like to resolve the issue, for that is the goal around which it has formed and mobilized. But it has not yet achieved its goal. What is it still lacking?

What it still needs is an uncontested set of directions for making its way from seeing the issue to resolving it. To close this gap, the community invites you and other aspiring authors to give it direction (a line of argument) from seeing to resolving. Slowly but surely, you've been working your way to the point where you can accept this invitation. For example, in the course of writing your analysis, you taught yourself about the different approaches to the issue from which positions can be formulated. You composed an analysis to help you discover and align yourself with one of these approaches for your own efforts. Now you can use your chosen approach to direct your search for a new line of argument.

Newness is an extremely important criterion by which communities judge authors and toward which you should aspire in your personal efforts as an author. Members of your community can judge that your line of argument is "interesting," "persuasive," and even "well argued." But if they can't also say that it is "new," they won't recognize it or be able to justify it as an original contribution.

Must you be a genius to say something new to your community? Not at all. Think of "community" as an open-ended concept, ranging in scope from a single classroom, to a regional interest group, to the members of an academic discipline, to the world at large, to the historical world spanning centuries. Newness is always relative to a community. Designing new positions is an art that you must practice across many small, familiar communities before you can expect to say something new to large, impersonal, anonymous ones. In fact, you have already practiced this art. You couldn't have survived the family dinner table or the summer campfire if you hadn't cultivated the art of saying new things to a (very small, very intimate) community. Newness is not beyond your reach.

To understand newness intuitively, think of the total knowledge a commuity needs to resolve an issue as divided between what it now knows and what it does not yet know but needs to know:

THE TOTAL KNOWLEDGE A COMMUNITY NEEDS TO RESOLVE AN ISSUE

Known information	The unknown

Total knowledge required for resolving the issue

The information your community knows is typically called "known," "given," "shared," "received," or "commonplace" information. When you target something new to say to your community, you intend to shift the boundary between what it knows and what remains unknown. You can plan to shift this boundary either to the left or the right. By shifting it to the right, you try to increase known information by filling in unknowns. By shifting it to the left, you try to decrease known information by showing that information your community takes as settled and beyond dispute is, in fact, unsettled and disputable.

A shift in either direction can mean "making progress" through the issue. A shift to the right means that the progress is straightforward and forward moving. A shift to the left means that the progress you advocate is more roundabout. You are asking your community to take a step backward before it can take two forward. Your community must go backward through the issue because, you believe, it has based some of its previous progress on information that is unreliable.

As an author, you can also plan to shift the boundary in both directions. You can plan to show your community that some settled information is really unsettled and that you are prepared to decide other information that has, until you, remained undecided. Intuitively, then, you aim to say something new when you try to shift the boundary between what your community knows about resolving the issue and what it does not.

We can sharpen these intuitions further by noticing that newness is a large goal composed of subgoals. In particular, your goal to say something new breaks down into two component goals—into the goal of **accountability** and into the goal of **freshness**. The following diagram illustrates this breakdown:

NEWNESS = ACCOUNTABILITY + FRESHNESS

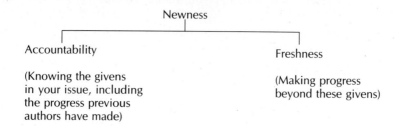

Newness

Accountability

(Knowing the givens
in your issue, including
the progress previous
authors have made)

Freshness

(Making progress
beyond these givens)

Let's consider each of these components in turn, starting with freshness. While a fresh position, overall, is unfamiliar, it can still have familiar parts, including points, an approach, assumptions, principles, milestones, faulty paths, return paths, and support. Nonetheless, the community recognizes that you have assembled these parts into a fresh combination, and hence a fresh line of argument.

Were freshness all there were to newness, it would be trivially easy to be new. You could be new simply by selecting familiar parts randomly and combining them into fresh lines of argument. You would be guaranteed to spout a position that your target community had never before heard. And yet your community would not recognize your position as new—and justifiably so. What's missing?

Newness requires freshness plus the second component, accountability. Beyond being fresh, communities expect you to be accountable to their current conversation. Your line of argument is accountable when it is accurately grounded in your community's current discussion and its sense of progress through the issue.

We consider people impolite when, unannounced, they barge into a serious conversation and try to change its course. To join an inner circle of conversers, you must *earn* your way into the conversation. You must justify your entry by showing that you made it after following the conversation for a good while, finding gaps, and only then deciding you had something to add that was fresh, worth people's time, and capable of filling a gap.

Like ordinary persons, members of a community also find it impolite when would-be authors offer positions that do not build on their current conversation and current sense of progress through the issue. No one will credit you with being new if you don't first account for and acknowledge the givens you find yourself moving beyond.

As an original author, you try to establish accountability and freshness in a set order. You typically try to reveal your accountability to the community as early as possible (in the introduction). You show you are familiar with, and motivated by, the very questions that motivate the community. You show you have done your homework tracing previous contributions and their effect on the community's progress. You then proceed (in the body) with your own position, saying what the community has never before heard, in order to advance its progress toward a resolution. If you are successful at executing this sequence of goals, your community will see you as both accountable and fresh—and consequently new.

EXTEND YOUR CONCLUSIONS INTO AN ORIGINAL LINE OF ARGUMENT

When you start to design your original essay, your line of argument looks like this:

AN EMPTY LINE OF ARGUMENT

$$\longrightarrow$$

Thus far, there are no points along your main path, no milestones, no faulty or return paths, and certainly no support or development for these paths. Now think about your general conclusions and general approach to the issue in relationship to this empty line. If you could place only one point along this line, what would it be? What *one* point, in other words, do you think your conclusions allow you to make that might be truly new? The name of this point should be familiar: it is your main point.

Your main point is also the "point" of your essay. All your other points should develop your main point. Your main point encapsulates your position in the issue. It also represents your readers' primary destination. You must focus your plans for freshness within this main point: If your main point is not fresh, neither will your essay be.

When you are trying to find something new to say at any milestone, list your givens (especially the points contained in previous or possible positions) at that milestone and *above* the line representing your main path. Save the space *below* the line for your explorations beyond the givens—for your search of something new to say. This visual convention allows you to check, at a glance, whether you are accounting for your givens and moving beyond them as well. Let's now turn to the steps you can work through to decide on your main point.

Search For Your Main Point at "Seeing the Issue"

Try to locate your main point at "seeing the issue." Start by listing your givens at this milestone. Fill in your empty line of argument under "seeing the issue" with the name of your approach, the previous authors and potential positions that have taken it, along with general names reminding you of the problem cases most commonly talked about in your issue.

For us, this meant filling out our empty line of argument in the manner below. Although these notes are brief, they were enough to remind us of a wealth of information in our notes about problem cases in the wilderness issue.

FILLING IN OUR GIVENS AT "SEEING THE ISSUE" IN WILDERNESS

Givens at "seeing the issue"

Psychological approach
(Taken previously by Swain)

Problem cases involving
   Parks
   Uninhabited land
   Wild terrain

——————————————————————————————————→

Once you've set up your givens at "seeing the issue," you are ready to explore beyond them for something fresh. Ask yourself, "Do my conclusions give me a reason to define a new approach? Do they give me a dramatically expanded set of problem cases through which to see the issue?" If you can answer yes to one or both of these questions, you will have found something fresh to say to your community about how to see the issue.

There is a clear advantage to looking for your main point at "seeing the issue" before any other milestone. When you say something fresh at this milestone, you have the opportunity to make the most radical change in your community. You are not only helping your community make progress toward a resolution, you also have the potential to teach it how to see the true dimensions of the issue through which they must make progress. You have the opportunity not only to address your community, but to surprise it, to show it that the issue they need to resolve is substantially larger than the issue they have so far discussed.

In brief, you should always try to place your main point at "seeing the issue" first because that is the milestone where you can *enlarge the issue.* Authors who enlarge issues in the attempt to resolve them make the most valued contributions. Before any community can resolve an issue, it must understand the issue's true proportions. Authors who enlarge issues teach their communities about these proportions.

To search for ways to enlarge your issue, use your conclusions to explore for new analogies or new frameworks. New analogies are concrete situations that have never been mentioned or anticipated as problem cases in your issue, but which you now see as needing to be included as problem cases—and whose inclusion as problem cases may justify your defining a new approach to the issue.

For example, after setting up our givens at "seeing the issue," we explored our conclusions ("Wilderness offers security and stability") for new analogies. We asked ourselves if we could locate fresh problem situations that arise in the tension between our goals of "progress" and our goals of "stability in the face of rapid change." We came up with answers such as efforts to preserve historical landmarks against bulldozers, to support costly restoration efforts against modern architecture, and so on. Because our approach to wilderness cast "progress" versus "stability" as the basic tension in the issue, it seemed to us that these urban problem cases (so far unfamiliar to the wilderness issue) were really part of a common issue with wilderness.

Frameworks are technical concepts and methods used by communities to see, define, and resolve the problem cases in an issue. New frameworks are frameworks that your community has not yet applied or anticipated applying to the problem cases in your issue, but which you see as relevant to apply. Usually, your search for new frameworks becomes relevant after you have found new analogies.

For example, after we linked problem cases in urban restoration with problem cases in wilderness, our thoughts immediately turned to the technical literature of urban planning. Did urban planners have a framework of concepts and methods for discussing problem cases that would perhaps also apply to conventional problem cases in wilderness? We did not pursue this lead, but if we had, we would have been able to add a fresh framework to the discussion, and we would most certainly have labeled a new approach—perhaps the "urbanological" approach. However, don't expect to add new frameworks to the discussion without committing yourself to mastering the framework you are planning to introduce.

After trying to enlarge the issue through new analogies and frameworks, our visual notes came to look as follows:

EXPLORING BEYOND THE GIVENS AT "SEEING THE ISSUE" IN WILDERNESS

Givens at "seeing the issue"

Psychological approach
(Taken previously by Swain)

Problem cases involving
    Parks
    Uninhabited land
    Wild terrain

———————————————————————————→

Our Conclusions:
"Wilderness offers security and stability."

Other situations valid as problem cases
    Landmark buildings
    Historic sites
    Museums

If your search for new analogies or frameworks fails, you cannot enlarge your issue. You forfeit the dramatic effect of unveiling one or more fresh problem cases, systematically connected to the issue, but fully unanticipated and unexpected. To achieve freshness without enlarging the issue, you must rely on assembling the parts of the positions you've explored into a fresh line of argument. In other words, you will recycle your line of argument by reorganizing and varying the details of old parts into an original line of argument.

Perhaps you want to raise problem cases that aren't dramatically new or unexpected, but still, in your estimation, have yet to be discussed in the detail you deem appropriate. A writer like Nash may have had this in mind when he decided to discuss problem cases in wilderness that may have been acknowledged previously, but not in the detail he offers. Or perhaps you notice a disagreement over which problem cases are most central to the issue and you want to argue on behalf of your own paradigms. Adopting an economic approach to the issue, for example, you may want to defend Tucker's paradigms over Nash's. Each of these instances gives you a reason to place your main point at "seeing the issue" through the recycling method.

Search For Your Main Point at "Choosing a Solution"

Suppose after seeking ways to enlarge or recycle issues, you fail to locate your main point at "seeing the issue." Shift your focus to the third milestone, "choosing a solution." Enumerate the solutions that have already been proposed and then explore whether your conclusions allow you to go beyond them. After listing the solutions that have already been given, you should nearly always find that you can use your conclusions to propose a solution that is your own.

For example, turning our focus to solutions, we listed the solutions already given to the wilderness issue. We then started with our conclusions and challenged ourselves to come up with a solution that went beyond the solutions we had been given. We felt that a solution which studied the human cost of losing wilderness would be consistent with our conclusions about wilderness. We felt that Swain, who shared our psychological approach to the issue, presumed to know that human cost. We felt that it was still unknown and a reasonable solution would need to determine how great the cost was. Here is what our exploration looked like:

EXPLORING BEYOND THE GIVENS AT "CHOOSING A SOLUTION" IN WILDERNESS

Givens at "choosing a solution"

"Promote access"
"Limit access"
"Blow up the dam"
"Develop wilderness"
"Create a renewable economy"

———————————————————————————————————→

Our conclusions:
"Wilderness offers
security and stability."

Our solution: "Study the
human cost of
losing wilderness."

If enlarging the issue at "seeing the issue" can be difficult, saying something fresh at "choosing a solution" is typically easy—sometimes too easy to be informative. You may recall that our natural inclination is to think of issues in terms of solutions. Should someone give you proposal A, B, or C, you can usually come up with proposal D, often a trivial variation of the others. Just because you can come up with such a minor variation does not mean that it has earned its way to the status of your main point.

A general rule about solutions: Never decide to place your main point at "choosing a solution" merely on the evidence that you can generate a new solution. On that evidence alone, you would always be fooled into placing your main point at solutions, even when you have almost nothing of interest to say about them. Demand two types of additional evidence before placing your main point at solutions.

First, convince yourself that there is widespread agreement at "defining the problem." Establish that most in your community take the problem definition as settled and are ready to move on to solutions. Second, inventory your own knowledge and make sure you have a great deal fresh to say about the positive and negative effects of previous solutions and the one you propose. Make sure you've gone into the cost, feasibility, and logistics of alternative solutions and the one you propose. Make sure you can speak at length about the comparative strengths and faults of each.

In our case, neither of these circumstances applied. It was clear that in the wilderness issue, there was no widely accepted problem definition. Nor did we have a great deal to say about the implementation details of our solution. We had no idea how a study of the human cost of losing wilderness would be carried out. We just felt one was needed. These observations suggested to us that we had to turn to "defining the problem" for our main point.

Search For Your Main Point at "Defining the Problem"

Thus far, we've indicated that placing certain main points at "seeing the issue" can fail because they are too hard to establish, and that placing other main points at "choosing a solution" can fail because they are too easy. Your third alternative, placing your main point at "defining the problem," is usually your best bet when the others fail.

Unlike the other milestones, "defining the problem" is hard to rule out for your main point; it's also hard to rule in. Consequently, it's best to look to the other milestones first. If you can rule the others out, place your main point at "defining the problem" by default.

Suppose you have now searched and eliminated the other milestones for your main point. You know you will place your main point at "defining the problem." List the problem definitions that have been given to you and then formulate one that goes beyond the givens. Make sure your fresh solution and your fresh problem definition are coordinated with one another. Your solution should eliminate either the X or the Y in your problem definition. Since our solution involved "studying the human cost of losing wilderness," we knew our problem definition involved a conflict between a goal (wanting to rely on wilderness for security and stability) and our knowledge (not knowing the price we would pay if we could no longer rely on it for these needs). Our search at "defining the problem" thus resulted in the following notes to ourselves:

EXPLORING BEYOND THE GIVENS AT "DEFINING THE PROBLEM" IN WILDERNESS

Givens at "defining the problem"

X: Free access   *but*   Y: We are loving wilderness to death.
X: Preserve wilderness   *but*   Y: Consume its resources. (etc.)

Our conclusions: "Wilderness offers security and stability."

Our problem definition:
X: We want wilderness protected because it offers security against rapid change.
but
Y: We don't know the human cost of losing wilderness.

For Class 13.1

Pick one from the following list of conclusions in the wilderness issue. Then use that conclusion to design a main point that goes beyond the points of any of the authors you have read on wilderness. Indicate whether you place your main point at "seeing the issue," "defining the problem," or "choosing a solution" and give your reasons why.

Possible Conclusions in the Wilderness Issue

1. Wilderness reminds us that "the best things in life" are still free.
2. Wilderness reminds us that everything now has a price.
3. Nature probably is too good for us after all.
4. There is no irony in our victory over wilderness.
5. You really can love wilderness to death.

For Your Notebook #28

In this notebook entry, using your conclusions on wilderness, decide on your main point and on the milestone at which you will place it. Take the following steps:

- Start with the conclusions you have drawn from exploring your issue.
- Using your conclusions, search "seeing the issue" for your main point.
- Using your conclusions, search "choosing a solution" for your main point.
- Using your conclusions, search "defining the problem" for your main point.

FILL IN YOUR LINE OF ARGUMENT AROUND YOUR MAIN POINT

Fill In Points at the Remaining Milestones

Once you have decided on your main point and where to locate it along your line of argument, draw in your points at the remaining milestones. If your main point is about defining the problem, fill in your points at "seeing the issue" and "choosing a solution"; if it is about choosing a solution, fill in your points at "seeing the issue" and "defining the problem"; and so on. Once you have your main point, filling in points at other milestones isn't hard at all. Just apply the following rules of thumb:

RULES OF THUMB FOR FILLING IN POINTS AT OTHER MILESTONES

1. If you locate your main point at "seeing the issue," fill "defining the problem" with an "X *but* Y" description that covers the cases you introduce or emphasize. Fill in a solution that eliminates either the X or the Y.
2. If you locate your main point at "defining the problem," fill in paradigms (at "seeing the issue") with tensions that your definition captures; fill in solutions that eliminate either the X or the Y in your definition.

3. If you locate your main point at "choosing a solution," fill in (at "defining the problem") an "X but Y" that your solution can remove or relieve; fill in paradigms (at "seeing the issue") with tensions that your definition captures.

These rules ensure that your main path flows from seeing to resolving in a tight logical chain. Your problem definition will capture the tension in your paradigms. Your solution will relieve that tension. For example, suppose we located our main point at "seeing the issue," based on the analogy between problem cases in wilderness and problem cases in urban settings (should we destroy or restore this old house?). We thus had to come up with a problem definition that would be sure to include these additional cases and a solution that would be sure to eliminate the X or the Y in our definition. We arrived at the following main path:

AN ORIGINAL MAIN PATH THROUGH WILDERNESS

Paradigms	X: We want to preserve these objects for stability *but* Y: We don't know the human cost of losing them.	Solution
Wilderness		"Study costs."
Old houses		(Eliminates Y)
Decayed landmarks		

$$\longrightarrow$$

Seeing the issue	Defining the problem	Choosing a solution

Search For and Distribute Faulty and Return Paths

Once you sketch your main path, you are ready to add faulty and return paths to it. As before, there are easy rules of thumb you can use to find your faulty and return paths:

RULES OF THUMB FOR ADDING FAULTY AND RETURN PATHS

1. To add faulty paths at "seeing the issue," discuss the problem cases that miss the tensions you see in your paradigms. To add return paths, indicate which tension-producing aspects you find missing from these problem cases. You will then be able to introduce your own paradigms as examples of cases conveying the tension-producing aspects you associate with the issue.

2. To add faulty paths at "defining the problem," discuss any problem definition that denies the X or denies the Y in your own problem definition. To add return paths, indicate that the first set of problem definitions misses the X; indicate that the second misses the Y. You will then be able to introduce your own problem definition as capturing both sides of the conflict.

3. To add faulty paths at "choosing a solution," discuss any solutions that would remove the problem as you define it, but not in the way your solution would remove it. That is, if your solution would resolve the "X *but* Y" by eliminating the Y, discuss as faulty any solution that would eliminate the X. To add return paths, indicate why X is part of the tension that can't be eliminated.

These rules ensure that as your main path progresses, you will bring into your discussion those faulty paths that can make your own directions less misleading to readers. Bear in mind the two reasons why you want to include faulty paths in your directions to readers. First, in many instances, your readers will expect you to do more than say what you think. They will also expect you to have read and to have contrasted your own position with that of a previous author or authors—simply because these authors are famous, or are assumed to have had the final word on the issue, or both. If you fail to mention these authors and contrast your position with theirs, your readers may think you haven't done your homework or that you are trying to reinvent the wheel.

Second, in many instances, you will find that the position of another author or authors, famous or not, provides a neat comparison and contrast with your own. You thus find that discussing this alternative position can only make your own clearer. You rely on other positions, that is, to provide a background against which to pinpoint the exact twists and turns of your own position. You supply this background for your own main path by indicating how these alternative positions fall short—why they are faulty.

If you wish to discuss more than one faulty path at a single milestone, make sure you do so at the milestone where you have placed your main point. Above all, you will want readers to follow your main point. Discussing multiple faulty (and return) paths as alternatives to your main point can help ensure that they do. Also, if you decide to include multiple faulty paths at a milestone, first discuss the ones that you judge to be most flawed (and farthest from your own position). Then move to those that you consider more reasonable, closer to your own direction. Then (when you have run out of faulty paths) move to, or reiterate, your own point.

By sustaining this movement, you will give readers the impression that you are narrowing the space of possible positions until your own point emerges as the last remaining and most plausible candidate. You will also make it easier for your readers to reconstruct the decisions that led you away from your faulty paths, onto your return paths, and back onto your main path.

Notice that faulty paths are not random positions you do not like. They are actual or possible positions that you want to make sure your readers realize you are not advocating. By concentrating faulty paths around your main point, you make your own path perceptually easier for readers to grasp.

Applying the above rules of thumb, we knew exactly the kind of positions we needed to function as faulty paths. At "seeing the issue," for example, we knew we could clarify the tension-producing aspects in our own paradigms by characterizing as faulty positions built on problem cases that overlooked these aspects.

We found our own paradigms could be broken into the following problem aspects:

ASPECTS OF OUR PARADIGMS IN THE WILDERNESS ISSUE

Agent: humans
Action: destroying objects with historical interest
Goal: to make "progress"
Result: things with secure ties to our past are destroyed.

The action and result aspects seemed most tension-producing for us. And yet many descriptions of the tensions in the issue overlook these aspects. We thus knew to search for problem cases (and positions built on problem cases) that lacked these aspects. By finding these positions and assigning them to faulty paths, we could throw into sharper relief for readers our own main path at "seeing the issue."

At "defining the problem," we knew we could place on a faulty path, as a point of contrast with our own problem definition, any position that denied either the X or the Y in our own formulation. In other words, we could assign to faulty paths positions that denied either of the following: (1) "Our goal is to preserve wilderness for its ties to our past"; (2) "We don't yet know the human cost of losing wilderness." By arguing that each of these positions lacked key components of the problem, we could then introduce our own problem definition as bringing these components together into a single definition.

At "choosing a solution," we knew we could place on a faulty path, in contrast with our solution, any position that resolved our "X *but* Y" in a way different from our own resolution. Since our resolution tried to eliminate the Y (our lack of knowledge about the human cost of losing wilderness), we knew we could stalk positions that argued for the opposite resolution (that we eliminate our goal to preserve wilderness because of the stable links to the past it offers).

Sketching out this strategy in notes to ourselves, we could now visualize on paper our line of argument complete with faulty and return paths. We offer our notes below. While still sketchy from the point of view of a final draft, they provide a fairly complete plan of how we intended to direct readers through the wilderness issue in an original essay.

FAULTY AND RETURN PATHS ADDED TO A MAIN PATH

Paradigms	X: We want to preserve	Solution
↓	these objects for	
Wilderness	stability	"Study costs."
Old houses	*but*	(Eliminates Y)
Decayed landmarks	Y: We don't know the	
	human cost of losing	
	them.	

————————————————————————————→ Our main path

Seeing the issue	Defining the problem	Choosing a solution
Faulty paths:	*Faulty paths:*	*Faulty paths:*
wilderness as economic resource	Positions that deny X	Positions that eliminate X
	(wilderness gives us a stable link to the past)	(that would try to eliminate our goal to preserve wilderness for purposes of stability with our past)
Coal deposits	and	
Minerals	Positions that deny Y	
Paper		
Return paths:	(we don't yet understand the human cost)	
Misses reasons why we want to restore stable links to the past	*Return paths:*	
	Show that both X and Y are essential to the problem	

❖❖

For Class 13.2

Using the main point on wilderness you designed in For Class 13.1, develop a line of argument around it. Use the rules of thumb in this section to fill in points at other milestones along your main path. Also use the rules of thumb we've provided to fill in faulty and return paths as well. Create a diagram showing your complete line of argument and be prepared to discuss it in class.

For Your Notebook #29

In this notebook entry, you'll design your line of argument around the main point that you've generated for your own issue. Take the following steps:

- Fill in your points at other milestones. Make sure your points at each milestone make a consistent line of argument with your main point.
- Fill in faulty and return paths at each milestone.

⬜⬜ 14 DRAFT YOUR
⬜⬜⬜ ORIGINAL ESSAY

In the last chapter, you visualized a line of argument for your essay—a main path, faulty paths, and return paths. An essay, however, is a line of argument fleshed out into prose. An essay leads readers through the subtle twists and turns of your line of argument. Besides main, faulty, and return paths, it includes various kinds of statements that allow you to support and amplify these paths, and that give your readers special guidance when you have to make your directions complex.

Your textual directions reach their climax (but do not necessarily stop) at your main point. Your main point, in other words, is the featured destination to which your directions lead. The line of argument you visualized in the last chapter functions as the outline of the body of your original essay. Besides the body, your original essay also has an introduction and conclusion. The function of each part is diagramed below:

THE FUNCTION OF THE THREE PARTS OF YOUR ESSAY

Raises question to be answered in body	Offers your line of argument as detailed response to question	Indicates progress made and progress remaining with your response
Introduction	Body	Conclusion

DRAFT THE INTRODUCTION

As shown above, your introduction raises the question that the body of your essay will answer. This question is sometimes called the *crux* or the question at the crux. It is the major question that you define when seeking to contribute to a community. It may or may not be the same major question that you attribute to the community when synthesizing previous positions. You find your crux by thinking of your line of argument as an answer to a question. You've worked hard thus far to find your line of argument. But if your line of argument is the answer, what is the question? When you discover the question that needs your line of argument as answer, you have your question at the crux.

244

The purpose of your introduction is to give your readers the background and incentive they need to understand the question at the crux and to seek an answer for it. Once they have this background and incentive, you can move on to the body, where you begin your answer. Often, you conclude the introduction with a *thesis statement*. A thesis statement does not give your response to the question at the crux (the entire body of your essay does that). Rather a thesis statement previews your response in a single statement.

The length of your introduction depends on how far away, in understanding or incentive, your readers are from asking and wanting to answer the question at the crux. The farther away your readers are from your question, the more information your introduction will need to supply to close the distance. Put yourself in your readers' shoes. Where do they stand in relation to your question and your response? Do they now have the incentive to ask the question you are asking? If not, give them the incentive. Are they now able to understand the question you are asking? If not, give them the information they need to understand it. Would they resist asking the question you want to ask? If so, consider what they would need to hear to reduce their resistance to it and then tell them.

What follows is a checklist of information your reader needs in order to understand your question at the crux and to want to hear your answer to it.

CHECKLIST OF BACKGROUND INFORMATION FOR AN INTRODUCTION

A. Historical accounts that transcend approaches in your issue
B. Problem cases that transcend approaches in your issue
C. The fact that there are different approaches
D. The approach you will be taking
E. History and problem cases associated with your approach
F. The major question occupying authors within your approach
G. The question you place at the crux
H. Your thesis statement to preview your response

The background information here moves from the general to the specific. Note that this is a checklist, however, and not a rigid sequence of how every introduction changes focus from the general to the specific. Usually, you won't want to proceed mechanically from the top of the list to the bottom. But if your readers know absolutely nothing about the issue, you will need to start with A and work your way straight down. If they are already familiar with your approach, you might start with D and work down. If they are aware of the major question dominating the community, you will need to move them from that question to your crux (if these questions are different). If they also know the question you place at the crux, you can begin an essay with "My thesis is that. . . ." When you and your readers share a deep background in the issue, introductions are easy.

When drafting your introduction, you might find it convenient to layer your introduction upward from the bottom of the list to the top. Start with paragraphs introducing items G and H—your question and response. This introduction should serve well for readers who share your knowledge of the issue, your approach to the issue, and your understanding of previous sources.

Now think about the readers this introduction will still miss. To pull in readers who don't know your sources, add a few more paragraphs in front of your original introduction with information from item F. You will thus be adding information about your sources and your relationship to them.

You still may lose readers who don't know the specific approach within which you are working. Cater to these readers by adding more paragraphs in front of the previous ones with information from items C–E. This will force you to bring out what you know about the specific approach you are taking.

Finally, there may be readers who know nothing about the issue at all, its history, or its problem cases. For the benefit of these readers, compose even earlier paragraphs with information from items A and B. With these additions, you aren't likely to exclude any literate adult from your discussion.

When you are writing for a general audience, assume that your readers don't share your knowledge of your issue or your sources. So for general audiences a longer, carefully prepared introduction is probably better than a shorter, abbreviated one. Since you move from the general to the specific in your introduction, increase the range of audiences you can address by composing from the bottom of the list to the top.

For Class 14.1

After exploring the wilderness issue, you've taught yourself about its history and standard problem cases. You've identified three approaches: an economic, a deprivational, and a psychological approach. You align yourself with the psychological approach. Your line of argument focuses its main point at "seeing the issue." Using the analogy of wilderness as a cultural landmark, your line of argument suggests that wilderness is a landmark that ensures stability in our lives against a background where all other landmarks (historic buildings, bridges) are being torn down. You identify this line of argument with your response. You identify your crux with the question "What explains our psychological need for wilderness?" You believe your line of argument responds to this question.

Now you need to draft an introduction to your line of argument. You consider every audience you want to reach, from the most to the least knowledgeable about the issue. The following list describes all the readers you want your introduction to catch somewhere along the way:

- Readers who know your question at the crux, but not your thesis
- Readers who know your sources, but not your question at the crux

- Readers who know your general approach, but not your sources
- Readers who know something about the issue, but not your approach
- Readers who know nothing about the issue

For each set of readers in the list, draft a one-to-three-paragraph introduction that you think would prepare them to understand your question at the crux and to motivate them to want to hear your response. As you move down the list, compose your introductory paragraphs in ascending order so that later paragraphs are written above earlier ones. As your paragraphs grow from bottom to top, check to see whether your introduction includes the wider circle of readers you intend for it.

DRAFT THE BODY

When you draft the body, you are writing down in connected prose your line of argument, your directions through the issue. Like any good directions, yours should focus on points where you think readers are most likely to misunderstand or misinterpret you, or at points that your readers must understand if they are to understand your main point. Rely on the stylistic techniques for signaling main and faulty paths we discussed in Chapter 3 to help readers distinguish the points you are making from the faulty positions you are only characterizing.

The most time-consuming part of drafting your essay comes when you work on supporting and developing your main point. Your main point is what you claim is new in your essay. It can therefore be the essay's weak link. For if it doesn't convince, neither will your essay. As such, your main point should attract the most traffic in your line of argument—the largest number of faulty and return paths, the most support and development, the most complex linguistic signaling. Your readers, wondering whether you have something new to say and what, will dwell on your main point to see what sort of case your essay is trying to make. When they evaluate the strengths and faults of your line of argument, they will take special note of what you do to defend and develop your main point.

Make sure you support your points—especially your main point—according to the external standards of your community. Different communities require authors to meet different standards of support before they are willing to recognize their new points as valid contributions. In the technical communities of mathematicians and scientists, for example, having a strategically sound and new point to contribute is only the beginning. Mathematicians must often cast their "new ideas" in theorems that can be proved before they are acknowledged to have contributed something new. Scientists typically design studies to test their "new ideas" as hypotheses before the scientific community acknowledges them to have said something new. And humanists must meet standards involving a high degree of plausibility, abundance, and converging support before their "new ideas" are recognized as legitimate contributions. When you learn to write for a specialized community, you learn special conventions for the type and amount of support you must marshal to have *your* "new ideas" recognized as contributions.

What if you are a freshman contributing to a classroom community under a strict deadline? Under such conditions, your community will require only "some reasonable support and amplification" in order for your new ideas to be recognized as contributions. For a student learning to write from sources for the first time, that requirement is probably enough.

Imagine a freshman on the wilderness issue who comes up with the following crux: "What is the psychological importance of wilderness to us?" and answers with the following main point: "Wilderness represents a stable landmark that offers us security in a world of change." Now imagine that the student, drafting that point, tries to offer "some reasonable support and amplification" as follows:

A STUDENT'S DRAFT OF A MAIN POINT IN WILDERNESS

I never knew my father's father, but I knew the tree he climbed as a boy and the street he lived on. It was important for my father to show me these landmarks because he wanted me to know his father. And I'm sure when I'm a parent I'll want my son or daughter to know about my father through a set of landmarks that touched his life.

But, nowadays, it seems harder and harder to identify landmarks that will last. My father's school has been leveled and turned into a parking lot. The house he grew up in is now part of a shopping mall. Now, as a college student, I find that even many of the landmarks of my own childhood have disappeared. The store where I used to buy candy is now a dry cleaners. I used to have my bike fixed at a place that is now a restaurant. A grave site is about the only place you can count on not changing . . . and perhaps a wilderness. If that is so, then we can understand the problem the preservationist is really trying to solve and why a solution is so important.

Oh, I suspect my readers are thinking I am guilty of the same sentimentalism that Tucker accused some pro-wilderness writers of showing. Am I not also glamorizing wilderness, turning it into a religion to be worshiped?

I don't think so. I am not trying to associate wilderness with Eastern mysticism. I am saying that wilderness now embodies a very powerful Yankee ideal—the ownership of and attachment to land. For our ancestors, land was plentiful if you were willing to destroy a wilderness to get it.

Now more and more land is being developed and fewer and fewer of us lay any real claim to it. People don't own land anymore. Banks do. Investors do. The cardinal rule of real estate these days is not to become attached, even when you do call yourself an owner.

In our transient society, people are just as likely to put roots in a profession as in a place, a neighborhood. To be unwilling to move, to be unwilling to uproot, is economic suicide. The steelworkers of western Pennsylvania discovered this lesson the hard way in the early 1980s. Laid off from their jobs, they at first refused to believe their life as steelworkers was over. Their parents had worked in the mills and so had their parents' parents. They had taken pride in their community. They had built schools. They had built churches. Their community mattered. How could the economic fluctuation of steel destroy all that?

But it did. And now most of these small mill towns are desolate ghost towns, their residents long since scattered, like the wind, across the country.

Wilderness used to be our great frontier, our great unknown. But now it is civilization that has become uncertain, mysterious. It is civilization that holds all the surprises. In the midst of this change, we've gradually transformed our wilderness into places for security, stability, comfort, relaxation, even attachment. These are the reasons we should grit our teeth when people look at our wilderness and see only a better parking lot.

The support and amplification are from the freshman author's personal experience. The standards of support are not high enough to justify publication in a scholarly journal. Perhaps a student newspaper would publish it. In any case, to its credit, an essay employing these arguments has a main point to make that is "new" (both accountable and fresh in relation to a handful of other authors) with at least "some reasonable support and amplification" as backing. As we mentioned, for freshman authors first learning how to contribute, this seems an appropriate standard.

If you are an advanced student or beginning professional contributing to a community outside the classroom (for example, the community of your disciplinary major), you'll be expected to meet the external standards of support that are specified by your community. To do this, you may need to acquire more background knowledge and to summarize and synthesize more sources in order to substantiate your main point. Moreover, you may need to rely on analytic tools (such as statistics, spreadsheets, mathematical models, experiments, computer simulations) more specialized than the techniques we discussed in analyzing.

Imagine, for example, that a more experienced author, an urban planning expert, came to the same personal insight about wilderness as our freshman writer. Also assume that the expert is trying to contribute to a scholarly journal that demands a "high preponderance" of support in accordance with the standards upheld in the urban planning literature. For our experienced author, the personal insight of relating wilderness to cultural landmarks would not be a cue to finish drafting. Instead, it would be a cue to open a search for sources on cultural landmarks, urban decay and restoration, and other topics the expert might need to meet the standards of his or her profession.

Once you've elaborated your main point to the standards required by your community, you should look for opportunities to add road signals to your text, especially around your main point, where your directions to the reader are likely to become unavoidably complex. Concessions, disclaimers, qualifications, and conditionals are such signals. They can greatly increase the accuracy with which you are able to give directions.

Concessions direct readers to "stay on my course" when you are developing a point and describing a fault in it ("Granted that . . . yet"; "Admittedly . . . but"). By conceding faults in your own points, you show your readers that you are aware of the imperfections in your own directions—and that there are no better alternatives. Also use concessions to urge readers to abandon faulty paths even in the face of their strengths. By conceding strengths in faulty paths, you show your readers that you have an open mind about alternatives—though your course remains best.

Compose *disclaimers* when you find yourself making accurate statements that may lead your readers to inaccurate inferences. Disclaimers ("I don't mean to imply that") block these inferences. *Conditionals* and *qualifications* modify statements that are too strong. Readers who will reject directions that claim too much ("X is true") will often accept them once they have been modified by a conditional ("If X is true, then . . .") or a qualification ("X is sometimes true").

DRAFT THE CONCLUSION

Your main point takes your readers beyond the community's current discussion, but probably not to a resolution. After you've introduced and elaborated your main point, your readers will want some perspective. They will want to know how far toward a resolution your point has taken them. They will want to know where it falls short. They will want to know something about the questions that still need to be asked to continue making progress toward a resolution of the issue.

What follows are four suggestions about what to include as you draft your conclusion. First, consider discussing how your line of argument needs further confirmation. It's rare when an author can answer the question at the crux with certainty; it's also rare when a community accepts a single author's answer as definitive without confirmation from other authors. Understand that no matter how high your standards of support, you are likely to need confirmation from later authors before the community will recognize your response as a definitive step of progress. It's thus a good idea, in the conclusion, to invite such further confirmation and to discuss what sort of confirmation is needed.

Second, discuss the parts of your question that remain unanswered. Your thesis attempts to answer the question at the crux. However, it's quite unusual for your response to fit your question as snugly as glove fits hand. Typically, your question is large, open-ended, and can be viewed from many angles. In order to support your response to it, however, you've had to narrow the response, focus it, and develop it from a consistent point of view. As a result, parts of your question are sure to remain unanswered. In addition, there are sure to be parts you have answered that deserve answers from approaches different from your own. Your conclusion is the right place to discuss what more can be done to make further progress in answering your question.

Third, discuss the next questions to answer. Assume for the moment that you can confirm your response and that your response offers complete coverage of your question. There still remain questions to ask and answer before a resolution is possible. What are these questions? Your readers will appreciate hearing about them in your conclusion.

Fourth, discuss the implications of your main point for later milestones. To visualize your line of argument, you had to place your main point at a particular milestone. Suppose your main point lies at the milestone "defining the problem." Then you've given your community some direction about how to abstract the tension from problem cases. But what are the implications of your direction-giving for solutions? You may have discussed solutions in your body, but only as a immediate follow-up to your problem definition. What if you want to discuss implications for solutions that involve the "big picture"—that point toward the full resolution of the issue? The conclusion is the right place to discuss such big-picture implications involving later milestones.

For Class 14.2

Draft a two-page essay from the line of argument you developed in For Class 13.2. Write an introductory paragraph for readers who are newcomers to the wilderness issue. Elaborate your line of argument just enough to mention your main, faulty, and return paths at each milestone. Offer "some reasonable support" for your main point (one or two paragraphs from your personal experience or background knowledge). Your main point should be "new" relative to the authors you've so far read on the wilderness issue. To work this exercise, do the following:

A. Outline the body.
B. Draft the introduction.
C. Draft the body.
D. Draft the conclusion.

Exchange your paper with a partner. Evaluate your partner's paper to see if it says something new (relative to Julber, Nash, and the others) under the criterion of "some reasonable support" offered for the main point.

For Your Notebook #30

In this notebook entry, you will outline and draft an original essay, of a length specified by your teacher. Elaborate your main point for whatever community standard you are trying to work within. If you are writing for classroom standards, offering "some reasonable support" may be sufficient (check with your teacher). If you are writing for the standards of a larger community, then perhaps a higher standard for support is called for. Take enough time to make sure that you have a new main point and a standard of support for it that is appropriate to your community. Work in the following order:

- Use your line of argument as the outline of the body.
- Draft the introduction.
- Draft the body according to the appropriate standard of support.
- Draft the conclusion.

Hand in a rough draft to your teacher, adviser, colleague, or some other reader for comments on two features of your draft: Do I have a main point that is new? Are my standards of support for my main point adequate for my community? Revise your draft only for these features until your reader can answer yes to both. When that happens, you will have a draft that has the minimally essential features for a contribution.

REVISE FOR PRECISION AND COHERENCE

Once you have roughed out a first draft, you are almost certain to confront a number of lingering problems: Your line of argument won't be entirely clear, even to you; you may find that important assertions along your main path are still lacking in support and development; you may wonder whether you are being fair to the authors or positions you've characterized as faulty; you may doubt in some places whether your return paths are supported well enough to coax your readers to return to your main path; and finally, you may sense that the contrast between your line of argument and your faulty paths is so slight or subtle that even you aren't quite sure of the difference that supposedly defines your effort as new.

These problems occur because in the effort to get everything down on paper, you can't get everything right. At some point, you have to use your draft to search for gaps or inconsistencies in your line of argument and then make repairs. All the strategies we have discussed so far, from summarizing to contributing, apply as much in the context of revising a draft as they do in helping you compose one. If you sense that your draft is unfair to an author or misrepresents beliefs common to a group of authors, you will appreciate, perhaps better than before, why skills of summarizing and synthesizing are important. If you find that your draft has no concrete issue to talk about, you will understand the importance of locating paradigms and then testing problem definitions and solutions against them. If you suspect that your draft excludes readers you want to include, you will recognize that you have yet to take advantage of all the options that are available to you in fashioning an introduction.

In fact, you will often find it simpler to work with these strategies backward from an existing draft. Revising a rough draft always gives you a perspective that you could not have had before the draft was written. Working from the hindsight of your draft, you can focus on how best to use these strategies to fine-tune or elaborate a line of argument that lacks precision or coherence.

To show you how this perspective works, we will follow Michele, an actual student, as she revised to improve the precision and coherence of a line of argument she had drafted on the wilderness issue. We begin with Michele's original draft. As you read it, ask yourself where you think her line of argument needs to be improved and how you would improve it. Then check your answers against the analysis of another reader, which follows the draft.

Michele's Draft on the Wilderness Issue

Our ancestors struggled to tame the American frontier and would not likely have envisioned a time when Americans would fear its disappearance and debate the terms of its continued existence. Some authors like Eric Julber and Roderick Nash agree that wilderness is an issue about "access" but fundamentally disagree for whom. According to Julber (par. 19), the public should enjoy full access to wilderness areas. According to Nash, wilderness access should be limited by a strict quota system (par. 20). What these authors fail to consider is that neither of their positions will be relevant if there is no wilderness to have access to. The issue of maintenance is more important than the issue of access.

Paul and Anne Ehrlich, on the other hand, take a different interest in wilderness. They are mainly concerned with preserving species and natural formations. They view the issue as ecologists and do not consider the economic implications of preserving wilderness. They thus miss the point that we live in a world of supply and demand, and that the natural resources provided by our wilderness areas are in great demand. As Edward Swain states, "In North America, wilderness areas are presently being destroyed through the consumption of nonrenewable resources in an effort to maintain our standard of living" (par. 19). Swain further contends that we will eventually be forced to create a "renewable" economy when our natural resources run out. But even Swain seems to overlook the fact that we have the technological capability to devise substitutes for virtually anything. We have already developed solar power in an attempt to diminish our need for gas and oil power. Why can't the same be done for all the natural resources for which we currently rely on wilderness?

Martin Krieger in his essay entitled "What's Wrong with Plastic Trees?" (cited in Swain) suggests that humans can adapt to a wildernessless environment. The flaw in his argument is that if we can adapt to plastic trees, then we can also adapt our technology so that we don't need plastic trees.

Unfortunately technology can never bring back what is lost. Extinction of species today is more serious than it was in the past because the same human activities that are causing extinction are the same activities that are preventing diversity from being regenerated (Ehrlichs, 31). When we lose an animal or plant species, it is gone forever.

Opponents to my argument will argue that there is plenty of wilderness and that a few thousand acres here and there are not worth worrying about. That may be true presently. But what will happen five years from now? . . . fifty years? . . . 100 years? How long can we chip away at our wilderness areas before we finally say that there isn't much wilderness left?

Perhaps this won't happen in our lifetime, or our children's lifetime. But our legacy to future generations will be one of barrenness that could be avoided if we act now to develop our technology to avoid raping the land for natural resources. William Tucker doesn't see the loss of our land as a problem and in fact is appalled that we import logs or natural resources when we have vast resources of our own (par. 15). His attitude itself is appalling.

The true problem we face is that while we want to preserve wilderness, we also believe there is no harm in developing some of our land for its natural resources. As the economic demand for this land grows, so will the temptation to apportion more and more for development. As long as we tolerate a definition of wilderness as a divisible economic commodity, we will always be tempted to divide it into smaller chunks and sell it to the highest bidder. One could also say that there is a desire by many people for Picassos. But we would find it appalling to cut a Picasso painting into chunks and distribute them to consumers. Instead replicas of the paintings are made and distributed. Of course the replicas may not be quite as good as the original, but people are satisfied because the natural beauty of the original is left intact. The same principle should be applied to our natural resources.

Perhaps the author who is closest to my position is Edward Abbey. As a purist, his solution is to leave the land alone as God and nature intended (par. 28). In fact, in his solution, he suggests that the Lake Powell reservoir be drained so that Glen Canyon can be restored. Because I am also a purist at heart, I too would like to see the land remain untouched. However, I will admit that, to be realized, Abbey's solution must be expanded to satisfy politicians and

economists. What I propose is to preserve the land by
turning to technology to provide substitutes for
natural resources.

    By using the same principle we apply in
replicating priceless paintings, we can use technology
to save the wilderness instead of destroying it.

When Michele submitted her draft to a reader for comments on the precision and coherence of her line of argument, the reader made the following analysis of problems he found. While the reader had much praise for Michele's first effort, we will focus on his critical comments, which are in italics:

A Reader's Critical Evaluation of Michele's Argument

    Our ancestors struggled to tame the American
frontier and would not likely have envisioned a
time when Americans would fear its disappearance
and debate the terms of its continued existence.

[*The introduction is too short. Michele would miss many general readers.*]

Some authors like Eric Julber and Roderick Nash
agree that wilderness is an issue about "access"
but fundamentally disagree for whom. According to
Julber (par. 19), the public should enjoy full
access to wilderness areas. According to Nash,
wilderness access should be limited by a strict
quota system (par. 20). What these authors fail
to consider is that neither of their positions
will be relevant if there is no wilderness to have
access to. The issue of maintenance is more
important than the issue of access.

[*An unconvincing return path. Michele does not make clear what the issue of maintenance is, so it's impossible to understand why she believes it is more important than the access issue. More support and development are needed both for these faulty paths and Michele's reasons for returning from them.*]

    Paul and Anne Ehrlich, on the other hand,
take a different interest in wilderness. They are
mainly concerned with preserving species and
natural formations. They view the issue as
ecologists and do not consider the economic
implications of preserving wilderness. They thus
miss the point that we live in a world of supply
and demand, and that the natural resources

provided by our wilderness areas are in great
demand. As Edward Swain states, "In North
America, wilderness areas are presently being
destroyed through the consumption of nonrenewable
resources in an effort to maintain our standard of
living" (par. 19). Swain further contends that we
will eventually be forced to create a "renewable"
economy when our natural resources run out. But
even Swain seems to overlook the fact that we have
the technological capability to devise substitutes
for virtually anything. We have already developed
solar power in an attempt to diminish our need for
gas and oil power. Why can't the same be done for
all the natural resources for which we currently
rely on wilderness?

[*Michele raises many faulty paths in this paragraph as well as her reasons for returning from them. But her characterizations both of faulty and return paths are too brief to follow her reasoning. Indeed, Michele had not fully explored her own thinking here in sufficient detail. What makes her argument especially difficult to follow is that she buries her own points by placing them on paths returning from the points she rejects. That is, we find out only what Michele believes by listening to her short replies to points she does not believe.*]

          Martin Krieger in his essay entitled "What's
Wrong with Plastic Trees?" (cited in Swain)
suggests that humans can adapt to a wildernessless
environment. The flaw in his argument is that if
we can adapt to plastic trees, then we can also
adapt our technology so that we don't need plastic
trees.

[*Michele offers yet another faulty and return path sequence, this time citing Krieger. Again, the characterizations pass by too quickly to follow where Michele wants to lead (if indeed she herself is sure). Her return path is almost impossible to understand at this point, but (as we will see) it anticipates her own position.*]

          Unfortunately, technology can never bring
back what is lost. Extinction of species today is
more serious than it was in the past because the
human activities that are causing extinction are
the same activities that are preventing diversity
from being regenerated (Ehrlichs, 31). When we
lose an animal or plant species, it is gone
forever.

[*Michele uses the paragraph above to offer her own point, citing the Ehrlichs for support. However, Michele leaves this point isolated and does not make clear how it fits in with other points along her main path.*]

Opponents to my argument will argue that
there is plenty of wilderness and that a few
thousand acres here and there are not worth
worrying about. That may be true presently. But
what will happen five years from now? . . . fifty
years? . . . 100 years? How long can we chip away
at our wilderness areas before we finally say that
there isn't much wilderness left? Perhaps this
won't happen in our lifetime, or our children's
lifetime. But our legacy to future generations
will be one of barrenness that could have been
avoided if we act now to develop our technology to
avoid raping the land for natural resources.

[*The wording "to my argument" in the above paragraph implies that Michele thinks
she has now presented the brunt of her main path argument—certainly her main point.
And yet, as we mentioned above, almost all of her points have been tossed out as brief
return paths leading away from positions she rejects. We understand from this paragraph
what Michele's solution would be—to develop our technology to avoid raping the land.
Still, Michele leaves us wondering how her position precisely grows out of and beyond
previous positions.*]

William Tucker doesn't see the loss of our land as
a problem and in fact is appalled we import logs
or natural resources when we have vast resources
of our own (par. 15). His attitude itself is
appalling.

[*Given that Michele now believes her positive argument has been revealed, the position-
ing of these two sentences is perplexing. She places Tucker on a faulty path and then
offers a short return. But the fault she associates with Tucker seems not to contrast at all
with any point along her main path. Michele has not followed the normal rules of thumb
(discussed in Chapter 13) for devising faulty paths. She seems instead to have generated
these sentences out of the blue. Her return path is nothing more than ridicule of Tucker
rather than a genuine reason for rejecting his position.*]

The true problem we face is that while we
want to preserve wilderness, we also believe there
is no harm in developing some of it for its
natural resources. As the economic demand for
this land grows, so will the temptation to
apportion more and more for development. As long
as we tolerate a definition of wilderness as a
divisible economic commodity, we will always be
tempted to divide it into smaller chunks and sell
it to the highest bidder. One could also say that
there is a desire by many people for Picassos.
But we would find it appalling to cut a Picasso
painting into chunks and distribute them to
consumers. Instead replicas of paintings are made

and distributed. Of course the replicas may not be
quite as good as the original, but people are
satisfied because the natural beauty of the
original is left intact. The same principle
should be applied to our natural resources.

[*Michele uses the paragraph above to present her (goal/belief conflict) problem definition.
Although there is no hard and fast rule that milestones must be presented in the natural
order of seeing, defining, and solving, Michele causes a bit of confusion here because she
offers her problem definition only after she has given away her solution. To appreciate
the fit between Michele's problem definition and her solution, we must connect her previously stated "technological" solution with the elimination of the belief (the Y) in
wilderness as a divisible economic commodity. Michelle also uses this paragraph to mention the principle of replicating works of art. She does not make clear, however, whether
she uses this principle as the logical extension and justification of her solution (Chapter
10) or as a new analogy (drawn from the field of art) to show us a fresh way of seeing
the issue (Chapter 13). She may have both functions in mind but each function emphasizes a different milestone as the location of her main point.*]

     Perhaps the author who is closest to my
position is Edward Abbey. As a purist, his
solution is to leave the land alone as God and
nature intended (par. 28). In fact, in his
solution, he suggests that the Lake Powell
reservoir be drained so that Glen Canyon can be
restored. Because I am also a purist at heart, I
too would like to see the land remain untouched.
However, I will admit that, to be realized,
Abbey's solution must be expanded to satisfy
politicians and economists. What I propose is to
preserve the land by turning to technology to
provide substitutes for natural resources.

[*In this paragraph, Michele develops her solution by indicating her ties to Abbey and
explaining why, despite being a purist, she moved beyond the purist point of view to
her technological solution. Apparently, Michele believes that readers might mistake her
solution for a "cold" attitude (like Tucker's) to wilderness and she wants to block this
misreading of her position. Still, the information Michele provides in this paragraph
pertains to her basic assumptions and approach to the issue and should probably have
come much earlier, perhaps in the introduction.*]

     By using the same principle we apply in
replicating priceless paintings, we can use
technology to save the wilderness instead of
destroying it.

[*In this final paragraph, Michelle comes back to the principle she had earlier stated. We
learn nothing more about it, however, so it functions as a useless and redundant conclusion.*]

After receiving feedback on the precision and coherence of your line of argument, make a list of what seem to you to be the most important problems. After working through her reader's analysis, Michele made the following list of the problems her reader had detected:

- I lose too many readers who know little about the issue.
- I have too few connected main path points (my constructive position remains underdeveloped).
- My distinction between issues of access and maintenance is unclear and so I have failed to contrast my position with that of Julber and Nash.
- My characterization of the Ehrlichs and Swain is too brief and so I fail to distinguish my own position from either of theirs.
- My technological solution comes through to the reader as a main path point, but it doesn't seem to grow out of earlier points I have offered or characterized as faulty.
- I offer my problem definition after my solution. My reader must strain to figure out how the latter resolves the tensions in the former.
- I say too much about my basic purist orientation too late into my argument— though this does give me a chance to state my differences with Abbey and imply my differences with Tucker.
- My conclusion doesn't conclude anything; it doesn't indicate where my line of argument stops and where the work needed for a full resolution begins.

After you compile your list of problems, decide which are most important and make a plan about what strategies you will have to work on to correct them. Michele thought her biggest problem was that she had been too brief and unclear both in accounting for her sources and in explaining her differences with them. She attributed this problem to the fact that her lens on the issue (her paradigms) was still fuzzy. She believed this fuzziness compromised her ability to carry through on her own line of argument and to distinguish it from others.

Since the lack of a clear lens seemed to Michele the major fault in her draft, she made a plan to redo her search for paradigms. If you recognize that you lack clear paradigms, you will sometimes find it a useful strategy to search for a single paradigm that crystalizes the issue for you. Using this strategy, Michele eventually came up with the following new paradigm, which she adapted from some of her background reading.

```
    The majority of federal lands around Yellowstone
Park are under lease for oil and gas exploration.
Several mines threaten the quality of Soda Butte
Creek, which flows into the park.  These development
projects threaten the existence of Yellowstone's flora
and fauna, including the grizzly bear.
```

Michele recognized that this paradigm was probably shared by Tucker and the Ehrlichs, both of whom saw an issue in the conflict between nature lovers and the energy industry. Because her paradigm would be well known and shared by previous writers, she understood she brought no novelty to the issue at the milestone "seeing the issue." She decided to search for something new to say at "defining the problem." She tested alternative problem definitions against her paradigm. She first tried the problem definition "We want to develop the wilderness and preserve it" based on a goal conflict. She observed that this problem definition fit her paradigm, but would fit the paradigms of most of the other authors as well.

Michele continued in search of a problem definition that could set her apart. She next tried the problem definition "We want to develop economically and preserve wilderness, yet we believe there are no solutions that would allow us to do both" based on a goal/belief conflict. This problem definition, she concluded, could not distinguish her own position from Swain's, for Swain's solution (create a renewable economy) seemed to her in keeping with this definition of the problem. After all, she reasoned, Swain's solution would eliminate the belief (the Y) side of the conflict.

Michele now considered whether she could find ways of separating her own understanding of the problem from Swain's. How did she part company from Swain? She found herself questioning Swain's sense of optimism that alternative sources of energy would be available to make "maintaining wilderness" and "developing economically" compatible goals. Swain, after all, had offered no direct support for the feasibility of these alternatives and neither, she recognized, had her other sources.

In light of these doubts, Michele revised her problem definition into "We want to develop our resources, but we don't yet know whether we can do so without threatening wilderness" based on a goal/knowledge conflict. As Michele saw it, this problem definition set her apart from Swain, who claimed confidence in the feasibility of alternative technologies rather than the healthy caution Michele thought needed to be exercised.

Having a problem definition that set her apart, Michele wondered whether she might now be able to classify her authors by approach and, perhaps, define an approach of her own based on her new problem definition. She considered authors in the order in which she was able to separate herself from them. She asked herself: What did Tucker and the Ehrlichs have in common that led me to move my problem definition away from theirs? She noticed that these authors shared a common pessimism about uniting the interests of energy development and wilderness protection. In Michele's view, both Tucker and the Ehrlichs seemed to assume, from different sides of the issue, that the conflict between the energy industry and nature lovers was inevitable and unbridgable. Michele called this group the "technological pessimists."

She next asked, where does Swain stand in relation to the pessimists? And why did I find myself moving away from his problem definition? Michele identified Swain as a "technological optimist." She next looked to her final problem definition for some hint of her own identity in the issue. She realized that, like Swain, she was concerned both with the economics of energy and wilderness protection. But instead of assuming that alternative-energy technologies were in the offing, Michele located at the center of the problem the feasibility of these alternatives. Can we expect a day when energy development poses absolutely no threat to our wilderness areas?

Michele realized that a technological optimist or pessimist would supply quick (and predictable) answers to these questions. She thought that only a person with her views would be open to the promise of a technological solution, but still "realistic" about the limits of that promise. She came to think of herself as a "technological realist."

Michele had now made much progress against her reader's criticism that she was unsure of her relationship to her sources. She now had a fairly precise understanding of what her position shared with theirs and what set it apart. She still recognized, however, that she remained open to the criticism that she had too few connected points along her main path. Despite a clearer plan for relating herself to her sources, she had no detailed support or elaboration to strengthen the constructive position that a technological realist might take. She thus found she had to make another revision plan. She returned to the library to see if she could find further support for the position she wanted to defend.

Michele's revised essay follows.

Michele's Revised Draft

The federal government owns over 700 million acres of land. This comes to approximately one third of all land in the United States. Of this vast acreage, about 80 million acres are presently designated as wilderness areas (<u>Nonfuel Minerals</u>, 94). An additional 174 million acres have been identified by the Bureau of Land Management as wilderness study areas. Wilderness study areas are lands that are candidates for inclusion in the wilderness area category. In 1964, environmentalists pushed through an act which prohibits exploring and mining within wilderness areas. The oil and mining industries would like these prohibitions lifted.

Consider the situation of Yellowstone National Park. The majority of lands around this park are under lease for oil and gas exploration. Energy companies are now challenging the "off-limits" status of the Teton Wilderness, a status it has enjoyed for over seventy years. The energy industries argue that they are moved only by desirable goals: economic growth, trade, employment, national security. The environmentalists argue in response that these goals are outweighed by the moral and aesthetic values encouraged by an untainted wilderness. Who is right?

Finding the victim in this war of values is not an easy thing to do, since both the oil and mining industries and the wilderness advocate can rightfully point a finger at the dramatic success of the other. The wilderness advocate can point to the world's insatiable appetite for energy. In this century, the demand for energy has increased by a factor of 10 over the last, a demand that coal and oil serve better than wind and wood. The energy spokesperson can point to the fact that areas designated as wilderness have grown from 9 million acres to 80 million in the last 25 years (<u>Nonfuel Minerals</u>, 94). In this war of values, we are dealing with two strong armies.

Some authors believe or at least hope that the war is winnable by one side or the other. William Tucker, for example, is rooting for the energy industry. He laments that environmentalists have used wilderness as an "all purpose tool" for interfering with economic activity. He believes that this interference is especially harmful "because of the many mineral and energy resources available on western lands that environmentalists are trying to push through as wilderness designations" (par. 11). Paul and Anne Ehrlich, on the other hand, lend their sympathies to the guardians of wilderness. Against the backdrop of a world with complex energy needs, they realize their stance is idealistic:

If the value of each endangered species or population must be compared one on one with the value of the particular development scheme that would exterminate it, we can kiss goodbye to most of Earth's plants, animals, and microorganisms. After all, dam X will be able to supply power to illuminate fifty thousand homes; freeway Y will make it possible to cut twenty minutes from the drive between Jonesville and Smith city; Sunny Acres Apartments will provide decent housing for two thousand people now condemned to existence in a slum; mine Z will create two hundred and fifty needed jobs. How can any organism win in the face of such arguments (par. 34)?

Nonetheless, they insist that we should sometimes sit back and reflect on whether our priorities are in order. "Might there not be some less destructive way to provide jobs than by opening a new mine?" they wonder (par. 35). Are we perhaps too attentive to short-term benefits in the face of long-term, environmental consequences? Certainly, the Ehrlichs do not project a tone of "technology-bashing" in the manner of Tucker's tone against wilderness. But they do seem to think that the long-term consequences of our favoring development at the expense of nature can be catastrophic, far worse than anything Tucker fears from granola-eating backpackers.

In comparison to Tucker and the Ehrlichs, Edward Swain explores the more optimistic possibility that the war can end with two winners. As Swain sees it, the hope that nourishes the future of our economy is also the hope that nourishes our dream of maintaining uncivilized lands. Proceeding from a psychological theory of individual freedom, Swain believes that the very existence of wilderness lands is essential for helping individuals maintain their sense of personal freedom. He further believes that our country's movement to an economy based on renewable energy sources is a foregone conclusion. He only wonders whether we will have the resolve to maintain our wilderness lands before the reality of a renewable economy comes to pass: "If we create a renewable economy before we eliminate wilderness," he writes, "we can provide the potential of an enhanced quality of life in the future" (par. 19). Our short-term conviction to maintain wilderness will yield two long-term wins: an economy with healthier consumption patterns and the "valued option" of "seeing wilderness and all its inhabitants" (par. 23).

Swain's position is based on a healthy vision of the future. But is it a realistic one? A renewable economy was part of our past. Wood was our major source of thermal energy until 1890 and was then replaced with wind and water, also renewable sources, in our industrial mills. We left the renewable economy behind early in this century when it proved insufficient to our growing energy needs. It remains insufficient. And Swain offers no evidence except a hope that it can be sufficient again.

Perhaps a more realistic approach would be to explore the feasibility of Swain's future instead of wondering only how to welcome it. What is the likelihood that our modern-day renewable energy sources—in particular, energy from the sun—will meet our growing energy needs? After reviewing some of the pertinent literature, I must report that the verdict is not yet in. The good news is that solar energy, unlike oil and natural gas, already exists. It doesn't need to be manufactured. This relieves any worry about unleashing energy-producing reactions in the manufacturing process (<u>Energy: The Next Twenty Years</u>, 468). In addition, some scientific

breakthroughs have been made. In 1972, a special
silicon crystal that is vital to the development of
solar energy became inexpensive to manufacture.
Because of this breakthrough, people can now use
solar energy to heat the water in their homes. This
is a small-scale achievement. A larger-scale
achievement would be to collect the solar energy from
outer space. This would make it easier to tap solar
power from space and would make clouds less a source
of interference (<u>How to Obtain Abundant Clean Energy</u>,
130-32). Researchers are now hard at work on this
problem.

    The bad news is that the research remains far
away from producing energies in forms and quantities
that we take for granted with our current fossil-fuel
resources. While solar energy is free, expensive
devices must be deployed to trap it and transform it
into usable energy forms. These devices do not yet
justify their cost. And while collecting solar power
from space has a promising future, it will be a long
time before it becomes a productive or profitable one.
The orbiting collectors being proposed are too heavy
to be launched from the earth. They would need to be
built in space. And the price for putting them into
space is currently too expensive (10,000 dollars/
kilogram) to make the effort viable (<u>Solar and Wind
Energy</u>, 15).

    We must conclude that alternative forms of
renewable energy remain promising but still very much
experimental enterprises. Swain's future seems
farther off than ever. And his hope that we can
remain patient until the advent of renewable energy
sources now only seems to test our patience all the
more. Still, I believe it is worth the wait. The
battle between energy and wilderness interests has no
just resolution. It is better to see the battle as

```
one between our goals for the future and our ingenuity
to get us there.  I believe we should trust our
ingenuity.


                        Works Cited
Katzman, Martin T.  Solar and Wind Energy. Totowa,
    N.J.: Rowman and Allanheld, 1984.
Landsberg, Hans.  Energy: The Next Twenty Years.
    Cambridge: Balinger, 1979.
McGown, Linda, and John Bockris.  How to Obtain
    Abundant Clean Energy.  New York: Plenum, 1980.
Mikesell, Raymond.  Nonfuel Minerals.  Ann Arbor:
    University of Michigan, 1987.
```

Study the differences between Michele's original draft and her revision. Notice that her introduction addresses a more general readership. She includes her paradigm case at the beginning so her readers have a concrete understanding from the start of her concern and how to share it. As readers, we know her introduction is asking, "What shall we do about such cases?" and we know she will use the body of her essay to give us her answer. Her characterization of faulty and return paths is more developed than before. That is, she lets other voices have their say so we have a better understanding of why she decided that they should not have the last word. She also takes the time to support and develop points along her main path more fully and in a more organized way. We thus can associate her with having a constructive argument to make and not simply a series of short replies to the constructive arguments of others.

REVISE FOR YOUR READERS

Now you have written a rough draft of your essay, you have had it reviewed for its basic argument, and you have revised it as necessary. But even if your essential argument is sound, you are likely to find that your essay is far from finished. Three problems in particular are likely to remain:

POSSIBLE READER RESPONSES

- You haven't said all you need to say to help readers follow the fine twists and turns of your directions. As a result, your essay sometimes jumps around, mystifying the reader.
- You sometimes say more than you need to say. As a result, your essay drags in spots, boring the reader.

- You sometimes make it hard for readers to predict what's coming by burying important information. As a result, your essay sometimes reads like a jigsaw puzzle, wearying the reader who tries to piece your meaning together.

You'll want to reread your essay looking for places where you mystify, bore, or weary readers. Better yet, you'll also want to give your essay to a real reader to see where he or she experiences these reactions. Ask your reader to go through your text and mark passages as follows:

READER'S REVISION CHECKLIST

- Put "?" over passages that seem unclear and in need of more elaboration.
- Put "wordy" over passages that seem to move sluggishly.
- Put "reorganize" over passages that seem to be poorly structured.

When you get your essay back, you can work on these problem areas. It's a good idea to work on elaborating, reducing wordiness, and restructuring in that order. You need to elaborate to make sure your essay captures all that you want it to capture. Once you are sure of that, you'll have a better idea of what is meat and what is fat that should be cut. And once your text is good and lean, you can work on a structure for it that helps the reader see the organization of your ideas as quickly and easily as possible.

Elaborate Your Text

A rough draft typically leaves out information that readers require. Locate these possible omissions by considering areas where your reader left a question mark. How you elaborate your text depends on the information you omitted. You can often discover what type of information you left out (and thus what to fill in) by judging your own reaction to the text. Here is a list of possible reactions to choose from:

REACTIONS REQUIRING ELABORATION

This is complex.
This is questionable.
This gives the wrong impression.
This makes me seem unfair.
This is a big leap.

Each reaction suggests a different problem and cure. "This is complex" suggests that your language is too compressed, that you need to amplify what you are trying to say with more words and sentences. "This is questionable" suggests that you are missing support for some statements. "This gives the wrong impression" suggests that you are using inappropriate words or leaving out disclaimers. "This makes me seem unfair" means that you are wording inappropriately, missing qualifiers, or failing to make important concessions. "This is a big leap" suggests that you are missing important transitions between your ideas.

Cut the Fat from Your Text

After expanding your draft to include all the ideas your readers need, determine whether you really need all the words you've used to present your ideas. Go through your draft and cut out whatever seems redundant, irrelevant, or unnecessary. Read your text aloud as if you were trying to communicate the main ideas to a listener. You'll find yourself dropping words, phrases, and even whole sentences. Whatever you leave out of these readings is probably fat that you can cut.

Restructure Your Text

When you have a draft that seems both complete and lean, you are ready to test and revise its structure so that the basic organization of your ideas is easy for readers to understand and anticipate. When you restructure, always work from the top down. That is, look for ways to restructure at the whole-text level, then the section level, then the paragraph level, then the sentence level, then the word level.

Ask yourself the following questions about the overall structure of your essay:

A CHECKLIST FOR RESTRUCTURING

Introductory paragraphs

- Does the introduction prepare readers to understand my question at the crux?
- Does it use a thesis statement to preview my response to this question?
- Does it give readers the right amount of background information?

Seeing the issue

- Does the text give readers a sense of the issue through historical accounts and problem cases?
- Does it inform readers about possible controversies associated with seeing the issue? about my own paradigms if there is a controversy?

Defining the problem

- Does the text give readers a sense of my problem definition? of alternative positions whose problem definitions I consider faulty?
- Are my reasons clear for rejecting the alternatives?

Choosing a solution

- Does the text give readers a sense of my solution? of alternative positions whose solutions I consider faulty?
- Are my reasons clear for rejecting the alternatives?

Main point

- Is my main point well supported and amplified?
- Does it meet the criteria of support required by my community?

Overall flow

- Does my text unfold as a set of directions from seeing to resolving with clear transitions along the way?

Trying to answer these questions at a whole-text level should give you a good plan for restructuring.

Look at your headings, if you have included them. Headings and subheadings are a potent way to signal your text structure to readers. Look for opportunities to forecast the structure of your text with headings and subheadings. (Caution: It is easy to overdo headings and subheadings, so don't be too eager to use them, particularly if your essay is short.)

Look at your paragraphs. Imagine that your readers are trying to gather the overall structure of your text just by skimming the first sentences of your paragraphs. While not all paragraph breaks will signal major shifts of ideas, all major shifts of ideas should be signaled by paragraph breaks. Scan the tops of your paragraphs to see if you can track the major shifts in your ideas as you progress through your line of argument. If you can't, then add sentences to describe them, and compose transition paragraphs or summary paragraphs telling your reader where you're going and where you've been.

Turn your focus to the inside of your paragraphs. Is the plan by which one sentence flows into another clearly evident? Is it immediately clear how all the sentences revolve around a central idea? Do the sentences all lead somewhere? If not, revise the paragraph until you can answer yes to these questions.

For particularly long, complex, or important paragraphs, try the following strategy: Write a sentence about what readers are supposed to know upon entering the paragraph. Write a second sentence about how you want their knowledge to change upon leaving it. Start from the top of the paragraph and rewrite each sentence so that all the sentences, taken together, form the "shortest line" between your readers' entry knowledge and the change in their knowledge you are using the paragraph to bring about. This strategy will teach you about the real work your paragraphs are doing. Sometimes you will find you have composed a paragraph that is doing no work at all. When that happens, cut it.

Turn your focus more inward still, to the inside of your sentences. You probably have a good reference handbook of style, grammar, and usage to help you revise sentences in isolation. Our purpose here is much more modest—to help you edit your sentences so that they minimize a reader's difficulty in following your text. In that spirit, we offer the following simple strategies.

Use the active voice. We use the active voice to indicate that a subject is doing something:

A Sentence in Active Voice

Many moved to the city.

In contrast to the active voice, we use the passive voice to indicate that something is being done to the subject:

A Sentence in Passive Voice

John was found in the library.

If you have a choice between putting a sentence in the active or passive voice, prefer the active. The active is less formal and more natural-sounding than the passive. You can sustain the active voice over many sentences, but a series of sentences in the passive voice begins to sound robot-like. Compare these two paragraphs:

Extended Use of Active Voice

Opponents of wilderness development say that the economic benefits of sacrificing live trees do not justify the moral costs. They take an approach that is more ethical than the approach of the fuel companies. Given the choice between saving a tree and keeping a house warm in winter, they would save the tree.

Extended Use of Passive Voice

It is said by opponents of wilderness development that the economic costs of sacrificing live trees is not justified by the economic benefits. An approach that is more ethical than the approach of the fuel companies is taken by them. Given the choice between saving a tree and keeping a house warm in winter, they would choose to have the tree saved.

The passive voice is not well suited to argumentative prose, and if you overuse it, you are likely to disrupt the flow of your sentences. Your line of argument through an issue represents a set of *actions* (what you think, believe, recommend) that you are taking in response to the *actions* of other authors (what they think, believe, recommend). The active voice is the preferred voice with which to discuss actions.

Use people as grammatical subjects. This strategy is a corollary of the active-voice strategy. Argumentative writing describes authors acting in response to the actions of other authors. Thus, it makes sense to try to make the subjects of your sentences refer to agents (human beings, authors) as much as possible. When you put agents in the subject slots of your sentences, you are making it clear to your readers that real people are accountable for the ideas you are putting forth.

Making Agents into Subjects

The Ehrlichs state that developers may cause great harm to the environment. They also assume that one can't predict in advance how much damage that really involves.

Putting "the Ehrlichs" (the name of agents) as subject helps this writer convey that these authors are directly responsible for the ideas. This sense of direct responsibility, however, is weakened when we remove "the Ehrlichs" from subject position:

Agents Not Used as Subjects

It is stated by the Ehrlichs that developers may cause great harm to the environment. It is further assumed by them that one can't predict in advance how much damage that really involves.

Finally, *use strong main verbs and introduce them early.* Compare the following sentences:

A Strong Verb Introduced Early

Swain never proves that protecting wilderness now will lead to a renewable economy.

A Strong Verb Delayed

That protecting wilderness now will lead to a renewable economy is never proved by Swain.

Sentences are easier to understand when you use a strong main verb and introduce it early. By a "strong" main verb, we mean a content verb as opposed to an auxiliary verb (is, was, be, has). Auxiliary verbs don't function as main verbs as well as content verbs. When you use an auxiliary verb, you often deprive yourself of the opportunity to use agents in the subject slot.

Consider the following contrast:

A Strong Verb

Roderick Nash laments that so many of our national parks are now being inundated by tourists.

An Auxiliary Verb

The lamentable fact, according to Roderick Nash, is that so many of our national parks are now being inundated by tourists.

Worse yet, if you consistently use auxiliary verbs as your main verb, you'll have to add awkward nouns to fill in for the information you lost by not having a stronger verb. The shape of many of your sentences will begin to fall apart as soon as you rely on an auxiliary verb for your main verb. Compare the following sentences:

A Strong Verb

We can't consistently protect wilderness from human intervention and at the same time intervene.

An Auxiliary Verb

Consistent wilderness protection free of human intervention is not possible if there is at the same time an intervention strategy.

Introducing a strong verb early into your sentences will make them easier to understand. Following this strategy, in turn, will open up more opportunities to use the active voice and express agents as subjects. Thus, the strategies we have discussed work together in a system of good editing habits.

For Class 14.3

Exchange drafts you wrote in For Class 14.2 with a partner. Your partner should mark your text as indicated in this section and give it back to you to revise. When you receive your text back, do the following:

A. Elaborate your text to include information your reader needs.
B. Cut the fat from your text to rid it of unnecessary or redundant information.
C. Restructure your text at the whole-text, paragraph, and sentence levels so that readers can readily see how you organize ideas.

For Your Notebook #31

Revise your original essay on your own issue. Solicit comments from other readers, and then revise:

- Elaborate.
- Cut the fat.
- Restructure.

⊞ GLOSSARY

accountability A property of an author's position. An author's position is accountable when it is well and accurately grounded in a community's current discussion and its sense of progress through an issue. See also *freshness*.

approach A name for a group of positions sharing features at one or more milestones, beginning with "seeing the issue."

argumentative text A text in which an author takes a position on an issue and tries to convince readers to accept and act on it.

aspects The components or factors that can contribute to the frustrations, tensions, and troubles in a problem case.

assumptions The implications of a position associated with seeing the issue in the terms in which the position frames it.

"choosing a solution" An argument for taking a specific action or accepting a specific belief.

common point of discussion A claim about some aspect of an issue to which multiple authors can be said to respond.

counterexample A concrete situation that does not fit some prior generalization.

"defining the problem" An argument giving the terms in which to understand a problem, usually stated as a conflict between an X and a Y.

faulty path The part of an author's line of argument containing points an author wants readers to avoid or reject.

freshness A property of an author's position. An author's position is fresh when, taken in full, it is unfamiliar or different, something never before heard in the author's targeted community. See also *accountability*.

grid of common points An array of all the major positions in an issue.

implication The extreme endpoints of a line of argument, often unstated, moving from seeing to resolving the issue. See also *assumptions*; *principle*.

line of argument A set of points that together make up an author's position on an issue.

main path The part of an author's line of argument containing points the author wants readers to accept and act on.

major split The dispute in an issue on which the most disagreement among authors is found.

milestone A division of the main path of an author's line of argument; a set of points that together make an argument for either "seeing the issue," "defining the problem," or "choosing a solution."

minor split A dispute among authors on the same side of a major split.

paradigm A problem case considered to be the most important or central to an issue.

point A statement of belief about the world that an author presents as true but that other authors might contest.

preliminary split A dispute over decisions that many authors in an issue take as settled.

principle The implications of a position that would follow were it applied consistently and rigorously as a solution.

problem case   A concrete situation whose existence raises discontent or dissatisfaction for a community.

problem definition   A formal way of representing the tension in a set of problem cases.

return path   The part of an author's line of argument that provides reasons for rejecting the points lying on faulty paths.

"seeing the issue"   An argument describing the problem cases or history of an issue, intended to convince readers to become committed to seeing it resolved.

synthesis tree   A tree depicting preliminary, major, and minor splits among authors.

APPENDIX ON REFERENCES AND DOCUMENTATION

WHEN TO CITE SOURCES

Start your research by gathering both informative and argumentative texts on your issue. Use the informative texts as background for your line of argument. Use the argumentative texts for background and for lines of argument to support or contrast with your own. Cite a particular text whenever you find your line of argument relying on it for *immediate* background, support, or contrast.

WHY CITE SOURCES?

Documentation allows your readers to retrace your reasoning. By knowing what has influenced your thinking, readers can evaluate whether you've been fair to these influences and, at the same time, whether you've made your way beyond them. More important, perhaps, your citations can give readers efficient search paths of their own, helping them select texts (possibly including your own) to develop their own lines of argument. Thus, through your citations, you provide for future authors what previous authors have provided for you. Citing sources ensures that the cycle of literacy (from reading to authoring) you have been practicing throughout this book will perpetuate itself indefinitely.

HOW TO CITE SOURCES

Of the many formats for citing sources, the two most common styles are those of the MLA (Modern Language Association) and the APA (American Psychological Association). Complete rules for the MLA style can be found in the *MLA Handbook for Writers of Research Papers*. For the APA style, consult the *Publication Manual of the American Psychological Association*. Your instructor will probably tell you which style to use. (Be sure you have the most recent edition of either manual.) We shall discuss some of the basics of these two styles and some of the essential differences between them, but first a word about the philosophy behind the direction in which scholarly citation seems to be headed.

277

TOWARD A PARENTHETICAL SYSTEM OF CITATION

Traditionally, the MLA endorsed the documentary notes system of citation—the use of superscript numbers ($^{1\ 2\ 3}$) to attribute ideas to external sources. Such numbers are linked to corresponding information at the bottom of the page (footnotes) or at the end of chapters or the end of the book (endnotes). But this system is easy to abuse in all kinds of writing, and some of the abuses particularly affect the writing of arguments. For instance, some authors have used their notes to carry on long-winded discussions that distract readers from the line of argument in the main text. Others have used their notes to "patch holes" in the main text. Both of these practices are wrongheaded. The line of argument in your main text should always stand alone at center stage. Introduce additional content in footnotes or endnotes only when you think it will supplement or enhance a reader's experience of your line of argument. Never use notes to distract your reader from your main text or to "repair" omissions in it.

To discourage such practices (and for other reasons), a few years ago the MLA developed a parenthetical system of citation, which it recommends for student use. (The APA has had its own parenthetical system for some time.) This system of citation works just as well as documentary notes in crediting ideas in your text to outside sources. However, unlike content notes, it does not tempt you to start discussions that are peripheral to your main text. The basic idea is that whenever you refer to material from a particular source, you place after the reference, in parentheses, the last name of the author of that source and the appropriate page number. For example, if you were quoting the previous sentence in an essay of your own, you would write: "The basic idea is that whenever you refer to material from a particular source, you place after the reference, in parentheses, the last name of the author of that source and the appropriate page number" (Kaufer, Geisler, and Neuwirth 278). A "Works Cited" list at the end of your essay would contain a full citation to this book, to which your readers could then refer.

The parenthetical system of citation can be used in conjunction with traditional footnotes or endnotes. In fact, used carefully, the combination of these two systems gives you the best of both worlds. Most of your citations will parenthetically (and efficiently) point to a fuller reference. On those few occasions when you have a choice tidbit to enrich your readers' experience of your line of argument, you can include it in a note. A genuine advantage of using both parenthetical and documentary notes is that you can more easily monitor your reason for using a citation—whether it simply credits an external source or whether it introduces information bearing on your line of argument but peripheral to it. Citation information of the first type is essential in serious scholarly writing; citation information of the second type is not.

As we have mentioned, the MLA now recommends parenthetical citations, although it continues to accept the use of documentary notes. We will consider next the MLA's parenthetical system (including a brief discussion of the increasing use of nontextual materials, like computer software, videotapes, and TV programs). We shall then discuss the APA style as an alternative parenthetical system. Following that is a short section on the use of documentary notes.

THE MLA FORMAT

In-Text Citations

Every parenthetical system is based on the inclusion of certain citation information in parentheses within the body of the text, but the information given varies from one style to another. The main differences between the MLA and APA styles are that the MLA's parenthetical citations (1) include page references but not the year of publication; (2) do not use commas before page references; (3) use titles to distinguish several works by the same author; (4) do not use the word "page" or "pages" or their abbreviations.

For example, suppose Thomas is a general source you have used to learn about the Wilderness Campaign of the Civil War. You can credit him in your own essay as follows:

```
The Wilderness Campaign occurred in May and June of 1864.
It consisted of a series of skirmishes between the Union and
Confederate armies.  General Lee led 70,000 troops into an
area called the "Wilderness" about 50 miles northwest of
Richmond (Thomas).
```

The citation information includes only the author's last name. This is sufficient if you won't be referring to any other books by Thomas and if the reference is so general that you don't need a specific page number. *Include only the information you need to lead readers unambiguously to your source.*

Now let's say you want to point readers not only to a source but to a specific page within that source. You include that information as follows:

```
The Wilderness Campaign occurred in May and June of 1864.
It consisted of a series of skirmishes between the Union and
Confederate armies.  General Lee led 70,000 troops into an
area called the "Wilderness" about 50 miles northwest of
Richmond (Thomas 870).
```

No punctuation separates the author information and the page number.

Sometimes it is convenient to incorporate citation information in your main text. If so, adjust your parenthetical citation accordingly:

```
The Wilderness Campaign occurred in May and June of 1864.
It consisted of a series of skirmishes between the Union and
Confederate armies.  According to Thomas, General Lee led
70,000 troops into an area called the "Wilderness" about 50
miles northwest of Richmond (870).
```

Thomas is mentioned in the main text, so the parenthetical information requires only a page reference.

Now suppose your full essay draws from two books by Thomas. One source, the one to be cited for this passage, is titled *Wilderness Campaign*, and the other is titled *Charting the Ohio River*. In this case, you need to cite the relevant title along with the author:

```
The Wilderness Campaign occurred in May and June of 1864.
It consisted of a series of skirmishes between the Union and
Confederate armies.  According to Thomas, General Lee led
70,000 troops into an area called the "Wilderness" about 50
miles northwest of Richmond (Wilderness Campaign 870).
```

End-of-Text References

Complete citations for all your references are listed on a "Works Cited" page at the end of your paper. The entries are arranged alphabetically by author and are double-spaced. Type the first line of each citation flush with the left margin, and indent subsequent lines five spaces. Use the author's full name, putting the last name first. Capitalize all major words in titles. If you use more than one work by the same author, list the works alphabetically by title. Give the author's full name with the first title, but substitute three hyphens for the name in subsequent entries, as in this example:

```
Shepard, Paul.  Nature and Madness. San Francisco: Sierra,
     1982.
---.  Over the River.  Columbus: Ohio State UP, 1983.
```

As the examples show, MLA-style citations are composed of three parts, separated by periods—author, title, and publication information. The publication information consists of the place of publication, followed by a colon(:), the name of the publisher followed by a comma, and then the date of publication. The MLA recommends using a shortened version of the publisher's name; there is a list of acceptable short forms in the *MLA Handbook*.

These general rules go far, but variations are inevitable because of the wide assortment of source materials you may be citing. For example, when there are two or more authors, invert only the first author's name:

```
Ehrlich, Paul R., and Anne Ehrlich.  Extinction: The Causes
     and Consequences of the Disappearance of Species.  New
     York: Random, 1981.
```

When citing a translation, insert the name of the translator between the title and the publication information:

```
Undset, Sigrid.  The Master of Hestviken: The Axe, the Snake
     Pit.  Trans. Arthur G. Chater.  New York: Knopf, 1934.
```

In an edited volume, add "ed." after the author's name to identify the "author" as an editor:

```
Krutilla, John V., ed.  Natural Environments: Studies in
     Theoretical and Applied Analysis.  Baltimore: Johns
     Hopkins UP, 1972.
```

When citing a source that has been published in multiple editions, indicate what edition you are citing in the slot between the title and the publication information:

```
Bagenal, T., ed.  Methods for Assessment of Fish Production
     in Fresh Waters.  IBP Handbook.  3rd ed.  London:
     Blackwell Scientific Publications, 1978.
```

When citing a chapter in a larger anthology or collection, include both the author and title of the chapter and the editor and title of the collection, and give the page numbers of the chapter:

```
Passmore, John.  "Nature, Intellect and Culture."
     Philosophy and Culture.  Ed. Venant Couchy.  Montreal:
     Du Beffroi, 1986.  52-80.
```

When citing an unpublished dissertation, put the title in quotation marks, indicate that you are citing a dissertation, and give the institution at which it was conferred and the year:

```
Bedient, P.  "Hydrologic Land Use Interactions in a Florida
    River Basin."  Diss. U of Florida, 1982.
```

To cite a volume that is part of a series, include both the total number of volumes and the one(s) you are citing. For example, if you used volume two of Cragg's three-volume series, you would reference it as follows:

```
Cragg, J. B., ed.  Advances in Ecological Research.  3 vols.
    New York: Academic Press, 1978.  Vol. 2.
```

When the individual volumes of a series have their own separate titles, reference both titles. In this example, the citation is to a chapter in one volume of a series:

```
McHugh, J. "Estuarine Fisheries: Are They Doomed?"  Uses,
    Stresses, and Adaption to the Estuary.  Vol. 1 of
    Estuarine Processes.  6 vols.  New York: Academic
    Press, 1976.  15-27.
```

Government publications are often given an alphanumeric designation to help identify the specific agency from which they originated and the specific document within the agency. Include them in your documentation:

```
Hern, S. C., V. W., Lamboer, and H. Jai.  Pesticides and
    Polychlorinated Biphenyls in the Atchafalaya Basin,
    Louisiana.  U.S. Environmental Protection Agency,
    Office of Research and Monitoring.  EPA-600/4-79-061.
    Washington: GPO, 1979.
```

If no author's name is given for a government document, put the agency's name in the author slot.

Encyclopedia articles may or may not have signed authors. When they do not, leave the author slot blank. The year or edition is the only publication information you need:

```
"Wilderness Road."  Academic American Encyclopedia.  1982 ed.
```

To cite an article in a periodical or journal that has continuous pagination over several issues, include the volume number, the year of publication, and the page numbers, punctuated exactly as in this example:

```
Arthur, John.  "Resource Acquisition and Harm."  Canadian
    Journal of Philosophy 17 (1987): 337-47.
```

For a journal whose issues are separately paged, include the number of the issue as well, separated from the volume number by a period but no space:

```
Loftin, Robert W.  "Psychical Distance and the Aesthetic
     Appreciation of Wilderness."  International Journal of
     Applied Philosophy 2.3 (1986): 15–19.
```

But for an article in a monthly magazine, it is enough to cite the date and the page numbers:

```
Sheffe, Edward D. "How to Eat Well in the Wilderness and
     Lose Seven Thousand Pounds." Backpacker Sept. 1982: 8.
```

When an article is unsigned, just leave the author slot blank:

```
"Don't Call It 'the Barrens.'"  Audubon July 1981: 72.
```

To cite information from a weekly publication, include the day as well as the month and year of publication. Notice that the day appears before the month:

```
"Two Tracks in the Wilderness."  New Republic 31 Dec.
     1983: 7.
```

To cite a newspaper article, include the edition and the section along with the date and page number. You would refer to section D, page 23, in the late edition of the *New York Times* or section A, page 17, in the national edition of the *Washington Post* as follows:

```
Dougherty, Phillip H. "Wilderness Publication Begins
     Accepting Ads." New York Times 18 April 1985, late
     ed.: D23.
Peterson, Cass.  "But We Thought They Like Backpacking."
     Washington Post 19 Feb. 1985, natl. ed.: A17.
```

Letters to the editor should be specified as letters:

```
Fitzpatrick, Donna, William W. Hopkins, Rod Schenker, and
     David Allison.  Letter.  Christian Science Monitor 30
     Dec. 1987, natl. ed.: 13.
```

A citation for a book review must include the author and title of the work reviewed as well as the reviewer's name. Here, Eder is the reviewer and Keeley is the author of the work reviewed:

```
Eder, Richard. Rev. of A Wilderness Called Peace, by Edmund
        Keeley. Los Angeles Times 28 April 1985, natl. ed.: 3.
```

REFERENCES TO NONTEXTUAL MATERIALS

In a world of growing use of technology, you may find it increasingly necessary to cite nontextual sources of reference materials: computer software, computerized or other types of information services, radio and television programs, musical recordings, cartoons, slides, and audio or video recordings of speeches, plays, and films. A complete discussion of how to cite these various non-print forms is available in *The MLA Handbook*. Here we offer some basic instruction about some of these forms and a few models for you to work from.

Computer Software

Include in your citation the writer of the software program, the title of the program, the label "Computer software" to identify the reference as software, the distributor of the program, and the year of publication. Underline the title of the program. Insert a comma between the distributor and the year. Insert periods between every other piece of information. To help readers understand the software further, you may also include, after the date, information about the hardware the computer runs on (Apple, IBM), the size of the program in kilobytes (10kb), the operating system it requires (DOS, Unix), and the form in which the program is distributed (cartridge, disk, diskette). Separate these items with commas and place a period at the end:

```
Doe, John. The Wilderness Simulation Game.  Computer
        software.  Carnegie Mellon University, 1988.
        Macintosh, Sun Workstations, IBM RTs, Micro-Vax, Unix,
        Mac operating system, 1000 kb, disk, diskette.
```

Computerized and Other Information Services

Cite these like any printed material, but include at the end the name of the service and its identifying number:

```
Dixon, Melvin.  Ride Out the Wilderness: Geography and
        Identity in African Literature.  Urbana: U of Illinois
        P, 1987.  ERIC 078 562.
```

Radio and Television Programs

State the title of the program (underlined), the network, the local station, the city, and the date of broadcast. When appropriate, include the title of the episode, in quotation marks, before the program title. If the program is part of a series, include the series title after the program title. Separate the station and the city with a comma. Use a period for all other separators. If you want to include the names of writers, directors, producers, or narrators, put them after either the episode title or the program title:

> Cry of the Wilderness. Dir. John Jay. Writ. and prod. Bruce
>   Feld. PBS. WQED, Pittsburgh. 5 June 1988.
> "Life in the Wilderness." Narr. Marlin Perkins. Wild
>   Kingdom. NBC. KSDK, St. Louis. 3 Mar. 1971.

Films

Include the title of the film (underlined), the director, the distributor, and the year of release. Separate the distributor and date with a comma. When appropriate, include the names of writers, producers, or performers after the title. Data about the physical characteristics of the film—running length—goes after the date:

> Hard Times in Wilderness. Dir. Jean Linn. United Artists,
>   1950. 92 min.

Performances·

Cite dramatic performances as you would a film, but listing the theater and city, separated by a comma:

> The Land. By Sally Fictitious. Dir. Terry Scott. Benedum
>   Theatre, Pittsburgh. 5 Apr. 1987.

Interviews

Name the person interviewed. If the interview is part of a larger work (a newspaper article or radio program), place the title of the interview, if any, in quotes. If the interview is the entire work, underline the title. If the interview is untitled, follow the name of the interviewee with the word "Interview." Close with the usual bibliographic information:

> Commoner, Barry. Interview. New York Times 14 Jan. 1980,
>   late ed., sec. 1:1.

Lectures and Speeches

Cite the name of the speaker, the title (if any) in quotes, the meeting or sponsoring organization, the location and date. If there is no title, label the event generically as a lecture, address, or speech:

```
Horner, Jack. "The Disappearance of the Dinosaurs."
     Carnegie Museum.  Pittsburgh, 22 June 1988.
Gould, Steven J. Lecture.  Carnegie Museum.  Pittsburgh, 23
     June 1988.
```

THE APA FORMAT

In-Text Citations

As we mentioned earlier, every parenthetical system includes certain citation information within the body of the text. Unlike the MLA style, however, the APA style (1) includes the year of publication; (2) uses commas before page references; (3) uses dates, rather than titles, to distinguish several works by the same author; (4) uses the abbreviations "p." or "pp." with page references.

Let's return to our example of citing Thomas on the Wilderness campaign. Compare these APA parenthetical citations with the ones previously given in the MLA style:

```
The Wilderness Campaign occurred in May and June of 1864.
It consisted of a series of skirmishes between the Union and
Confederate armies.  General Lee led 70,000 troops into an
area called the "Wilderness" about 50 miles northwest of
Richmond (Thomas, 1982).
```

```
The Wilderness Campaign occurred in May and June of 1864.
It consisted of a series of skirmishes between the Union and
Confederate armies.  General Lee led 70,000 troops into an
area called the "Wilderness" about 50 miles northwest of
Richmond (Thomas, 1982, p. 870).
```

```
The Wilderness Campaign occurred in May and June of 1864.
It consisted of a series of skirmishes between the Union and
Confederate armies.  According to Thomas (1982), General Lee
led 70,000 troops into an area called the "Wilderness" about
50 miles northwest of Richmond (p. 870).
```

In the APA style, do not use titles to distinguish several works by the same author; use the year of publication instead. Should you need to cite two works by the same author published in the same year, distinguish them by adding the small letters "a" and "b" after the year. For example, suppose you want to cite a book by Thomas published in 1982, but you know that in a later passage you will be citing a second book by Thomas also published in 1982. You call the first reference "(1982a)" and cite it as follows:

```
The Wilderness Campaign occurred in May and June of 1864.
It consisted of a series of skirmishes between the Union and
Confederate armies.  According to Thomas (1982a), General
Lee led 70,000 troops into an area called the "Wilderness"
about 50 miles northwest of Richmond (p. 870).
```

End-of-Text References

APA references consist of four major parts separated by periods: author, date, title, and publication information. Type your citations on a page titled "References" at the end of your paper. Arrange the references alphabetically by author and double-space them. Make the first line of each entry flush with the left margin and indent subsequent lines three spaces.

Use the full last name of the author, but—unlike the MLA style—only initials for the author's first and middle names (with a space between the two initials). The date is enclosed in parentheses. Capitalize only the first word in titles; leave all other words in the title lower case. An example of a single-author book following this format is as follows:

```
Shepard, P. (1982).  Nature and madness.  San Francisco:
Sierra Book Club.
```

When you have two or more authors, invert all the names, insert commas between the last names and the initials, and use the symbol "&" before the final name:

```
Ehrlich, P. R., & Ehrlich, A. (1981).  Extinction: The
causes and consequences of the disappearance of species.
New York: Random House.
```

In case you have two references by the same author published in the same year, we've already suggested what to do:

```
Ehrlich, P. R., & Ehrlich, A. (1981a).  Extinction: The
causes and consequences of the disappearance of species.
New York: Random House.
```

```
Ehrlich, P. R., & Ehrlich, A. (1981b).  After extinction.
    New York: Random House.
```

To cite an article in a periodical with continuous pagination over several issues:

```
Arthur, John.  (1987).  Resource acquisition and harm.
    Canadian Journal of Philosophy, 17, 337-347.
```

Notice that the title of the article is not put in quotation marks and the volume number is now underlined rather than put in parentheses. The page numbers are separated from the volume number with a comma rather than a colon. To cite separately paged periodicals, put the issue number, in parentheses, immediately after the volume number (leaving no blank space):

```
Loftin, Robert W. (1986).  Psychical distance and the
    aesthetic appreciation of wilderness.  International
    Journal of Applied Philosophy, 3(2), 15-19.
```

Cite a monthly periodical by putting the month in parentheses after the year, with a comma between them:

```
Sheffe, E. D. (1982, September).  How to eat well in the
    wilderness and lose seven thousand pounds.  Backpacker,
    p. 8.
```

Add the day's date for a daily newspaper:

```
Dougherty, Phillip H. (1985, April 18).  Wilderness
    publication begins accepting ads.  New York Times,
    p. 23.
```

DOCUMENTARY NOTES

In-Text Citations

Start with the superscript number [1] and number your notes consecutively throughout your entire essay. Place the number at the end of the text unit (paragraph, sentence, clause, word) that best encompasses the scope of the information you are citing. (To type superscript numbers, position the number slightly above the line.)

End-of-Text References

Documentary notes—that is, footnotes or endnotes in a "Notes" list at the end of your essay—differ only slightly from the references in a "Works Cited" list. Recall that a "Works Cited" reference has three main parts, separated by periods: author, title, and publication information. The biggest difference is that a documentary note has four parts: author, title, publication information, and page numbers.

The publication information in a documentary note is enclosed in parentheses. Instead of periods to separate the parts, a comma is inserted between the author and title, and a period appears only at the end. Authors' names are not inverted but appear with the first name first. Most striking, perhaps, the indentation follows the familiar paragraph pattern. That is, the first line of each entry is indented five spaces and subsequent lines are flush with the left margin. When your paper has both notes and parenthetical citations, insert your "Notes" list *before* the "Works Cited" list (MLA style) or *after* the "References" list (APA style).

Compare this "Works Cited" entry:

Shepard, Paul. <u>Nature and Madness</u>. San Francisco: Sierra, 1982.

with the following "Notes" entry:

[1]Paul Shepard, <u>Nature and Madness</u> (San Francisco: Sierra, 1982) 101.

Document an edited volume in a footnote or endnote as follows:

[3]John V. Krutilla, ed., <u>Natural Environments: Studies in Theoretical and Applied Analysis</u> (Baltimore: Johns Hopkins UP, 1972) 54.

A chapter from an anthology:

[12]John Passmore, "Nature, Intellect and Culture," <u>Philosophy and Culture</u>, ed. Venant Couchy (Montreal: Du Beffroi, 1986) 87.

A reference from a multivolume work:

[6]J. B. Cragg, ed., <u>Advances in Ecological Research</u>, 3 vols. (New York: Academic Press, 1978) 2: 134.

A government document:

> [3]S. C. Hern, V. W. Lamboer, and H. Jai, <u>Pesticides and Polychlorinated Biphenyls in the Atchafalaya Basin, Louisiana</u>, EPA–600/4–79–061 (Washington: U.S. Environmental Protection Agency, Office of Research and Monitoring, 1979) 345.

An unsigned encyclopedia article:

> [2]"Wilderness Road," <u>Academic American Encyclopedia</u>, 1982 ed.

or one that is signed:

> [4]John Thomas, "Wilderness Campaign," <u>Academic American Encyclopedia</u>, 1982 ed.

A periodical:

> [8]John Arthur, "Resource Acquisition and Harm," <u>Canadian Journal of Philosophy</u> 17 (1987): 337–47.

An article in a monthly journal:

> [5]Edward D. Sheffe, "How to Eat Well in the Wilderness and Lose Seven Thousand Pounds," <u>Backpacker</u> Sept. 1982: 8.

A weekly magazine:

> [9]"Two Tracks in the Wilderness," <u>New Republic</u> 31 Dec. 1983: 7.

A newspaper:

> [11]Phillip Dougherty, "Wilderness Publication Begins Accepting Ads," <u>New York Times</u> 18 April 1985, late ed.: D23.

A review:

> 4Richard Eder, rev. of <u>A Wilderness Called Peace</u>, by Edmund Keeley, <u>Los Angeles Times</u> 28 April 1985, natl. ed.: 3.

CONTENT ENDNOTES

Even in the APA style system, you may have a "Notes" page at the end of your manuscript for content notes—notes that supplement your line of argument. Keep such content notes brief and to a minimum.

⊞ INDEX

A 8
B 9
C 0
D 1
E 2
F 3
G 4
H 5
I 6
J 7